A PROSPECT OF GRAY'S INN

A PROSPECT

OF

GRAY'S INN

Second Revised Edition

BY

FRANCIS COWPER

of Gray's Inn, Barrister-at-Law

Illustrated by Jacqueline Geldart

LONDON
Published by GRAYA on behalf of Gray's Inn
1985

Published by GRAYA on behalf of Gray's Inn

First published 1951 Stevens & Sons Ltd
Second edition 1985 Graya with the assistance of
Ashford Press Publishing

British Library Cataloguing in Publication Data

Cowper, Francis
   A prospect of Gray's Inn.——2nd ed.
   1. Gray's Inn——History
   I. Title   II. Gray's Inn, *Benchers*
   344.2'006'0421   KD504.G7

   ISBN 0-420-47330-0

Printed and bound in Great Britain by
Biddles Ltd, Guildford and King's Lynn

Contents

Foreword

by The Right Hon. Lord EDMUND-DAVIES,
*formerly a Lord of Appeal in Ordinary
and Treasurer of Gray's Inn, 1965*

I count it a privilege to welcome the appearance of this new and revised edition of "A Prospect of Gray's Inn". Written by Francis Cowper, whose long devotion to the Inn has in part been recognised by his election as an Honorary Master of the Bench, it first appeared in 1951 and has for some years been out of print.

Repeated requests from home and abroad have led to the production of the present volume. It tells of the modest beginnings and varying fortune over the centuries of one of the four Inns of Court in this country, and it brings the story up to 1985. It is an absorbing tale, elegantly told by a master of the art of writing history, its learning leavened throughout by the author's wit and flavoured by many disclosures of his deep affection for "Domus".

In a Foreword to the first edition, the Hon. Sir William McNair wrote: "Gray's Inn has been fortunate in her historians and Francis Cowper's book is worthy to take its place with Fortescue and Douthwaite". That is equally true of this new edition and I warmly commend it.

"Fantastic forms, whither are ye fled?"

Charles Lamb
"The Old Benchers of the Inner Temple"

Author's Preface

IN composing the continuation of the story of Gray's Inn from 1951 onwards I have been constantly tormented by the omissions which the inexorable limitations of space impose. From the recesses of memory, from the pages of *Graya,* the magazine which, year by year, records the happenings within the Inn, there rise the ghosts of men and women, lively, varied, vigorous, intelligent, amusing, who in their time filled the foreground of its life; echoes of the songs they sang in Hall, of the stories that set the tables in a roar; memories of events that were seen as notable milestones once, but have now receded into the perspective of a vanishing road. To some it has been possible to refer; others have perforce been passed over in silence. If the full story of Gray's Inn could but be told, every page could be expanded into a chapter. Nor was there room to record even all those now living who have made their contributions, outstandingly recognised or unobtrusive, to the honour and well-being of the Society. Of the living and of the ghosts from the past alike I ask pardon for silences which are not intended as a slight.

In this edition's new chapter I have adhered to my original plan not to treat the Inn as a closed club of lawyers but to place it, as far as possible, in the context of the changing scene around it, visual, social, national. In that context it is easier to perceive its mission, the personalisation of the life of the Bar and the Bench, creating a sense of common purpose in the simultaneous pursuit of public justice and fairness to the client, as opposed to the mere careerism of a loose association of legal technicians concerned only to pass through a qualification factory on the road to personal enrichment and treating the misfortune of litigation as if it were a growth industry. Litigation for litigation's sake would be much like war for war's sake, beneficial only to mercenaries. So an Inn of Court is not a business geared to profit but a fellowship existing to promote and perpetuate within itself a public opinion in which the course of justice and the due benefit of the client are paramount, a spirit transcending that selfishness always sprouting in the human heart. At different stages in their history the Inns of Court have stabilised that spirit, sometimes more, sometimes less, effectively, but it is their continuing purpose and justificaiton. If they are not the fortresses protecting the free and lawful man from the exercise of arbitrary power, there are no others.

The Inns are not businesses existing to maximise their own incomes for their collective aggrandisement or that of their individual members. Of course they must maintain their solvency, if only from common honesty and common prudence. They must live within their means, cut their coat according to their cloth, without prodigality and without running into debt. Good fellowship can be maintained with great simplicity and without ostentatious grandeur, provided the spirit is right. It does not demand a diet of champagne and oysters. Good husbandry is enough. What is essential is loyalty to a common end and the singleness of purpose to maintain its continuity in terms of personal service. Doom is on the House, the Church, the college, the club, the country, treated as a milch cow, when the accepted habit is to take all, give nothing, cadge on the common resources and leave essential tasks to unattached hirelings. True economy lies in the willing rendering of the personal services of all within the fold. That is the region in which profit and loss are determined.

Gray's Inn holds within itself all the possibilities of renewing its strength as it did after 1945. Communication between its members can make itself effective, through the meeting ground of the body called GIBBS (Gray's Inn Bench, Bar and Students) as well as AGIS (Association of Gray's Inn Students). A small Management Committee of Benchers has been formed to meet the immediate need for swift decisions in a time of financial anxiety. The corporate sense renewed after the disasters of the last war is still alive and must not be ignored. Perhaps it might coalesce into an intermediate body of barristers below the Benchers participating in the responsibility for the day-to-day life of the Inn. Such a body did once exist.

I wish to express my gratitude to all who have helped me in the production of this edition, for the encouragement given me by Master Lord Edmund-Davies, one of my oldest friends, the dynamic Master Stephen Terrell Q.C., Master Charles Sparrow Q.C., and all my other colleagues on the committee of *Graya,* particularly David Barnard, Geoffrey Hawker and Mary Burke, whose late husband Charles was prominent in Hall and in the inception of the magazine. I owe thanks too for the encouragement given me by Master Sir William Mars-Jones, Treasurer in the year in which I suffered a grave operation, who, with Lady Mars-Jones, kept up my spirits with exhortations to persevere with this work. I owe another debt of gratitude to Mrs. Theresa Thom, the Society's Librarian, for her help on all occasions and especially for her kindness in contributing her particular skill in drafting the index. I thank too the Library staff, especially Mrs. Claire Butters, for help received. I also offer heartfelt gratitude to Miss Sheena Currie who in typing my often illegible manuscript used her head as well as her hands. I am most grateful too to Jacqueline Geldart for allowing me to use her drawings of Gray's Inn as illustrations.

Finally, I thank Master Sir John Vinelott, chairman of the Management Committee, and his colleagues for the financial support they have accorded the publication, an instance of the corporate spirit which animates Domus, our House.

FRANCIS COWPER

14A GRAY'S INN SQUARE.

GRAY'S INN.

May 1985

List of Illustrations

Gray's Inn Hall, The Gallery

Gray's Inn Chapel

Gateway into Gray's Inn Road

Gray's Inn Hall, South Side

The Garden Gates, Field Court

No. 1 South Square, Gray's Inn

The above illustrations are by Jacqueline Geldart

View of Gray's Inn and Holborn c1600

(from the map of London of Ralph Agas, reproduced by permission of the Guildhall Library.)

GRAY'S INN HALL, THE GALLERY *by Jacqueline Geldart*

GRAY'S INN CHAPEL *by Jacqueline Geldart*

GATEWAY INTO GRAY'S INN ROAD by *Jacqueline Geldart*

GRAY'S INN HALL, SOUTH SIDE *by Jacqueline Geldart*

THE GARDEN GATES, FIELD COURT *by Jacqueline Geldart*

No. 1 SOUTH SQUARE, GRAY'S INN *by Jacqueline Geldart*

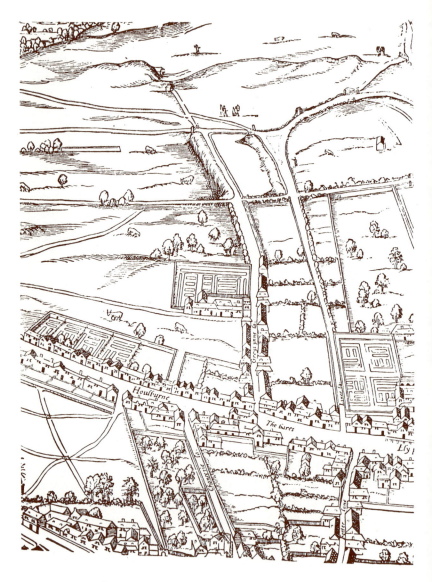

VIEW OF GRAY'S INN AND HOLBORN *c.*1600

1

In the Beginning

ON the western edge of mediaeval London where the suburbs ended at the outworks of Temple Bar and Holborn Bars and the open country of fields and scattered villages began, the guilds of the lawyers formed a closely knit and well-defined community. Along the Thames, which had given it birth, the commerical city, crowded within the circuit of its walls, raised a cluster of spires and towers to the crowning spire of old St. Paul's Cathedral on its hill. Round the bend of the river and linked with the City by the waterside palaces and gardens of the magnates of Church and State, lay royal Westminister, seat and burial place of Kings, its tremendous Abbey matched by the vast Hall where the Lord Chancellor and the Judges of England had their Courts. Between the two and independent of both, the Inns of Court and Chancery were taking shape. Independent likewise of the Universities of Oxford and Cambridge, they themselves constituted at once a legal university and an autonomous professional organisation unique in Christendom.

Through the heart of this legal quarter Chancellor's Lane or Chancery Lane, tortuous, muddy and sometimes impassable, climbed from the Temple by the river past Serjeants' Inn, past Henry III's former asylum for Christianised Jews which the Master of the Rolls had converted to the uses of his department of the law, past the Bishop of Chichester's old house which had become Lincoln's Inn, up to the higher ground of Holborn. On the opposite side of the great thoroughfare ('very full of pits and sloughs and perilous and noisesome to all that repaired and passed that way') Gray's Inn, outermost of the legal houses lay

1

among fields against the distant background of the Hampstead and Highgate hills.

Approach it another way, say in the middle of the fifteenth century, passing out of the City walls through Newgate, the gatehouse already a prison visited periodically by the Judges, onto the ancient highway which carries travellers to Oxford and the west and the condemned to the gallows at rural Tyburn. Where St. Sepulchre's stands on the right, with the Norman priory and hospital of St. Bartholomew behind it, beyond the open ground of Smithfield and its horsepond, the road drops steeply into a deep hollow to cross the Fleet River which, fouled by the horse and cattle market, flows south under the westward walls of the City to join and pollute the broad silver Thames. Up the long, heavy hill on the further bank the road passes St. Andrew's Church on the left and, opposite, the stone-built palace of the Bishops of Ely with its famous gardens and strawberry beds. Here begins the world of the law. Beyond St. Andrew's stands Davy's Inn and, beyond the corner of Fetter Lane, Barnard's Inn, where the signs of the Fleur de lys and the Angel on the Hoop used to stand over the street. Furnival's Inn lies almost opposite and on the left again just by Holborn Bars, where the posts and chains across the street mark the end of the City's jurisdiction, Staple Inn, where the lawyers have taken over the former business centre of the wool merchants.

Beyond the Bars cottages and little low gabled houses and shops straggle irregularly along the highway for a short distance more, and by Staple Inn a small island of buildings makes a bottle-neck in the thoroughfare, just at the point where a side lane, in no better condition than the main road, branches off to the north. Behind the houses on the right just past the lane a large meadow drops a little below the level of the highway and, where the ground begins to rise again beyond its stands, low-built but solid, an irregular group of ancient buildings enclosing a single quadrangle, with a gate opening eastwards onto the lane. This was the Manor of Purpoole with pasture and ploughland and windmill and dovecot and is now Gray's Inn.

Of the mediaeval Inn and its origins all impressions are of necessity blurred and shadowy, for the connected and continuous

2

story of regular records in minute and account books starts abruptly in the reign of Elizabeth and the lost annals of earlier times can be supplied only from fragments surviving at second hand, or else by deduction and inference. Great figures loom in the mist of that obscurity, dominantly the de Greys who gave the Inn its name and in the ownership of whose family it remained till 1506—Sir Reginald de Grey servant and friend of Edward I, soldier, administrator and judge, Justice of Chester, Constable and Sheriff of Nottingham, the first of his line to hold the Manor of Purpoole by title derived from the Dean and Chapter of St. Paul's; Sir John de Grey his son, a man cast in the same mould, Lord of Ruthin, Justice of North Wales, Constable of Caernarvon Castle, by whose provision the manor house in Holborn enjoyed the services of a chaplain from St. Bartholomew's in Smithfield. Their giant shadow lies across England from the Welsh and the Scottish borders to their ancestral lands beside the Thames at Grays Thurrock in Essex. In that England what we call the Judges' circuits were still, as has been said, rather the King's raids and ordinary civil government might have to be conducted by a sort of civil war. But, as the conceptions embodied in the reforms of Edward I, the English Justinian, worked themselves out in a gradually evolving system, the living pattern of a whole new legal world began to assume recognisable shape. As Maitland has declared: 'No English institutions are more distinctively English than the Inns of Court . . . . Unchartered, unprivileged, unendowed, without remembered founders, these groups of lawyers formed themselves and in the course of time evolved a scheme of legal education, an academic scheme of the mediaeval sort, oral and disputacious . . . . What is distinctive of mediaeval England is not Parliament, for we may everywhere see assemblies of Estates, nor trial by jury, for this was but slowly suppressed in France; but the Inns of Court and the Year Books that were read therein, we shall hardly find their like elsewhere.'

As the half light of that dawn grows clearer in the fifteenth century other figures stand out against the background of Gray's Inn, shadowy and remote for all their judicial scarlet, but moving in the familiar paths of an established profession, Walter Cheyne and John Fineux, Chief Justices of the King's Bench, Walter Moyle, Justice of the Common Pleas, Humphrey Starkey, Chief Baron of the Court of Exchequer, ghosts now rising from forgotten monuments. Yet among them one stands clear in a radiance of his own, William Gascoigne, Henry IV's great Chief Justice, legendary pattern of judicial intrepidity. He is claimed both by the Inner Temple and Gray's Inn.*

In Gray's Inn families took root and flourished in the law. The son of John Markham, Justice of the Common Pleas, was another John, Chief Justice of the King's Bench, who a full century after was still remembered as one who 'did eschew corrupt judgments, judging directly and sincerely after the law and the principles of the same', and Gray's Inn at any rate should remember the elder John who was on the Bench at the hearing of that curious case in 1400 when its chaplain brought an action for assault and battery and the defendent pleaded that the battery was provoked by an unclerical assault committed by the plaintiff himself. From the Wars of the Roses to the Great Rebellion the Fairfax family were linked with the Inn, from Guy Fairfax, Judge of the King's Bench under Edward IV, whose son William sat in the Common Pleas under Henry VIII, to their descendants in the seventeenth century, Ferdinand the father and Thomas the son, who won another sort of fame as generals of the armies of the insurgent Parliament. William Yelverton, Justice of the King's Bench, to be met with more than once in the Paston Letters, was of that great line which, from the fourteenth century to the seventeenth, lived and prospered in the Inn. And in those letters too there is a casual, intimate glimpse of Thomas Billing, Serjeant-at-law and later on Chief Justice of the King's Bench, giving some sensible advice to one of the Pastons' acquaintances not to beggar himself by wasting his goods on men and livery

*Note on Chief Justice Gascoigne: When Gascoigne became a serjeant in 1388 he was set down as a member of the Inner Temple, yet his arms stand in the great bay window of Gray's Inn Hall. It is possible that he was originally a member of Gray's Inn. Sir Thomas More's Inn of Chancery was New Inn, subordinate to the Middle Temple, though he proceeded to Lincoln's Inn. In the 19th century, though Lord Chancellor Chelmsford had been called to the Bar by Gray's Inn, he soon migrated to the Inner Temple and his Gray's Inn connection has been ignored.

gowns and horses and harness, for 'I would ye should do well, because you are a fellow of Gray's Inn where I was a fellow.'

In the early sixteenth century under the rising star of the Tudors, the stream of life in the Inn flowed on, fed from many springs. There the learned and laborious Anthony Fitzherbert, later Chief Justice of the King's Bench, toiled to compile the Grand Abridgment. There the Hales family graduated to judicial honours, John as Baron of the Exchequer, James, his son, as a Judge of the Common Pleas, and Christopher, their kinsman, as Master of the Rolls. Noblemen and prelates were flocking to grace the books of the Society and in its ranks were found the new men who during the reign of Henry VIII changed the face of England. There was Thomas Cromwell, Earl of Essex, son of a Putney publican, self elevated to rank with the ancient nobility, but formed by business, money lending, political manipulation and the law into the instrument by which a whole social order was overthrown. His young protegé Thomas Wriothesley followed him in the royal service, to become Secretary of State, Lord Chancellor and Earl of Southampton. New to statecraft, he was not new at Court or in the Inn, for his uncle, Sir Thomas Wriothesley, Garter King-of-Arms at the Field of the Cloth of Gold, had been a member of the Society before him. Far different from both of these, Charles Brandon, handsome, flamboyant and extravagant, reckless and ruthless in self-advancement, radiated in court and camp the piratical glamour of the eternal adventurer. His rather obscure father had borne the standard of the King's father on the field of Bosworth, where the first royal Tudor picked from a bush of thorn the crown of the last Plantagenet, and he made himself Duke of Suffolk, brother-in-law to the King and almost his alter ego. He too was of Gray's Inn and men of his circle filled the Society. In 1901 his forgotten arms, carved in stone over the great north door of the Hall, were found beneath the plaster with which they had been covered up during the rebuilding under Mary and Elizabeth, when his descendants by Henry's sister (Lady Jane Grey was one of them) were still a potential danger to a precarious succession.

The extant records of Gray's Inn open in 1569. Elizabeth had just completed her first decade as Queen and it was a year of crisis at home and abroad. The Treasury was distressingly low and in January, after all the organs of Government publicity had been vainly employed for a whole year to cajole a surprisingly reluctant nation into investing its savings in ten-shilling tickets in an alluringly advertised state lottery 'without any blanks, containing a great number of good prizes,' failure had to be admitted and the prizes reduced in value to one-twelfth. The Netherlands were in revolt against the Spaniards, and France was in the throes of civil war. Wranglings with the Spanish Government had carried England to the utmost limits of what the jargon of another age called 'non-belligerence'. Exports from Spain had been cut off and English privateers retaliated unofficially by preying on her shipping. Non-intervention in France did not prevent a party of English volunteers, including a young gentleman called Walter Raleigh, from fighting on the Protestant side. More remotely there was difficulty over the negotiation of a commercial treaty with Russia. The Queen of Scots, newly arrived in England as a political refugee, was becoming an embarrassing centre of intrigue and unrest. There was disorder in Ireland and, in the north of England, the first rebellion of the reign flared up under the Earls of Northumberland and Westmorland to restore, as they proclaimed, the religion of their ancestors and remove ill counsellors from the Queen, though it was perhaps the Government's seizure of a copper mine on Northumberland's estate that had brought his resentment to a head. The revolt collapsed and the Earls fled. Northumberland was a member of Gray's Inn and in that year's accounts appears the item 'for taking down the Earl of Northumberland's arms and setting up glass in their place 8s. 8d'.

Against this background as the curtain rose on the continuously recorded history of Gray's Inn, four members of the Society were playing a conspicuous part; Sir William Cecil, who became Lord Burghly, the Queen's first minister, dominating the Society as he dominated the realm; Francis Walsingham, a young man rising under his patronage to a commanding position in the direction of foreign affairs; Sir Nicholas Bacon, Lord Keeper of the Great Seal; Sir Gilbert Gerard, the Attorney-General, afterwards Master of the Rolls. In power and influence they stood foremost amid a brilliant membership that adorned and would continue to adorn the Society throughout the Queen's long reign. In that galaxy were men as diverse as Lord Howard of Effingham, who commanded the fleet against the Spanish Armada, and the incomparable Sir Philip Sidney, who, with his father and so many of his kindred, maintained a long traditional association with the Society.

Yet, if Gray's Inn was great upon the national stage it was small enough in physical compass. The only entrance was from Gray's Inn Lane through an ancient gate beside an old iron-bound tree. Over the gatehouse the Yelvertons, privileged by long association with the Society, had their lodging. The quadrangle within, unplanned and irregular, covered no more than what is now the southern extremity of Gray's Inn Square. The red brick Hall, 're-edified' between 1556 and 1560, at a cost of £863 10s. 8d., and the Chapel, its ancient fabric rather incongruously topped by chambers newly piled above it, filled the whole length of the south side save for the rooms wedged between them where the Office of the Duchy of Lancaster was afterwards established. The tall louver towering with its cupola above the ridge of the Hall's new roof dominated the Inn, dwarfing the smaller glazed turret which crowned the little Chapel, while the great bay window at its upper end, filled with armorial glass, shone with a blaze of magnificence amid the grey stone of the older buildings. At the lower end of the Hall, the ornamental porch stood fresh and bright, only just completed, crested with Dunstable stone and adorned with coats of arms in Caen stone. Opposite, a double range of ancient stone buildings ran cloistered along the north side of the quadrangle, inwards the Lower Gallery, and, rising behind it, the Upper Gallery with the square House Buildings at its western extremity and at the back little private gardens fenced in for the ground floor chambers. The quadrangle was closed on the far side by buildings which came right up to the Hall. In those directly opposite the gateway the Bacon family had their lodging and there too on the first floor in a single large room was the library where the great books in their black leather bindings with metal corners and bosses stood chained to the presses. These buildings must have been extremely substantial if not very lofty, since in 1588 Francis Bacon and his brother Anthony were given leave 'to raise and erect new buildings as well over their aforesaid lodging as also over and above the library,' and they added two storeys accordingly. Behind, where the Walks are now, was open ground on which grew many elms and into it a cart track came up from Holborn along the line now followed by the court of Fulwood Place. There were no other courts, only a few straggling buildings and some out-houses for coal and stabling.

By this time the Society was rapidly outgrowing its accommodation. In 1574 there were 124 chambers for 220 members and it was normal for even the Readers (or Benchers) to share quarters, to the extent that in 1579 it was ordered that 'henceforth no fellow of this House shall make choice of his bedfellow but only the Readers.' The Inn had to expand and this was achieved partly by erecting chambers above existing buildings — over the Chapel, over the library, over the 'pastry house' by the west end of the Hall and the Duchy of Lancaster Office by the other end — and partly by the device of granting long building leases to individual members.

Gradually two spacious courts took shape north and south of the original quadrangle. Laid out piecemeal and according to no preconceived pattern, with houses of different shapes and heights and proportions, partly brick and partly timber-framed, these new courts had none of the geometrical regularity of a Georgian square. Indeed, their general character must have been somewhere between a cathedral close or a village green. Each building had its own personal history, so that the new courts were a sort of architectural portrait gallery of the members of the Society, a purely domestic portrait gallery for the most part, in which the sitters were not heroically posed against any background of national achievement.

It is 1579 and the north court has taken shape round a piece of ground covered with elms and walnut trees. It has just been decided that it shall be 'reduced to the uniformity of a quadrant.' Walter Ashton has built on a site 16 feet by 30 feet in what will be the north-east corner. Daniel's Buildings already stand opposite on the west but a little further south. William Daniel is 'a very honest, learned and discreet man', according to Lord Burleigh, and James I will one day make him a Judge of the Common Pleas. South of Ashton's Building Edward Ellis is putting up a long range of chambers beside the lane, on the garden which Robert Shute formerly enjoyed with his lodging just north of the gate house. Shute has lately left the Inn on taking the coif as a serjeant. He is already a Baron of the Exchequer and will soon be a Judge of the Queen's Bench. He was Reader in 1568 and took a ticket in the famous lottery, evidently on behalf of the Society, with the motto: 'Et mihi et multis'. It won 1s. 2d.

So far the portrait gallery records decorous professional worthies of secondary eminence or no eminence at all; Stanhope's Buildings along the north side of the new court reflect a somewhat different personality—Edward Stanhope, Member of Parliament, first for Nottinghamshire and then for Yorkshire, Surveyor to the Duchy of Lancaster, Recorder of Doncaster, Member of the Council of the North, and in 1588 Treasurer jointly with Daniel. In 1579 he is ripe for the office of Reader but he pleads public employments and begs to be excused till the following year, the learned Daniel performing the Reading in his place. Next year he pleads ill-health, agreeing to pay a fine of £40 for his default but secures his admission to the ranks of the Benchers as if he had read. Now, early in 1579, an extensive range of chambers has been planned 'between Mr. Ashton's Buildings and the further part of Mr. Daniel's Buildings towards Gray's Inn Field on the woodyards that be now there, the whole buildings to be 22 feet wide and to leave an entry to lead to the privy of 10 feet wide and to reserve Mr. Ashton's upper light by means of a side roof with a party gutter'. In February a building lease for sixty years is granted to Walter Strickland, a barrister who built one of the new chambers over the Chapel, but sickness and public employment do not prevent Stanhope from taking over the lease and somehow completing the work by July.

The site is not the choicest in the Inn. Beyond it to the north lies the privies on a piece of ground, half rubbish heap half kitchen garden, let for 20s. a year to the panyerman, the servant primarily concerned with marketing and supplies. There sewage is buried (doubtless to the benefit of the produce) and chamber pots are emptied by custom from adjoining windows. It lies lower

9

than the ditches which are supposed to drain it and is often half covered with water. The pleasantest feature about it is the number of elm trees which grow there in profusion. For the benefit of the new buildings the panyerman is dispossessed and Stanhope is granted a sixty years lease of the ground, undertaking to raise the level and drain it. What he actually did is only told in 1605, two years after his death, when a long-suffering Society has at last decided to take action. He had raised the ground by turning it into a public rubbish tip for 'the scavenge of the streets and the like noisome stuff, whereby he did not only extremely annoy the House but did also perform the raising of the said ground without any manner of charge to himself and contrariwise not without benefit and gain at the scavengers' hands'. Instead of turning the place into 'a fair and level pasture to the beauty and pleasure of the said House', he had cut it up into little plots which he let out for bleaching clothes. He had erected 'stables for guest horses' and 'certain base and beggarly cottages', letting them to 'base and beggarly people', and finally he had 'felled and wasted seventeen goodly tall timber trees' out of thirty-seven. In view of these 'manifold abuses' the Panyerman's Close was forthwith resumed into the hands of the Society, which set about repairing the damage.

The south court started as a large meadow roughly rectangular with the open kitchen drain running across it and a gate called the Field Gate in the north-west corner, where a passage into Field Court afterwards went through. Building here had started early and Fuller's Buildings three storeys high were already standing on the west side in 1572 when Humphrey Purefey was given leave to put up a four storey house with a double staircase 'from Mr. Fuller's Building to the Field Gate over and upon the new coalhouses,' which had been erected three years before with wood houses and a brick larder. He crowned it with a tower which had to be pulled down five years later. Howland's Buildings lay beyond Fuller's to the south of it, with Cage's and Gooderick's next, forming the angle of the south-west corner and the Irish Rents adjoining Gooderick's, where the Irish members lodged together.

Edward Stanhope had a finger in the development of this

court too and in 1570 he completed a house, in which he occupied chambers, in the extreme south-east corner, on an irregular plot of ground beyond the last buildings then standing on the east side along the highway. Fifty-four feet to the west stood 'certain ancient buildings of Gray's Inn called 'Hales his buildings' and a mud wall running between them shut off the bottom of the long narrow garden coming down parallel with the lane from behind the Bishop Inn near the Holborn end of it. Eight years later, more sensitive here than as regarded the Panyerman's Close, Stanhope complained that this wall was 'very noisomely used' and was allowed to build along the line of it on a site fourteen feet deep. He also found the kitchen drain detrimental to amenities and obtained leave to cover it over at the Society's expense.

For all its sprawling extensions, the Inn was still to all intents and purposes a house and Gray's Inn Fields, until the Walks were laid out, were literally fields separated from the buildings by a wall through which individual members more than once made back doors from their chambers, while the Benchers repeatedly ordered that they should 'be dammed up and the wall well and sufficiently made by those that enjoy the same doors'.

In two years between 1598 and 1600 the wilderness of grass and elm trees was reduced to order and civilisaton by a young philosopher with very clear and detailed opinions on the subject of landscaped gardens. Favoured son of Sir Nicholas Bacon and nephew of Burleigh, Francis Bacon became a Bencher at twenty-five and was still under forty when he undertook the task. Till then the principal amenity of the Fields appears to have been a seat near an ash tree. Now elms and birches and cherry trees, oziers, quickset and privet hedges, woodbine and eglantine, standards of roses and cuttings of vine, pinks, violets and primroses here combined to weave the garlands of repose. The total expense incurred on behalf of the Society amounted to the then substantial sum of £60 6s. 8d. and ten years later, during his term as Treasurer, Bacon, then Solicitor-General, completed his work at the cost of a further outlay of £250, planting sycamores and elms and birches and beeches, laying out a bowling alley, adding roses and sweetbriar and setting up wrought iron gates.

On a small artificial mount in the midst of the high bank

11

along the western side of the Walks, a cluster of slender pillars supported the roof of a square open summer house adorned with the gilt griffin of the Society, memorial of a strange friendship and monument of Jeremy Bettenham 'viri innocentis abstinentis et contemplativi'—so the inscription on it ran. In that relationship Bettenham was by far the elder, already a student of the Inn when Bacon was in the cradle. Perhaps the younger man, toiling with such restless assiduity at the foundations of the career in which he was to raise himself to the Woolsack as Lord High Chancellor and to the peerage as Baron Verulam and Viscount St. Albans, found in Bettenham a repose deeper than the promptings of his own ambition. 'Knowing myself by inward calling fitter to hold a book than play a part, I have led my life in civil causes for which I was not very fit by nature and more unfit by preoccupation of my mind', he confessed. Not so Bettenham, well content, as the records of the Society attest, to be 'a diligent keeper of learning in the House' and 'no great gainer by the law'. He used to say 'that riches were like muck; when it lay upon a heap it gave but a stench and ill odour, but when it was spread upon the ground then it was cause of much fruit'. He said again 'that virtuous men were like some herbs and spices, that give not their sweet smell till they be broken and crushed'. Bacon remembered and recorded these words when in failure and disgrace, he withdrew 'for quiet and the better to hold out' to the sanctuary of the Inn which he had dominated in his glory and where now his spirit could walk in the realms of the mind and his ageing feet in the familiar paths of the garden he had created.

After half a century of internal expansion Gray's Inn had reached the point of almost bursting its skin, and a single outlet in a side road was totally inadequate to its needs. In 1593 a strip of land was acquired for a new gatehouse in Holborn with an approach entering the south court just east of the Irish Rents. In the highway into which the new gate opened the signs of an expanding metropolis were everywhere apparent in the 'many fair houses builded and lodgings for gentlemen, inns for travellers and suchlike, almost (for it lacketh but little) to St. Giles in the Fields'. Gray's Inn Lane was 'furnished with fair buildings and many tenements on both sides leading to the fields' and in 1599 the Society bore the cost of paving the highway alongside its property there. All round the Inn buildings were going up — towards the City the great new timber-framed front of Staple Inn and the hall behind; across Gray's Inn Lane at the back of Furnival's Inn the mansion rebuilt by the Earl of Bath and afterwards occupied by Fulke Greville, Lord Brooke; in Chancery Lane the Cursitors' Office 'built with divers fair lodgings for gentlemen, all of brick and timber' by Sir Nicholas Bacon.

On the confines of Gray's Inn itself the scene had likewise changed. Bentley's Rents had sprung up on a site behind Fuller's Buildings, a sort of annexe to the Inn, which Richard Bentley had erected on his own ground about the middle of the sixteenth century to relieve the congestion in the lodging of the members, and a passage between Howland's Buildings and Fuller's Buildings connected it with the new south court. By the end of the century Bentley's Rents and most of the property south of the Walks had passed into the possession of Sir George Fulwood, the husband of Richard Bentley's granddaughter. Here in 1580 he built a residence known as Fulwood House, somewhat overshadowed perhaps by the magnificence of the mansion which the widow of a gentleman named Richard Allington had built next door and which, says Stow's Survey, comparing it with its neighbours, 'passeth the rest in largeness of rooms'.

Fulwood, who had a good deal to do with the Society, was admitted to it in 1589 and it was from him that the land was purchased for the making of the new gate. The transaction led indirectly to a somewhat heated controversy. At the time of the purchase a cart track turning out of Holborn beside a forge, crossing Fulwood's property and entering Gray's Inn Fields, had hitherto been the only alternative approach to the Inn and for a little while more it remained open. Then Fulwood, feeling that his land was ripe for modern development, decided to build houses on both sides of the way. The Benchers thereupon in February 1596, sensing a menace to their amenities ordered 'that a brick wall shall be made from the end of Mr. Purefey his buildings directly to Mistress Allington's mud wall', that is roughly along the line of the future south side of Field Court. Fulwood, who was gentleman usher to Lord Keeper Puckering, immediately complained to his master that a public right of way was being stopped up and the Benchers received a summons to explain their position. In the course of the ensuing correspondence they insisted that it could not be a public right of way because they had paid eight shillings a year for the use of it and when they bought the land for the new gate it had been expressly agreed that Fulwood himself might stop it up; moreover he had actually erected barriers and steps and so 'turned it from a cart and horse way to a foot way of his own authority'. However, their chief objection was that 'a wholly alley of tenements' would involve 'great nuisance to the healthful situation of our House, which is all the commodity we had to recompense the remote standing of our House out of the way for gain and practice' and also grave hindrance in the government of the Society, which unanimously wished the closing of the passage 'except, it may be, some young men that seek all ways of liberty'.

Fulwood delivered a long reply in the course of which he claimed that he had Mr. Bacon's advice for the barriers and steps but that he had now removed them. He also indignantly protested that a passage twenty feet broad and open at both ends could not justly be called an alley and that the worst of his houses would be 'very fit for a gentleman of good sort to dwell in'. They would not be 'several chambers for young men to lodge in or for ale-houses' but 'fair tenements for gentlemen with their households to inhabit'. Moreover, 'betwixt Gray's Inn and the nearest part of any of the said buildings which I intend to erect there will be a garden and orchard of about 40 foot broad replenished with trees and most assuredly can be no way noisome but very healthful unto them by reason the stables and other annoyances by them before disliked of I have now removed'. There is no record of the final issue of the dispute, the course of which was doubtless affected by the death of Puckering in April of the same year. Probably it was a compromise. In 1639 there is a record of the carpenter's account for the making of a 'new gate in Fulwood's Rents end' but that way in always remained under the control of the Society.

Still, the wall was there closing the Inn on that side and not very long afterwards another court began to rise behind it. In

1619 Thomas Page, Steward of the Society, was granted a building lease of a plot of land just west of the gate into the Fulwoods' property and on that he eventually erected a building facing east and running from their boundary to the edge of the Walks. But first some opposition from another neighbour caused a certain amount of difficulty. Robert Rich, second Earl of Warwick, now lived in Mrs. Allington's house and with it occupied a piece of the Society's property at the back of Page's plot, walled in and laid out as a garden. In deference to the representations of the Earl, who had lately been admitted a member, the Benchers agreed to a modification of the building line and in November, 1622, Page, who had by that time built up to one storey was instructed to pull down his work and start again on a slightly different site. He took the risk of ignoring the order and hastily completed a block three storeys high above the ground floor with two staircases and a covered passage running through it from front to back, one window's breadth from the Walks. In the following June the Benchers not only accepted the accomplished fact but granted him some more ground between the building and the gate to Fulwood's land, to erect shops, for little shops sprang up in many odd corners of the Inn, a barber's here, a sempster's or a spectacle maker's there, and, under the new gateway into Holborn, a scrivener's.

Page's building was of brick and the rosy glow of brickwork was just beginning to spread itself all over the Inn. In February, 1604, after a fire on the west side of the north court had called forth the usual levée en masse of helpful neighbours from as far afield as Newgate Street with buckets for water and ropes and hooked poles to pull apart the timber-framed buildings involved or endangered, the members who had lost their chambers were given leave to 'build them anew to their own liking so as they perform the first storey of brick'. In 1626 Ralph Cowper, a Bencher of five years' standing, was granted the old chambers north of the ancient gatehouse 'to be by him new builded with brick' and from 1628 onwards Sir Richard Osbaldestone, King's Attorney for Ireland and one of the Benchers, was busy planning and erecting a long continous range of chambers with a low cloister and three staircases, starting from the other side of the gate and running behind the east end of the Chapel into the south court. The undertaking marked the start of the planned architectural development of the Inn, for 'to the end that henceforth no disorderly building may be,' it was ordered that 'an able and sufficient architect' should be retained 'not only for building the said intended building but likewise to make a module of all the House how the same shall be hereafter builded'.

Apart from the grand sweep of major planning, there had to be minor adjustments. There were negotiations with the officials of the Star Chamber Office and others whose lodgings stood on the building site and who had to be assured of future accommodation, and there were unforeseen misadventures, as when the workmen on the job accidentally broke through the party wall of the Yelvertons' chambers over the gateway doing 50s. worth of damage to panelling and glass. Their clumsiness violated the sacred seclusion of the rooms where, since the start of Elizabeth's reign alone, three generations of Yelvertons had succeeded one another: Christopher, Speaker of the House of Commons and Justice of the Queen's Bench; Henry, his eldest son, successively Solicitor-General, Attorney-General and Justice of the Common Pleas, and finally another Christopher, his eldest son. In 1614 Henry, then Solicitor-General, 'in respect of the great charges bestowed upon his lodging over the gate and in respect of the long continuance of the same lodging in the ancestors of Mr. Solicitor' had been secured in its enjoyment for a fresh term of sixty years. It was his father, the elder Christopher, who, when he bade farewell to the Society in 1589, on taking upon himself the degree of serjeant-at-law, declared: 'I cannot, gentlemen, take leave of you without some grief because I have lived so long amongst you with so great liking, for, as the tree that is deeply rooted is not soon transplanted, so the course that hath been long settled is not easily altered . . . for I do acknowledge myself deeply and infinitely indebted unto this House for the singular and exceeding favours that I and mine ancestors have received in it and for the great preferments that we have attained to by it for, two hundred years ago at the least, have some of them lived here and from hence have risen to serve in honourable room, and since that time there was scant any age wherein some of us have not been of this Society and thereby grown to best place here and to good calling in the commonwealth'.

The venerable structure of their home in the Inn was to stand for some time more, a wedge of solid antiquity between the modern buildings, with Matthew Walbank, the bookseller and publisher, carrying on business within the passage of the gateway itself, and a little booth standing just outside for the widow of a former porter to support her family by selling fruit.

Nearby, the Chapel too had lately been changed, but not radically, by a measure of reconstruction carried through between 1619 and 1624 by Sir Eubule Thelwall, an energetic Welshman, in London a Master in Chancery and a Bencher of the Inn and later a Member of Parliament, and at Oxford Principal of Jesus College, where he built munificently and was revered as a second founder. The chambers over the Chapel had been and remained a problem. Though as early as 1571 all except one over the west end had been ordered to be removed because of danger to the fabric and disturbance of the services, Thelwall unfortunately reproduced the same excrescence in his own work and by 1631 the question had arisen 'whether the buildings lately built upon the Chapel be weak or not likely to stand and whether the underpropping of the said buildings will be any defacing of the buildings'.

From the middle court a narrow passage ran along the front of Osbaldestone's new buildings passing, just before it entered the south court, the end of a tiny blind alley, shut in by the south wall of the Chapel and by a cluster of buildings huddled round it, and leading to the door of the Duchy Office. This adjoined the east end of the Hall and before the age of uniformity, William Gerard, cousin to the late Master of the Rolls and Clerk to the Duchy of Lancaster, to whom it had been granted in 1593, had built a roof-top chamber above it for his son Gilbert. By 1629 Sir Gilbert Gerard, baronet, as he now was, had yielded his little eyrie to Doctor Sibbes, Preacher to the Society, and was engaged in substantial building operations on his own account. Sir Thomas Denny, lately Treasurer, was reconstructing the chambers along the south side of the little alley, widening it by pushing the building line two feet further back, while west of his site and south of the Duchy Office, Gerard was closing its south-west corner with a building of his own. Both worked subject to the stipulation that they were not to darken the two great windows then lighting the Chapel from that side.

All over the Inn the ordered encroachments of bricks and mortar were consolidating their conquest. At the southern extremity of the great irregular huddle of buildings west of the Hall, Humphrey Davenport, another Bencher, was demolishing old chambers and reconstructing them in the new style, while, in the south court, perhaps the most picturesque if not the most substantial of the Elizabethan buildings were about to fall to the housebreaker, the 'hanging buildings' built on the site where the mud wall had been so 'noisesomely used' as to offend the susceptibilities of Stanhope. His ghost had been laid in the Panyerman's Close but it kept appearing in other corners of the Inn. His buildings in the north court had developed flaws as early as 1610 when the occupants of the chambers at the west end complained that, 'being weakly built and much decayed', they would fall down unless a supporting structure were added to buttress them. A dozen years later more reconstruction work had to be done in that quarter by Thelwall. As for the kitchen drain in the south court, which Stanhope was supposed to have covered up at the Society's expense in 1578, it was still a nuisance to be dealt with in 1631. Neither had the 'hanging buildings' been wholly satisfactory. Perhaps their overhanging storeys projected too boldly in defiance of the law of gravity. At all events, in 1607 it was ordered 'that the gentlemen of the hanging buildings shall support their several chambers, now ready to fall, with fair, sufficient and seemly pillars well and artificially and uniformly wrought without disgrace or unseemliness in show to the court wherein they are'. In 1632 Richard Higgons, a Bencher, demolished them and in the following year the lines of his new building were laid down to conform to a scheme for a regular range of chambers along the south side of the court with a gallery or cloister beneath. Next year he was joint Treasurer with Sir John Bankes and under them the whole court was gravelled and properly drained with cobbled gutters.

Although the early Stuart Inn has long since joined the

Elizabethan Inn and the mediaeval Inn deep in the ghostly realm of oblivion, its bone structure laid out on the map directly suggests its kinship with the Georgian Inn that came after, and, by the middle of the seventeenth century, Coney Court in the north, Holborn Court in the south, Middle Court between, and the Steward's Court to the west started to assume the lineaments of a familiar face.

2

Life with the Lawyers

LIFE within Gray's Inn, while the system which created it was still
active and vigorous, not yet changed and remoulded to fit the
fashions of an altered way of life in an altered social scene, was
an intimate and spontaneous blend of the scholastic and the
professional, autonomous and self-contained, yet a living and
essential part of the whole outer world of legal practice and the
administration of justice. The newly admitted member qualified
first as an inner-barrister and then as an utter-barrister; the
utter-barrister was called to the Grand Company of Ancients;
the Ancient served in the office of a Reader and so joined the
ranks of the Benchers. At each stage his professional ability and
his personal qualities were rigorously proved by the judgment of
his fellows, and the obligation to learn from his seniors merged,
as he advanced, with an equally peremptory obligation to instruct
his juniors. Below the Inns of Court in the legal hierarchy were
the Inns of Chancery, subordinate and preparatory, where the
chief study was to become familiar with the form of the writs
and other documents issued from the King's Chancery. Above
them were the Serjeants' Inns, the abodes of the ancient order of
the coif, the servientes ad legem summoned by the King to serve in
the superior obligations of the law—final apotheosis of the accomplished advocates—from whose ranks alone the common law
judges could be chosen.

In constitution the lesser Inns of Chancery were microcosms
of the greater Inns of Court. Thus Staple Inn, ruled by its Principal
presiding over the Ancients or Grandfellows, reflected the same
pattern as Gray's Inn, where the titular head was called the
Treasurer, the governing body Benchers and their meetings

'pensions', because pension meant in its Latin derivation 'expenditure', the regulation of which was their primary business. In 1577 it was ordered 'that a good and substantial chest shall be bought ... to remain in the pension house with two locks for the keeping of the books of account and pension rolls and the books of orders taken in pension.' The same meaning crops up again in the title of the Pensioner, in Gray's Inn one of the Ancients chosen to supervise the routine administration of payments and receipts. In the sixteen-thirties the office was gradually fused with that of the Under-Treasurer, which was finally put on a permanent footing in 1685, the holder of the office being a member of the Society and quite distinct from the Steward.

Maitland has described the manner of men who made and carried on the Inns: 'These lawyers are worldly men, not men of sterile caste – they marry and found families, some of which become as noble as any in the land; they are in their way learned, cultivated men, linguists, logicians, tenacious disputants, true lovers of the nice case and the moot point. They are gregarious, clubbable men, grouping themselves in *hospices*, which become schools of law, multiplying manuscripts, arguing, learning and teaching, the great mediators between life and logic, a reasoning, reasonable element in the British nation'.

John Stow in his Survey of Elizabethan London gives a concise account of the system of the Inns. 'The Houses of Court be replenished partly with young students and partly with graduates and practisers of the law; but the Inns of Chancery being, as it were, provinces severally subjected to the Inns of Court, be chiefly furnished with officers, attorneys, solicitors and clerks, that follow the Courts of King's Bench or Common Pleas, and yet there want not some others being young students, that come thither sometimes from one of the universities and sometimes immediately from grammar schools, and these having spent some time in studying upon the first elements and grounds of the law, and having performed the exercises of their own Houses (called bolts, moots, and putting of cases) they proceed to be admitted and become students in some of these four Houses or Inns of Court, where continuing by the space of seven years or thereabouts, they frequent Readings, mootings, boltings and other learned exercises, whereby, growing ripe in the knowledge of the laws and approved withal to be of honest conversation, they are either by the general consent of the Benchers or Readers, being the most grave and judicial men in every Inn of Court, or by the special privilege of the present Reader there, elected and called to the degree of utter-barrister'.

The orders promulgated by the judges in 1596 for the government of the Inns of Court add precision to the picture of their internal arrangements. They are essentially collegiate institutions and accordingly none must be admitted till a chamber is available for him; meanwhile he is to remain at an Inn of Chancery. Nevertheless some members continue to lodge outside in the neighbourhood. None must be called to the Bar unless he be 'of at least seven years continuance and have kept his exercises within the House and abroad in the Inns of Chancery'. No more than four are to be called each year in any Inn of Court 'two in Easter Term and two in Michaelmas Term where by the order of House the Benchers call barristers and, where the Reader by order of the House do call, then only two by the Summer Reader in his Reading and two by the Lent Reader in his Reading'. Those called must be 'fittest for their learning and honest conversation and well given'. Similarly the Readers must 'be chosen for their learning and their duly keeping the exercises of their House, for their honest behaviour and good disposition and such as for their experience and practice be able to serve the commonweal'. The Reader must continue his Reading for three weeks and must read at least thrice a week. The lavish hospitality expected of him by custom and immemorial tradition is a heavy burden to his office and will long continue so, both in the entertainment of those he invites to his own table in the Hall and in the provision of special extra dishes or 'exceedings' for the others. Official discouragement is constantly seeking to abate the extravagance and now it is laid down that he may invite but few to his table and those the Ancients attending his Reading; on Sundays he may entertain a few strangers, provided 'excess of diet be not used'. He may have not more than eight serving men to wait on him or fewer if he chooses. Benchers and barristers are bound to assist him and the obligation may be enforced by penalties and forfeitures; if he is not properly assisted 'then such by whose default that defect groweth shall be removed both from the Bench and Bar'. Double Readings, when a former Reader is called upon to read again, 'shall be strictly observed . . . according to the ancient orders of every House'. Benchers are occasionally elected without having read; they must be 'fittest both for their learning, practice and good and honest conversation' and these direct calls to the Bench are to be 'very sparingly' made. Fresh regulations appear from time to time. In the first year of James I it is directed that none shall be admitted to the Inns of Court 'unless he be a gentleman by descent'. In 1631 the period of preparation for call to the Bar is extended to eight years but practice is permitted within three years of call instead of five.

The professional discipline to which the young student had to submit himself, rigorously selective in all the Inns of Court, was most severe of all at Gray's Inn. Its prestige, illuminated by the eminence and power of the men who directed its fortunes or had risen from its ranks to authority in the State, steadily expanded its membership throughout the reign of Elizabeth, to exceed by far that of any of its sister Societies. In the later part of the reign the new student would find himself one of about three hundred fellows mostly lodging within the House and eating together in the common hall. If he had come from Barnard's Inn or Staple Inn, the Inns of Chancery subordinate to Gray's Inn, he might claim admission at a reduced fee, taking his place in Hall at the clerks' mess and waiting on the rest of the company, as sizars did at the universities. Otherwise he paid the full fee and joined the masters' mess.

The probation before him was long as well as arduous and call to the Bar represented only the start of the final preliminary to practice. The inner-barrister or junior student became an utter or outer barrister but even after he was sworn in open Hall he was still no more than a learner. So it was ordered in June, 1580, 'that none shall come to any bar at Westminster to plead or set his name to any plea unless he hath been allowed an utter-barrister by the space of five years before and continued that time in exercise of learning or read in an Inn of Chancery by the space of two years before at the least'. There was then no conception of reading for the Bar in the sense of book learning sucked in from a printed page and thrown up again in a written examination. Learning came more by the ears than by the eyes and was proved not pen in hand but by word of mouth. In the beginning was the word. The training was essentially practical in that it was achieved by actual practice. It was education by personal emulation.

Of the two central features of the system, Readings and moots, the manner of both has been left on record. The two 'learning vacations' in which the Readings were delivered began on the first Monday in Lent and the first Monday following Lammas, the first day of August. The previous Sunday the Reader went in state attended by liveried servants to hear a sermon at Paul's Cross, and on the appointed day, about eight o'clock in the morning he came into the Hall, where the whole company were assembled, there to 'read some one such Act or statute as shall please him to ground his whole Reading on for all that vacation, and that done, shall declare such inconveniences and mischiefs as were unprovided for and now by the same statute be redressed, and then reciteth certain doubts and questions which he hath devised that may grow upon the statute, and declareth his judgment therein. That done, one of the younger utter-barristers rehearseth one question propounded by the Reader and doth by the way of argument labour to prove the Reader's opinion to be against the law, and after him the rest of the utter-barristers and Readers, one after another in their ancienties, do declare their opinions and judgment in the same, and then the Reader who did put the case endeavoureth himself to confute the objections laid against him and to confirm his own opinion, after whom the Judges and Serjeants, if any be present declare their opinions . . . and this manner of Readings and disputations continueth daily two hours or thereabouts'. This was but a reflection of what went on in the courts in Westminister Hall. Hear Bolland in his *Manual of Year Book Studies:* '. . . the Justices intervene occasionally to give a ruling, . . . to tell a story, . . . to quote the Bible, the classics or a continental brocard. And the Serjeants are quite as ready tongued.

They all have the resources of the highest culture of the Middle Age to draw upon and in that Hall . . . the most highly cultured life of the Middle Age is finding its fullest expression in argument and repartee, in illustration and criticism, in apt quotation, in gibe and sarcasm . . . '.

The utter-barristers took their name from their place at the moots argued in Hall, outermost on the students' form, which was called the bar. The manner of mooting in Tudor times has likewise been clearly recorded. The Reader with two Benchers would enter the Hall every evening after supper during the Reading, coming first to the central table called the cupboard. Then 'one of the utter-barristers propoundeth unto them some doubtful case the which every of the Benchers in their anciencies argue and last of all he that moveth: this done, the Readers and Bench sit down on the bench in the end of the Hall whereof they take their name and on a form toward the middle of the Hall sitteth down two inner-barristers and of the other side of them on the same form two utter-barristers. And the inner-barristers do in French openly declare unto the Benchers (even as the serjeants do at the bar of the King's Courts to the judges) some kind of action, the one being as it were retained with the plaintiff in the action and the other with the defendant, after which things done, the utter-barristers argue such questions as be disputable within the case (as there must be always one at the least) and this ended, the Benchers do likewise declare their opinions how they think the law to be in the same questions, and this manner of exercise of mooting is daily used during the said vacations'.

Outside the period of the Readings, moots were carried on with penalties for default, as a regular routine, some in the Hall, others for the junior students in the library where the Ancients and utter-barristers presided. There were also the less formal 'bolts' or putting of cases. Orders regulating these exercises, which had to be properly performed before call, constantly recur in the records of Gray's Inn. Thus in January, 1570, it is ordered 'that from henceforth in Hilary, Easter and Midsummer Term the moots shall be kept three days in each week viz. Monday, Tuesday and Thursday . . . and that the cause be always assigned upon Sunday after supper; and that upon the other days not appointed for the mooting it shall be lawful for the utter-barristers to keep bolts and when they shall sit other students shall be bound to put cases, according as hath been a custom in Michaelmas Term'.

It reads solemnly enough but cheerfulness would keep breaking in and the occasions tended to become convivial. At any rate in June, 1613, it was found necessary to order that 'whereas banquets and suppers are given to excessive charge in respect of and for moots in the term and vacation times, from henceforth no suppers banquets or charges shall be made or spent for or in respect of any' under penalty of £5. There was no decorous hushed lecture-room atmosphere about these moots; one suspects that they were treated in some ways rather as sporting events. Certainly at one time it was deemed necessary to order that no member of the Society should make any rude noise in Hall at exercises.

It was chiefly through the educational system that the Inns of Chancery were linked with the particular Inn of Court to which they were appurtenant. Thus both Staple Inn and Barnard's Inn looked for their Readers to Gray's Inn, each having a choice of three utter-barristers put forward by the Benchers who, if the Principal and Ancients failed to make a selection, themselves proceeded to an appointment. The utter-barrister so called upon was under a duty to act unless formally excused on adequate grounds. As Reader he took precedence over the Principal but had no jurisdiction over internal discipline. His duties as defined in 1579 were 'to keep the Readings and moots according to the ancient orders heretofore therein used, that is to say, in the term time to read the Tuesday and the Thursday and to keep the moots on the Wednesday and Friday and in the Reading times their grand moots and their afternoon moots according to the ancient customs'. He could count on the assistance of junior members of his own Inn, since to have 'gone abroad to grand moots six times' was one of the qualifications for call to the Bar.

The restrictions imposed on the number of calls involved such serious delay, even for those who had duly performed their exercises and paid their dues to the Society, that it was a standing temptation to relax or evade them and observance oscillated between severity and indulgence. Thus, while at Gray's Inn at first it was the Reader who usually selected the names for call, other calls were made by the authority of the Benchers, though not indiscriminately. In 1629 it was ordered that calling to the Bar should be by Pension only and not by the Reader, but the practice in the matter did not remain fixed and settled. At Gray's Inn at any rate, despite the Judges' regulations of 1596, four calls at a Reading rather than two seems to have been normal. Indeed, in June 1608 there was an express order made 'that no Reader hereafter shall call above four utter-barristers at his Reading and if any shall call hereafter more utter-barristers than four he shall pay for every of them which he shall call above four forty pounds apiece'. Soon afterwards there was a melancholy sequel, for Henry Fleetwood, the Reader in the following Lent, having exceeded the prescribed number by three, it was discovered that each of the additional men had entered into a bond to indemnify him in respect of the fine thereby incurred. The Benchers reacted indignantly cancelling the bonds in open Hall, revoking the calls and expelling the guilty trio from the Society in a cloud of obloquy, 'because they have dared insolently and corruptly . . . to lay so great a scandal upon the House as if the Bar should be bought for money'. Having spent their wrath on the inferior offenders, they were able to deal more leniently with Fleetwood, who was first fined £120 and put out of commons and then six months later readmitted on payment of £10.

After call, but not immediately, came public practice and in the space of about ten years' time the maturing advocate, growing ripe for the office of Reader, was called to the Grand Company of Ancients, perhaps with a batch of some thirty of his contemporaries. Some reached it by a shorter road than seniority, the sons of judges for example and persons of distinction placed in the Inns of Court, as Fortescue said, 'not so much to make the laws their study, much less to live by the profession, having large patrimonies of their own, but to form their manners and preserve them from the contagion of vice.'

Serving the office of Reader, the normal condition precedent to attaining the status of Bencher, at once an honour and an onerous duty, was coveted by some and evaded by others according to temperament. In June, 1596, Christopher Molyneux sought and was refused it because he was 'not sufficiently learned in the laws', because of 'his want of discretion' and because he was 'not sociable, by reason whereof many of his fellows . . . have found themselves greatly discontented'. His rejection is the more remarkable because in that very month the Society had experienced unusual difficulty in finding a Reader. 'Mr. Walton . . . having shown cause why he could not read at this time' was excused. Mr. Vernon called upon instead 'certified that by reason of great infirmity and sickness' he could not read either. 'Mr. William Gerard although it be known that he is and hath been a long time very sickly, yet in respect of his worthiness and reputation' was called in to fill the gap, 'if it shall please him to accept thereof, the which is not doubted if his health will serve him'. But he too failed in the crisis and at last a Reader was found in Francis Bracken. Ill-health was a favourite excuse with those who wished to avoid their Reading. Refusal without due cause attracted a fine of anything up to £50.

So in his Reading the Ancient was translated to the Bench of the Society. 'The hour glass of my puisne time is run', began Robert Callis in 1622, 'and I am now come to take possession of your Reader's place. . . . These six and twenty years complete I have had continuance here . . . and herein I acknowledge Gray's Inn to be the best patron of my fortunes and yourselves the best companions of my forepast and present life.' He had questioned, he said, whether he should decline but, putting charge and care in one scale and resolution in the other, he undertook that burdensome place for the maintenance and preservation of the honour of the House.

It was small wonder that some did shrink from the ordeal. The sustained intellectual effort of subtlety in disputation before an audience which spent all its time sharpening its wits in the same sort of argumentation, was matched by the financial strain of a munificent hospitality which all the official discouragement in the world could not keep within bounds, when sociable impulses and gargantuan appetites set the standards for the public opinion of the table. So in a blaze of erudition and a glow of conviviality the new Reader left his old companions. Hence-forth, wearing a gown with a velvet welt at the back in Hall and in the Courts, he was set apart from the rest of the Society, taking his place as the junior in that small circle of little more than a dozen men in whom lay the direction of the fortunes of the Inn.

For the ordinary member life was cheerful in Gray's Inn, and indeed in all the other Societies, so cheerful that there was constant danger of club life superseding study and in 1630 the judges had to lay down explicitly that they 'were ordained chiefly for the profession of the law and in a second degree for the education of the sons and youth of riper years of the nobility and gentry of this realm and in no sort for the lodging and abode of gentlemen of the country, which if it should be suffered would be a disparaging of the said Societies and turn them from Hospitia into Diversoria'.

The great panelled Hall was the heart of the common life of Gray's Inn, at once refectory and lecture room, centre of ceremony and recreation and symbol of the continuing tradition of the men who made it. The huge gallery of Spanish chestnut, intricately carved, filled the lower end, like the poop of some vast galleon. From the hearth in the centre of the rush-strewn floor the smoke of the fire rose curling through the high dark beams and out by the louver far overhead. Above the small Tudor panels of the wainscot the coats of arms in the rich windows wrote a whole history of achievement in colour and light. There the members met daily for breakfast, dinner in the early afternoon and supper, for they might not eat in their chambers. The fare was ordinarily plain, mutton or beef, roast or boiled, bread and cheese, with oysters not regarded as a luxury, while the usual drinking was claret and beer. Festivals brought varieties, like eggs and green sauce on Easter Day, and at Reading times there would be special delicacies provided at the Reader's expense, venison perhaps, or salmon. In the Lent Reading in 1633 the chief cook lost his place for spoiling the salmon 'by putting the same in a stinking tub in sowce'.

The table appointments, as set out in an inventory of 1580, were unostentatious to the extreme limit of simplicity. A heterogeneous collection of pewter platters and dishes provided for basic requirements. Most of the candlesticks were pewter —a few were brass—and so were sixteen of the salt cellars. Two more were of silver and, apart from these, there seems to have been no other silver but a dozen spoons. The seven table cloths for the upper tables and twelve for the rest, ranging from the finest Holland for the Benchers down to whitened canvas for the least privileged, and the three dozen and three table napkins hardly seem excessive. In point of dress academic sobriety was enforced. The royal proclamation of 1574, enjoining a general austerity of apparel, applied, of course, to the Inn and was promulgated there. 'The monies and treasure of the realm' had been flowing far too freely abroad to purchase silks, satin, damask and cloth of gold, and their use was now stringently restricted except for buttons and facings 'for comliness only'. But apart from this the Society itself discouraged clothes 'of any light colour'. Hats, cloaks, boots, spurs, swords or daggers were barred in Hall. Gowns must be worn even in the suburbs and the fields and it was only by special dispensation that Francis Bacon as Solicitor-General and Sir Roger Wilbraham as Master of Requests were excused from wearing formal caps at table. In Hall there were occasional lapses from good manners to censure. Impatient self-service at the dresser had to be restrained and members were forbidden to 'take meat by strong hand from such as shall serve them'.

If the temporal life of the Inn centred round the Hall, the Chapel stood for the regulation of its spiritual affairs. Due attendance, prescribed by constantly reiterated orders, was the test of conformity to the Church by law established. Members 'shall resort to the lecture every Sabbath day' under pain of a fine. They 'shall receive the Communion in the Chapel of this House every term in the year once', under increasing penalties for each default—fine, suspension, loss of chamber and finally expulsion. 'The gardener in time of divine service is not to suffer any gentleman of the House or others to be in the Walks but to keep the door shut during that time'. From Elizabeth to Charles I these regulations were not relaxed and with other matters of discipline they came primarily within the purview of the Bencher appointed Dean of the Chapel. Apart from major points of doctrine, there were lesser points of good manners and etiquette to supervise. As in Hall, boots, cloaks and hats were forbidden. Members must take their places in the pews on either side of the Communion table and in the body of the Chapel in strict order of seniority — Benchers, Ancients, utter-barristers and others. Strangers might only come in by invitation and women and boys not at all. At the western end there was one gallery and after 1631 another in the south-east corner, which the Earl of Warwick was allowed to erect for himself and his friends, so as to be near the pulpit 'for the better hearing of the sermon'. So within the ancient walls, unchanged in essentials by Thelwall's structural alternations and the simplification of the furnishing under Elizabeth, the Society gathered for the worship and doctrine of the new England, coming in from the Middle Court by the two old rounded doors and sitting beneath the same great windows which had lighted the devotions of their ancestors.

The appointments of the chambers, designed as they were for sleep and study only, were no more elaborate than those of the Hall. A letter from one of the Rigby family, which had a long tradition of membership in the Society and occupied chambers in Seckford's Buildings just west of the Hall, gives some notion of the furnishings and interiors round about 1622: 'The covers of the windows in the inner chamber, all the forms in both chambers and studies, the little thick table removable and the bedstead in the study are not to follow the chamber; but, the great bedstead in the inner chamber and the great table belong to the chamber, as also the cover of both the study windows. The writing-desk ought not to go with the chamber, for I had it from my father and I know not how he came unto it'.

If you lived simply enough, even so large an establishment could be run without a very elaborate staff. The number of servants fluctuated from time to time but in the reign of James I there were the steward and his assistant, the panyerman, primarily concerned with the marketing, the master butler and three junior butlers, and in the kitchen a chief cook, a second cook, a washpot and a couple of turnbroaches. The steward and the chief butler were both officers of responsibility and importance and might be members of the Inn. Thus Sir William Segar, Garter King-of-Arms, admitted in 1618, had a son Thomas, admitted in 1638, who became steward in 1658, while Simon, son of Thomas, admitted in 1655, was second butler in 1677, chief butler two years later and also library keeper. The steward and the chief butler with the chief cook to keep them company stood on a markedly higher level than their subordinates, so that in 1612 when it was ordered that 'none of the servants of the Society then unmarried . . . shall continue his place longer than he shall live sole and unmarried', those three were excepted. First in the hierarchy of the celibates were the junior butlers. About this time the office of fueller, formerly discharged by a Bencher, fell to one of them. Literacy became indispensable and in 1639 it was ordered 'that no man be admitted to any of the butler's places hereafter unless he be a sufficient clerk to write and read'. In an outer orbit the porter and gardener performed their respective functions. Besides his strictly vocational duties the gardener had to keep 'boys, girls, rude and beggarly people' out of the Walks and see that nobody dried clothes on the rails and hedges of the bowling green, while the porters besides having charge of the gates and excluding 'beggars, boys and dogs' had to keep 'clerks, strangers, laundresses, mechanics, boys and girls' out of the Hall and buttery at meal times and during moots.

Besides these fixed retainers there was a motley assortment of casual helpers and hangers-on (sometimes swollen to inordinate numbers), the personal servants that the Benchers and some few privileged Ancients were allowed to keep in commons, and the ancient and honourable sisterhood of laundresses, already engaged in doing charwomen's work for the individual members. Ancient it was meet that they should be, for in 1581 it was prudently laid down that they must not come into the gentlemen's chambers until they were over forty nor send in their maids of whatever age they might be. There were odd jobs about the Inn which the Society itself entrusted to outsiders. The Hall table-cloths were washed under a yearly agreement by one of the laundresses. The cleaning of the courts was done by special arrangement. Thus in 1571 it was ordered 'that for making clean the sinks, the channels, the gutters, the Hall and the privy, there

is allowed Robin Dogstayle alias Holden per annum 26s 8d.'
Similarly when in 1585 it was decided that 'the nethermost court
of Gray's Inn' was to be 'handsomely kept with gravelled walks
round about it and a cross walk through the midst both ways
and the four quarters set about with privit borders and con-
tinually kept in good order', Richard Brooks, a labourer of Gray's
Inn Lane, was put in charge of the work and it was directed
'that no gentlemen of the House shall suffer their servants or
laundresses to throw or lay oyster shells or any other filthiness
out of the chambers into the said court upon pain to be put out
of commons' if Brooks complained.

For the gentlemen of the Society the regular disciplinary
sanction was to be temporarily put out of commons or suspended.
For the servants there were the stocks. An order of 1579 marks
the difference. 'If any fellow or companion of the House shall
from henceforth cast or lay any excrements or other filth at or
near the new rails of late made in Gray's Inn Field he shall for
every such fact be put out of commons . . . and if any laundress
. . . shall lay or cast thereon any urine, rushes, dust or other
filth . . . he out of whose chamber the same was brought thither
shall forfeit for every such offence 6s. 8d. . . . and if any servant
to any companion of this House shall therein offend he shall be
put to the stocks in or near the same place and there shall
continue by the space of three whole hours'. For the incorrigible
among the members the last resort reluctantly invoked was
expulsion from the Society. James Necton, for example, had a
chamber in the Inn but failed to keep commons in Hall for two
years together, was twice summoned before the Benchers and
refused to appear, saying he 'would come to one of their chambers
but not otherwise, as is testified by one of the butlers who
warned him'. There was nothing else for it. In 1601 he was
expelled and his chamber seized.

Financially the Society had few resources and led a rather
precarious hand to mouth existence in dependence on the dues
payable by the members but generally in arrears. One of the
earliest entries in the extant Pension Books is an ultimatum to
George Gascoigne, poet, dramatist, precursor of the English
novel, soldier, adventurer, the brilliant, erratic, extravagant

descendant of the great Chief Justice, that unless he pays his debts to the Society he will be 'put out of the fellowship'. But the Benchers are indulgent. One member pleads sickness and his debt is forgiven; another that he has been on Her Majesty's service as Sheriff of Shropshire and his is reduced. Towards the end of the Queen's reign the situation becomes acute. 1597 twenty-one members are warned by name to pay their dues within a fortnight under pain of expulsion. In 1599 it is decided that 'as divers of the gentlemen of this House, as well as ancients, utter-barristers as others, are indebted unto this House . . . by reason whereof the brewer and baker and others . . . are unpaid and some of the officers of this House to whom they have given credit are like to be greatly impoverished to the great discredit of the whole Society', members must enter into bonds with two sureties for payment of their debts. Next year six Ancients and utter-barristers having failed in due payment are 'utterly disgraded from their ancienties' or 'disabled to be called to the degree of ancients'. Finally in 1614 the Society adopts the simple device of requiring members on admission to enter into a bond of ten pounds for payment of their dues.

Besides money difficulties, there are other troubles great and small. In George Yard, east of the Holborn entranceway and parallel to it, there is an offensive sink, a nuisance to the chambers in the south court. A neighbouring tavern in Gray's Inn Lane permits 'disordered persons to remain and continue tippling . . . at unreasonable hours of the night' and one of the chambers gets its windows broken. In the jumble of rambling buildings round the unlit, tree-shaded courts there are sometimes burglaries and even murders. In 1598 Richard Anger, Treasurer for the third time and one of the wealthiest members of the Inn, is strangled in his chambers and his body is found a month later in the Thames. Richard, one of his sons, is hanged for the crime. The 'sad accident' which the Pension Books record in 1651, in laying down more stringent regulations for the closing of the gates and the patrolling of the Inn, is in plain terms the murder of Thomas Tisdale, the Under-Treasurer, in his chamber. Two men and a woman are eventually brought to trial and execution for the crime and in 1656 the zeal which a member of the Society has devoted to that end is noted and recompensed by a letter recommending him as fit to practise at the Bar in Ireland.

Wider calamities likewise cast shadows over the Inn. The recurrent outbreaks of the plague which sweep the City may break the rhythm of the Society's life, driving the members for safety to Hertford or St. Albans. In 1595, a year of great dearth and scarcity, the price of eggs soars to a penny each and of fresh butter to seven pence a pound 'and so the like of fish and flesh exceeding measure in price, such were our sins deserving it', and the Society steeled itself for strict economy. The poor, of course, were always there. To them, by ancient custom, went what was left over from the meals in Hall and in addition thrice a week alms were distributed at the gate in Gray's Inn Lane, with special consideration for 'the poorer sort of aged and impotent persons'.

The Society's contacts with the other Inns were, of course, most intimate with Staple Inn and Barnard's Inn, with which its relation was a mixture of trusteeship and educational supervision. It interfered little with internal discipline but in 1596 when the Principal of Staple Inn, supported by his Ancients, finding himself in conflict with the butler there, guilty of 'divers great misdeameanours' but backed by the 'unruly youths' among the members who wished 'to live without governance', dismissed the butler, some of the Benchers of Gray's Inn intervened in the quarrel and dismissed the Principal. The dispute went up to Lord Keeper Egerton and, though the Principal was ultimately reinstated, the jurisdiction of the Benchers was apparently made good.

Since the start of the 16th century there had been no night affrays with swords and cudgels between the students of Gray's Inn and Lincoln's Inn, its nearest neighbour, and with the Inner Temple Gray's Inn maintained an 'ancient amity, familiarity and friendship'. Aloof above them all reigned the Serjeants' Inns, the one at the foot of Chancery Lane and the other in Fleet Street by the Inner Temple, abodes of the Judges of the Common Law Courts and of their fellow serjeants still at the Bar whom they addressed as 'Brother'.

The summons to the immemorial order of the coif was final

and insistent as that of death itself. He who assumed it died to
his Inn of Court and for him its bell tolled as at a passing. The
group of new serjeants entered upon their state with robes and
ritual, with gold rings and gowns and liveries bestowed by them
broadcast and ceremonial gloves received, with a mighty slaughter
of deer and oxen and sheep and pigs and capons and pullets and
pigeons and swans and larks and pikes. At Ely House or Lambeth
Palace or one of the Inns of Court the highest in the Kingdom
and all the world of the law gathered to honour them in the
smoke of a great feasting which might last for a week together.
Thus in 1552 the feast was held at Gray's Inn. At the high table
sat the Lord Chancellor and members of the nobility; at the next
the Lord Mayor, aldermen and sheriffs, at the next the judges and
senior serjeants; at the next the newly created serjeants, two and
two. There were served 'ten dishes to the first course and eight to
the last course and after wafers and ipocras'.

At the heart of the great transition was the personal leave
taking between the departing serjeant and his former fellows.
For all who so left Gray's Inn, let Sir John Finch speak at his
farewell in the Hall when he assumed the coif in 1634 and took
the way that led him to the Chief Justiceship of the Common
Pleas, the office of Lord Keeper and a place in the House of
Peers: 'This is the first time that ever I did with unwillingness
appear in this place to direct my speech to you. Now, methinks,
all my words . . . have so many wings to carry me from hence,
where I have lived above half the age of a man and . . . I had
here ended my days, where I had ever the most comfort in
spending of them, but I have heard a voice from above. . . . The
sweet harmony between all the worthy members of this honourable Society has been the music that to me was ever most pleasing.
. . . I may truly say and I say it with much joy of heart, all the
other Inns of Court are not able to meet you on equal terms in
the lists of honour'.

3

Masques and Revels

T HE story of the beginnings of any one of the four Inns of Court
would be only half told were nothing said of that side of their
life which blossomed into masques and revels but, so far have we
drifted from the mood and spirit which created them, that the
modern mind is as ill-equipped to apprehend them as blind men
to visualise an elephant. An author who has written learnedly and
usefully on the subject has observed rather stiffly that the
spectacular settings and magnificent costumes displayed even in
the strictly professional ceremonials of the Readings 'show clearly
the fondness of the four Houses for the histrionic', a meiosis as
remarkable as if one said that St. Lawrence on the gridiron
evinced strong religious convictions. The reality may be better
understood in the fundamental difference between any mediaeval
miracle play and any modern 'super spectacle'. It is just that one
was a family party and the other only a public performance,
that the audience which was part and parcel of the one is separate
and apart from the other, a chance gathering of outside spectators
of a theatrical conjuring trick. If the schoolboy smiles at the
notion of the Elizabethan gallants watching Shakespeare's plays
from the stage, it is because he takes for granted a black line
dividing players and public, lest drab reality intrude on glamorous
illusion. But a truer picture of the early theatre and especially
of masques and revels like those at Gray's Inn would reverse the
image, rather as if the prince and princess, the fairy queen and
the demon king, Harlequin and Columbine and Clown were to
leap the footlights and sweep the audience into their own world
in one vast transformation scene, itself a scene within a scene,
since the world of the masque was itself a microcosm or reflection

39

of the whole of society. The mood of that society was, as it has never been since, the mood of the artist, moulding and colouring everything it touched in a direct living contact with persons and things apprehended through the five senses, a contact not yet refined and sophisticated by the man of taste or deflected by the man of business. Nor had the man of science yet reduced meals to the chemical formulae of 'nutritional intake' or analysed into abstractions the plain and palpable realities of earth, air, fire and water.

The creative exuberance of that mood was volcanic and its visual effect that of an eruption of all the colours of the rainbow and of all the shapes of fancy, as thick as snowflakes and as various. That spirit touched nothing that it did not adorn, shoes on the feet and ships on the sea and sealing wax on the charters, the robes of the lawyers, the vestments of the priests, the accoutrements of the fighting men, even the garments of the butcher, the baker and the candlestick maker in the high festivals of their guilds and townships. Sharply distinguished as sable and gules from argent and or, its sense of solemnity matched its sense of fun in the customs of a thousand manors and the usages of a thousand guilds, devising the mournful pageantry of funerals and the boisterous rites of the long Christmas season. Nothing human was alien to it any more than to Chaucer—religious gravity or Hogarthian grossness—and May Day and Michaelmas, All Saints and All Fools, Holy Week and Corpus Christi, the fires of St. John and the loves of St. Valentine clothed the very calendar with colour. All this implies not an assertion that all men were artists then—the Pastons, for example, would hardly qualify—and that none have been since, but that artistry was the determining factor in giving form to the social scene. Life, of course, could and did take in death, disease and poverty, war and pestilence, and the seven deadly sins are always with us; but, then, the artist as such is no more concerned to be a moral reformer than to be a gentleman or a sanitary inspector or a business executive, and the wonder of that age was, as Swift expresses it in another context in a ruthless poem, to see

> 'Such order from confusion sprung,
> Such gaudy tulips raised from dung'.

So, even above the carnage of civil strife the roses blew upon the banners as at a tournament, and the devouring plague from Asia stalked sable and sinister, like a figure in a masque, under the name of the Black Death.

When the age of the artist died and the age of the man of taste was born the transition, as in all human affairs, was gradual as the change from day to night through twilight. Yet if the world of the artist withered in England, it was because Henry VIII had cut the tap-root. Professor Chambers has recalled the riches of architecture and craftsmanship which at the start of his reign amazed foreign travellers even from Italy and has noted how by his 'deliberate destruction of most of the works of art existing in England, all English arts and crafts were arrested, some (the beautiful art of coloured tiles for example) were quite destroyed'. Again: 'When Henry came to the throne every Englishman, even the poorest, had many chances of seeing masterpieces of craftsmanship and, if he was a craftsman, of learning from them. When Henry died most of these things had been destroyed and the possibility of rejoicing in works of art had become the perquisite of the aristocrat. . . . From Henry's revolution onwards the beauties of England are not the abbeys but the country seats of the gentry jealously surrounded by fine red brick walls'.

This has been a long parenthesis, but without it the masques and revels and ceremonies, which were an integral part of the life of all the Inns of Court and in which Gray's Inn especially excelled, would seem mere lunatic eccentricity to a generation which, accepting drabness as normal, has forgotten a whole scale of human values and a whole range of human pleasures.

The Gray's Inn masque of 1526, circumstantially recorded together with its unfortunate sequel in the offence taken by Cardinal Wolsey, was still basically a morality play of moral qualities personified. Here it is:— 'This Christmas was a good disguising played at Gray's Inn which was compiled for the most part by Master John Roo, Sergeant-at-Law, twenty years past and long before the Cardinal had any authority. The effect of the play was that Lord Governance was ruled by Dissipation and Negligence which caused Rumor Populi, Inward Grudge and Disdain of Wanton Sovreignty to rise with a great multitude to expel Negligence and Dissipation and to restore Public Wealth again to her estate, which was done. This play was so set forth with rich and costly apparel, with strange devices of masques and morrishes that it was highly praised of all men saving of the Cardinal, which imagined that the play was devised of him and in a great fury sent for the said Master Roo and took from him his coif and sent him to the Fleet and after he sent for the young gentlemen that played in the play and them highly rebuked and threatened and sent one of them called Thomas Moyle of Kent to the Fleet but by the means of friends he and Master Roo were delivered at last. This play sore displeased the Cardinal and yet it was never meant to him'. Before becoming a serjeant Roo was a member of Gray's Inn.

Here was a sad end to a merry Christmas but Christmases came round again none the less cheerful. The celebrations regularly revolved round the mock court of one of the junior members elevated to rule as sovereign for the season, and most magnificent of all was the reign of 'The most high and mighty Prince Henry, Prince of Purpoole, Archduke of Stapulia and Barnardia, Duke of High and Nether Holborn, Marquis of St. Giles's and Tottenham, Count Palatine of Bloomsbury and Clerkenwell, Great Lord of the Cantons of Islington, Kentish Town, Paddington and Knightsbridge, Knight of the Most Heroical Order of the Helmet and Sovereign of the same, who reigned and died A.D. 1594'. The part was played by an accomplished young man called Henry Helmes.

On the 20th December his reign began and he was solemnly enthroned in the Hall attended by an elaborate retinue of officers of state, ecclesiastical, legal and military: the Archbishop of St. Andrew's in Holborn, the Bishop of St. Giles in the Fields, a Lord Chancellor, a Lord Chief Justice and other Judges, a Lord Privy Seal, a Lord High Constable, a Chancellor of the Exchequer, a Cup Bearer, a Master of the Revels, a Chief Ranger, a Captain of the Guard, a Pursuivant at Arms, in brief a faithful reflection of a royal court completed by trumpeters and yeomen of the guard and townsmen in the prince's livery. His King-at-Arms in a rich surcoat proclaimed him. His Champion in full armour challenged any who disputed his title. His Attorney-General made a flattering speech. Then the homagers and tributaries were enumerated, with their tenures and services. Alphonso de Stapulia and Davillo de Barnardia held the Archdukedoms of Stapulia and Barnardia by grand serjeanty and castle guard, with the right to relieve all wants and wrongs of all ladies, matrons and maids within the archduchies. Marotto Marquerillo de Holborn held the manors of High and Nether Holborn and must render one milk-white doe for each of the Prince's pensioners. Lucy Negro, Abbess of Clerkenwell, held the nunnery of Clerkenwell and its lands of the Prince by night service in cauda and must find a choir of nuns with burning lamps to chant Placebo to the gentlemen of the Prince's privy chamber on his coronation day. Ruffiano de St. Giles's held the town of St. Giles's by cornage in cauda and must render two ambling, easy-paced jennets for the Prince's two pages of honour. So they went on down to Markasius Burticanus and Hieronymus Paludensis de Knightsbridge, who held the village of Knightsbridge by villeinage in bare tenure and must provide men to clean all channels, sinks, creeks and gutters within the cities of the Prince's dominions. A parliament was summoned. A subsidy was raised. A general pardon was issued of 'all treasons, contempts, offences, trespasses, forcible entries, intrusions, disseisins, torts, wrongs, injuries, overthrows, overthwartings, cross bitings, coney catchings, frauds, conclusions, fictions, fractions, fashions, fancies' and so on and so forth, followed by clause after clause of equally fantastic exceptions, notable among which was the exception from pardon of all persons who should have 'any occasion, chance, opportunity or possible means to entertain, serve, recreate, delight or discourse with any virtuous or honourable lady or gentlewoman, matron or maid, publicly, privately or familiarly, and shall faint, fail or be deemed to faint or fail in courage or countenance, semblance, gesture, voice, speech or attempt or in act or adventure or in any other matter, thing, manner, mystery or accomplishment, due, decent or appurtenant to her or their honour, dignity, desert, expectation, desire, affection, inclination, allowance or acceptance'. After this the Master of the Revels was summoned and all danced far into the night.

So it went on from day to day. Holy Innocents' Day saw the

arrival of the Ambassador from Templaria with his train, but the Hall was overcrowded and, confusion ensuing, the guests departed in dudgeon, so that 'it was thought not good to attempt anything of account, except dancing and revelling with gentlewomen. And after such sports a comedy of errors (like to Plautus his Menechmus) was played by the players. So that night began and continued to the end in nothing but confusion and errors; whereupon it was afterwards called the Night of Errors'. Thus casually Shakespeare and his 'Comedy of Errors' crossed the stage of Gray's Inn. The great discouragement of this mischance provided matter for the next night's entertainment in the trial under a commission of oyer and terminer of 'a certain sorcerer' charged with being its author. He in defence alleged negligence of the Prince's council and great officers of state and in the end he was freed and pardoned.

Reconciliation with the Templarians was effected early in the New Year. To the altar of the Goddess of Amity came couples representing the friendships of antiquity, Achilles and Patroclus, Pylades and Orestes, Scipio and Laelius and lastly Graius and Templarius, whose incense offered on the altar first gave out a smoke that choked the flame, but after mystical ceremonies and hymns by the Arch-Flamen and attendant nymphs, burnt brighter and more clear than that of all the rest. The Templarian Ambassador and some of his train were then invested with the insignia of the Order of the Helmet, the statutes of which were published to them. The Knights must not bear arms against the Prince; they must not be inquisitive towards any lady 'whether her beauty be English or Italian or whether with care-taking she have added half a foot to her stature'. They must not wager on 'strange returns or performances, as to hop up the stairs to the top of St. Paul's without intermission'. Returning from abroad they were not to report any extraordinary exploits as to have ridden through Venice on horseback or sailed by the Cape of Norway in December. Each was to 'endeavour to be much in the books of the worshipful citizens of the principal city next adjoining to the territories of Purpoole and none shall unlearnedly and without looking pay ready money for any wares'. No Knight walking in the streets was to 'bear his hands in the pockets of his

great rolled hose . . . if it be not either to defend his hands from
the cold or else to guard forty shillings sterling being in the same
pockets'. No Knight must pawn his collar of knighthood for a
hundred pounds. After this a Privy Council was held, rival
counsellors advocating to the Prince war, the study of philosophy,
the gaining of fame by buildings and foundations, absoluteness of
state and treasure, virtue and gracious government and finally
immediate sports and pastimes. The Prince adopted this last
counsel till he could consider the others. Next day the Grayans
and Templarians rode, magnificently arrayed, through Cheapside
and Cornhill to Crosby Place, where the Lord Mayor entertained
them sumptuously.

On Twelfth Night, Envy, Malcontent and Folly were brought
in captives, their attempts against the state of *Graya* having been
frustrated by the Goddesses Virtue and Amity. Next a stately
masque was danced and afterwards, to the sound of trumpets,
there entered an embassy from the Emperor of Russia begging the
Prince's aid against the Tartars. He was graciously received and a
banquet was served but letters now brought other tidings:
Knightsbridge was being despoiled by three foreigners Johannes
Shagbag, Robertus Untruss and James Rapax and by various
former soldiers maimed in the wars against the Amazons. There
were plots and insurrections in Stapulia, Barnardia and Low
Holborn. Graver still, the merchants of Purpoole, sailing for
Clerkenwell, Newington and Bankside had been beset in the
narrow seas by a huge armada of French Amazons. In the straits
of the Gulf of Clerkenwell a merchant of St. Giles's had had a hot
skirmish with the Admiral of the Amazons named the Rouse-
Flower, 'when the merchant, having gained the wind, came up
with her in such close manner that he broke his bowsprit in her
hinder quarter, notwithstanding which the fight continued more
than two hours, when the merchant, finding his powder spent,
was forced to grapple . . . till seeing no hope of escape she fired
her powder and burnt herself. The ship was of incomparable
burden. Her chief lading was conchinella, musk, guaiacum,
tobacco and le grand vezolle. The chief of account that were
blown up were Catherina Dardana, Pecta de Lac and Maria de
Rotulis. The rich carrick of Newington coming to the rescue of

the Admiral was so close at fight when she was fired that the flame of the wild fire caught hold of their captain's inner cabin'. The Prince gave commands to deal with these disorders, declared his intention of going himself to Russia and led off the dance which closed the revel for the time being.

Candlemas approached and on the 28th January, as the Benchers were sitting at dinner in Hall, the Prince's King-at-Arms entered to the sound of the trumpet, announcing his return by water. On the 1st February he and his train came up the river in fifteen barges with standards and streamers and music and ordnance. At Greenwich Palace he sent two gentlemen ashore with a letter to Sir Thomas Heneage for the Queen, begging her leave to wait on her at Shrovetide, and received a favourable answer that she 'liked well his gallant shows'. At the Tower the guns fired a salute for him and a hundred 'choice and great horses gallantly appointed' were ready for all his company to mount. So he rode to Gray's Inn where he was received with trumpets and the firing of a salute and so inaugurated the Candlemas revels.

At Shrovetide the Prince redeemed his promise and he and his suite presented the Masque of Proteus to the Queen—Esquire, Proteus, Thamesis, and Amphitrite blending together ancient Greek mythology and the domestic English scene. When Proteus with his trident struck the Adamantine Rock it parted and the Prince and his Knights emerged to dance 'a new devised measure'. At the end of the entertainment, when the courtiers would have continued dancing, the Queen exclaimed; 'What! shall we have bread and cheese after a banquet?' declaring that Gray's Inn was 'an House she was much beholden to for that it did always study for some sports to present unto her'. That night there was tilting at the barriers, the last echo and reflection of the mediaeval tournament. The Prince bore away the prize and the Queen presented him a jewel of rubies and diamonds.

Year by year the same elements went to make up the Christmas and Shrovetide festivals at Gray's Inn, poetry and parody, pageantry and plays, masques and music, dicing and drinking and feasting. Sometimes the Lord of Misrule went too far in enforcing his jurisdiction and a 'rag' came near to becoming a riot. Soon after the great frolic of the Prince of Purpoole an order was made that no member at Christmas should assume the title of Lord nor might he 'break open any chamber or disorderly molest or abuse any fellow or officer of this House' on pain of expulsion. 'I trust', wrote the Puritan Lady Bacon in that very year of 1594 to her son Francis, 'that they will not mum nor masque nor sinfully revel at Gray's Inn.' Vain hope! Francis, who in his *New Atlantis* adorned his college professor with jewelled gloves and peach-coloured velvet shoes and his attendants with white silk and satin and blue velvet and fine plumes, always took a leading part in organising these entertainments. These were very much domestic occasions. In 1566 Gray's Inn presented George Gascoigne's comedy of mistaken identities called *The Supposes,* a prose translation from Ariosto's verse. 'I suppose you are assembled here', says the prologue, 'supposing to reap the fruit of my travails and, to be plain, I mean presently to present you with a comedy called *Supposes,* the very name whereof may per-adventure drive into every of your heads a sundry suppose to suppose the meaning of our supposes. . . . But understand this our suppose is nothing else but the mistaking or imagination of one thing for another; for you shall see the master supposed for the servant, the servant for the master, the freeman for the slave, the bondslave for a freeman, the stranger for a well-known friend and the familiar for a stranger.' The same year Gascoigne collaborated with Francis Kinwelmarsh, another member of the Society, in a translation called *Jocasta* of a play by Euripides, presented at the Inn with an epilogue by Christopher Yelverton. In the revels of Christmastide 1587-88 Thomas Campion, the poet composer, admitted to Gray's Inn in the previous year played a part and the Prince of Purpoole, was young William Hatcliffe whom Leslie Hotson identifies as Shakespeare's 'Mr W.H.' In the same year Yelverton and Bacon helped in the production of the blank verse tragedy *The Misfortunes of Arthur* by Thomas Hughes, afterwards a Knight and a Bencher, presented before the Queen at Greenwich by the gentlemen of Gray's Inn. Contemplating such a community, well might poor Lady Bacon exclaim: 'Alas what excess of bucks at Gray's Inn! And to feast so on the Sabbath! God forgive and have mercy upon England!'

Under James I the fame of the Gray's Inn masques endured

at Court. In 1613 the Society was invited to participate in the wedding celebrations of the King's daughter Elizabeth and the Count Palatine and joined with the Inner Temple to prepare the Masque of the Marriage of the Thames and the Rhine. In a fleet of richly decorated barges and galleys they sailed for Whitehall but their joint venture was at first as unlucky as in the entertainment of 1594 on the Night of Errors, for the great Hall was so crowded that it could not be cleared for them and 'the King was so wearied and sleepy with sitting up almost two whole nights before that he had no edge to it'. Bacon begged that they should not be so disgraced and they were invited to return in four days' time. Their show opened with classic formalism presenting Iris and Mercury, sea-green nymphs, sky-coloured Hyades and flame-coloured Cupids, till Flora brought in the rustic dance of Pedant, May-Lord, May-Lady, Serving-man, Chamber-maid, Country Clown, Country Wench, Host, Hostess, He-Baboon, She-Baboon, He-Fool and She-Fool. The comic interlude over, twelve Olympic Knights in carnation satin embroidered with silver stars emerged from two golden pavilions and closed the entertainment with dancing and a farewell song by the priests attending them.

The King was so well pleased that next year during the marriage celebrations of the Earl of Somerset and the Countess of Essex Gray's Inn presented at Whitehall the famous Masque of Flowers. It followed the same pattern, a mythological opening in which Invierno or Winter, an old man covered with frost and snow and icicles, and Primavera or Spring, a nymph naked to the waist, bedecked with flowers and cloth of gold, introduced a contest in song between old Silenus, the friend of Bacchus, and his crew, upholding the transcendant power of wine, and the barbaric Kawasha and his company championing the Indian weed tobacco. When they had done, a dance of an assortment of comic characters was followed by a magical transformation scene disclosing a lovely and elaborate garden under a night sky with 'transparent lights of variable colours' and enchanted flowers which the garden goddesses, singing a charm, changed into men. In 1618 the gentlemen of Gray's Inn were again at Court presenting the Masque of Mountebanks, a satire in the same mould on the frauds of quack doctors and the sophistries of intellectual quacks, the theme giving ample scope for 'witty ribaldry which made the company merry'. On Twelfth Night 1623 the Christmas revels at Gray's Inn ended with a wild prank at which King James was not amused. Borrowing four cartloads of small cannon from the Tower of London, the young men fired them all off in the middle of the night. 'The King, awakened with this noise, started out of his bed and cried "Treason! Treason!" and that the City was in an uproar; in such sort . . . that the whole court was raised and almost in arms.'

The masque had by now passed well beyond the sphere of its popular origins into the upper region of Court compliment. In 1634 the Triumph of Peace, presented jointly by the four Inns of Court as a mark of loyalty to the Royal House in the face of the rising tide of Puritanism, reached unprecedented levels of magnificence and elaboration with scenes and settings devised by Inigo Jones himself. In the procession to Whitehall twenty footmen in crimson liveries with silver lace bore torches and cleared the way for a cavalcade of a hundred gallant young horsemen, twenty-five from each Inn, richly apparelled in costumes which alone had cost ten thousands pounds. Behind them pageantry mingled with parody till the long procession closed with the four Roman chariots of the grand masquers. Gray's Inn went first, its chariot of silver and crimson richly carved bearing four 'proper and beautiful young gentlemen' in rich cloth of tissue sewn with silver spangles, while liveried footmen bore huge flambeaux beside them, lighting the painting and the spangles and the costumes so that 'hardly anything could be invented to appear more glorious'.

Peace supported by Justice and Law provided the theme of the entertainment presented, but the dances and mimes had all the inconsequent variety of a modern revue. Comic speculators displayed their inventions, a method of boiling one pot with the steam of another, a diving suit to walk under water and a device for ships to sail against the wind. There was a dance of birds, a mime of two thieves robbing a horseman and being caught by a constable, another of three satyrs attempting to deflower four nymphs who were rescued by four huntsmen; a scene of a

49

fantastic knight attacking a windmill. When all was done Peace crowned with olive descended from a cloud, when Law in legal purple and Justice in a white robe joined her to sing an ode to King Charles and his Queen. The grand masquers as their sons then danced before them and finally, after another comic interlude in the irruption of a crowd of low life characters, Dawn in the figure of a beautiful maiden called them all from the revels. Had the King and the company but known it, there lay before them the dawning of a stormy and terrible day.

4

The Religious Crisis

SUCH with its daily life, its work and its recreations was Gray's Inn during the sixteenth century and a little after. But at another level the great changes in the life of the nation were producing effects within the Society which cannot be passed over in silence, first the religious revolution of the Reformation and then the political revolution of the Great Rebellion.

When the Reformation burst upon the mediaeval Church the age of the saints was long past. The Crusade had long turned into a tournament. Fra Lippo Lippi was more in evidence than Fra Angelico. If it was not true that the clergy no longer believed in monastic asceticism or the works of public charity and service which flowed from it, it can be said that most people believed in it rather for others to practice than for themselves. ('Let Austin have his swink to him reserved.') The tremendous convulsion of the ages of faith, which had thrown up the great cathedrals and monasteries and churches, like mountains reared by the very force of the belief that could conceive and execute them, had long been still. They yet stood vast and splendid, from one end of England to the other, but another great convulsion was at hand in which far the greater number of them were to be shaken down and engulfed in oblivion.

Yet up to the very breaking of the storm the Church seemed as strongly established as ever. Gray's Inn was linked with it by many ties. From 1516 the Society held its property of Shene Priory, into whose ownership it had then come five years after passing out of the hands of the de Greys. There was still subsisting the arrangement made two centuries earlier by Sir John de Grey, whereby the Priory of St. Bartholomew in

51

Smithfield bound itself to provide a chaplain to celebrate Mass in the chapel of the Manor of Purpoole for the souls of John and his ancestors and of all the faithful departed. In St. Andrew's Church on Holborn Hill as well, the members of Gray's Inn maintained a chapel where a priest said Mass for them and where some were buried. But the connection was more intimate still and in the reign of Henry VIII there were admitted to membership William Atwater, Bishop of Lincoln, and five great monastic dignitaries headed by John Islip, Abbot of Westminster, and with them William Bolton, Prior of St. Bartholomew's.

The end was not far off. In 1533 the Statute of Appeals forbade appeals from English courts to be carried to Rome. In 1535 the first actual blows were struck in King Henry's revolution and Sir Thomas More, his former Chancellor, John Fisher, Bishop of Rochester, and the first six of the Carthusian monks from the Charterhouse beyond Smithfield to be called to choose between the old world and the new, laid down their lives. They fell and Thomas Cromwell rose. He had been Master of the Rolls. Now he became Keeper of the Privy Seal, a Baron and, greatest of all, the King's Vicar-General in spiritual matters, sitting in synods above all the prelates of the realm and in Parliament taking precedence above the peers and the high officers of the Crown.

An Act passed early in 1536 for the dissolution of the lesser monasteries contributed decisively to the accumulation of the discontents piled up by the religious and social changes threatened and accomplished. In October the north of England rose as one man under Robert Aske of Gray's Inn. Wearing the badge of the Five Wounds of Christ and unfurling the crimson and white banner of St. Cuthbert of Durham they set out to march on London and have, as they said, all the vile blood out of the King's Council. This was the mighty Pilgrimage of Grace. The Duke of Norfolk, commanding the royal forces, reported that he could not stand against the rebels, for most of his own common soldiers thought the cause of their opponents 'good and godly' and at the last moment Aske was invited to London to confer with the King, who received him with marked courtesy and reassuring words. At Christmas general pardons were sent into the North and the insurgents finally dispersed. Then the King struck. In the new year the leaders were arrested, arraigned before a special commission and condemned to death, and Aske himself was executed at York. Lord Hussey, another Gray's Inn man, son of Chief Justice Hussey, who had also been a member of the Society, suffered a like fate at Lincoln. Thirty-five years later there was more blood spilt in the same cause in the northern capital. In 1572 Thomas Percy, Earl of Northumberland, sold by the Scottish Regent to the English Queen, after his flight from the wreck of the abortive rising of 1569, a fainter echo of Aske's lost crusade, for which his own father had perished, yielded up his life too at York, refusing to purchase pardon by renouncing his faith, and his arms were torn from the window where they had stood in Gray's Inn Hall.

Meanwhile the King's work went on and in 1539 the dissolution of the greater monasteries began. For the Society of Gray's Inn the first palpable result of these changes was that after Shene Priory was suppressed it held its property of the Crown to which the yearly rent of £6 13s. 4d. was now payable. At the same time, inheriting the obligations of the Priory of St. Bartholomew, which had fulfilled its undertaking to provide a chaplain for the Inn by a yearly payment of £7 13s. 4d., the Crown became liable to an equivalent claim by the Society. This amount being shortly afterwards reduced to £6 13s. 4d. by a decree of the Court of Augmentations, the final result was that the two obligations balanced each other.

It was in 1539 that the final internal effect of the religious changes appeared in the records of Gray's Inn. Three and a half centuries delayed, royal absolutism was taking vengeance on St. Thomas of Canterbury, who in his death had thwarted the political intentions of an earlier King Henry. Now it was commanded 'that all the images of Thomas Becket, sometime Archbishop of Canterbury, in any windows either in churches or chapels should be obliterated' and the execution of this command was entrusted to Edward Hall, one of the Benchers, better remembered as a chronicler though he was also Common Serjeant of the City of London. He was ordered to take out one of the chapel windows 'wherein the picture of the said Archbishop was gloriously painted and place another instead thereof in memory of Our Lord praying in the Mount'.

It is interesting to note the reflection of the religious changes in the fittings and furnishing of the chapel. Under Edward VI in 1552 all traces of Catholic worship were effaced by the sale of 'one vestment, with a cross of red velvet, a holy water stock of brass, two candlesticks, a little bell of brass, a vestment of silk spect with gold and a pair of organs, which being accordingly sold there remained in the Chapel a chalice, a surplice, a Bible of the largest volume, a psalter, a book of service, an altar cloth, a table, a lanthorn of glass, a chest'. A year later Mary had come to the throne and the Benchers were hurriedly providing for a fresh religious turnabout by a series of purchases recorded as follows:

' For nine ells of Holland for three altar cloths	12s. 6d.
For seven ells and a quarter of lockram for an albe	7s. 3d.
For three quarters of an ell for a corporas	3d.
For five pieces for the albe and the ephode	1s. 8d.
For tape for the ephode and girdle	2d.
Two cruets	1s. 8d.
For making the albe, ephode, towels and corporas	1s. 2d.
For ciii foot of oaken board for the altar	3s. 8d.
For six double quarters	2s. 0d.
For nails	5d.
For carriage	6d.
For making the altar	2s. 8d.
For a painted cloth to hang before the altar	1s. 8d.
For hemming the altar cloths	4d.
For a desk	1s. 0d.

Elizabeth came and her reign brought fresh changes: the screen was removed, a pulpit was provided and new stalls were made. In Catholic worship all had centred round the altar; henceforth it was to the pulpit that the people would turn. The change of attitude was reflected in the creation of the office of Preacher to the Society in 1574. Thenceforth the chaplaincy was relegated to a position of secondary importance till, towards the end of the 17th century, it disappeared. It was clearly an office for the unambitious, whereas the Preachers present a long line in which were many churchmen and scholars destined afterwards to be bishops or heads of colleges. The very form of the appointment of the first Preacher, Dr. John Cherke, Fellow of Peterhouse, strikes a new note. He is to hold the office 'if it be not otherwise misliked by the Privy Council or the Archbishop of Canterbury or the Bishop of London'.

Through its members Gray's Inn played a divided part in the great religious revolution. Thomas Cromwell, the disciple of Machiavelli, the chief destroyer of the old England and founder of the new, was of the Society. Charles Brandon, Duke of Suffolk, mercurial and indomitable, and in his own way among the foremost in the new fashions, for he appropriated no fewer than thirty religious houses, was also an ornament of the Inn. So too was Sir Humphrey Wingfield, Speaker of the House of Commons when the Acts of Supremacy and Succession were passed, and also Thomas Wriothesley, Secretary of State under Cromwell and afterwards Lord Chancellor and Earl of Southampton. Below them in the hierarchy of the new men were lesser figures such as Simon Fish, the formidable pamphleteer, one of the actors who incurred Wolsey's displeasure over the masque of 1526 and whose 'Supplication of Beggars', advocating wholesale confiscation (or, in modern idiom, 'nationalisation') of all Church establishments, including the London hospitals, as the one remedy for social evils, exercised a very powerful influence at Court and drew from Sir Thomas More a reply called the 'Supplication of Souls'. The whole machinery of government had passed to the new order and in Gray's Inn none stood forth against its champions. At their level there is on the rolls of the Society only Stephen Gardiner, Bishop of Winchester, striving by every means as Mary's Lord Chancellor, to restore that state of things which under her father he had helped to undermine.

In Gray's Inn, as in the rest of England, the old religion went underground, and nowhere could there be a better hiding place than an Inn of Court, where intellectual freedom, independence of outside interference and professional and personal comradeship were deep-rooted traditions. The receiving of Holy Communion in the Chapel was made the test of conformity to the established religion, but the very frequency with which orders imposing penalties for default were reiterated bears witness to the laxity of their enforcement. In a State paper of 1577, when Elizabeth had been almost twenty years on the throne, four of the sixteen Benchers of Gray's Inn were set down Papists as well as six out of eleven of the 'barristers of name for their practice'. Their survival was not due to any lack of outside pressure in a Society in which Lord Burghley and Lord Burghley's sons and grandsons held a dominant place. Another State paper of 1569 records the interrogation of three members of the Inn by commissioners inquiring whether they had duly attended divine service on Sundays, whether they had received Communion according to law and whether they had heard Mass, matins or evensong in Latin or been shriven after the Popish manner. One excused his non-attendance at church for two years, 'by reason of his business and clients' causes'. Another pleaded a scruple of conscience. A third claimed intermittent attendance. Two admitted that they had not received Communion for two or three years. The other thought he had only received it once since the beginning of the Queen's reign and 'he cannot precisely say that he received once'. As to the third question, each under a different formula took refuge in that silence which had been Sir Thomas More's last resort and which now was best expressed by Richard Godfrey of Norwich, described as 'well practiced, rich'. 'He sayeth that he believeth he is not compellable by the laws to answer this interrogatory; if he hath heard Mass he sayeth he is not impeachable by the laws of the realm, as his case standeth'. In a State paper of 1577, which recorded twelve members as having been expelled from the Inn on account of their religious views, Godfrey and another were set down as having been readmitted after expulsion. Twenty-four were noted as not known to come to church, thirteen as coming very seldom and being backward in religion, while three more were described as 'Jesuits beyond the seas'. The net was tightening and in November, 1581, Godfrey was given a fortnight to conform and 'show his reconciliation'. He would not surrender to the ultimatum and in the following May 'the chamber which was Mr. Godfrey's' was disposed of. Then there was the case of John Smythe who in 1579 was ordered to be put out of commons 'for his contemptuous and opprobrious words' to the Benchers and who was not to be readmitted until he had publicly confessed his offence and taken the Oath of Supremacy. It is not recorded that he ever did so.

But secret adherence to the old religion went further in Gray's Inn than the avoidance of religious tests. In 1585 the authorities in a letter to the Benchers warned them that 'we have understood that not only some seminary popish priests have been heretofore harboured in Gray's Inn but also have had their assemblies and Masses and so have perverted divers young gentlemen insomuch as sundry of them . . . do no at this present frequent divine service and sermons nor repair unto the Holy Communion'. Confirmation of this was soon forthcoming in a confession wrung from John Hambley, a priest executed in 1587 under the statute 27 Eliz. c. 2 which made it treason for a priest ordained by the authority of the See of Rome to be within the Queen's dominions and felony to help such a one. He admitted 'he said one Mass on Easter Day was twelve months in a chamber being in Gray's Inn . . . and that there were present nine or ten persons as he supposeth, all gentlemen, some of Gray's Inn and some not . . . that the said Mass was by him said within Gray's Inn at the coming in of the court coming from the upper part of Holborn and turning in the court on the left hand chamber there, near the corner of the said Gray's Inn court, where he said the said Mass, where there was provided for him vestments, alb, amis, maniple, stole and girdle, wine and singing cakes, a Mass book, a super altare and altar cloths . . . that is six or seven of the company did communicate'. Afterwards he had talked with one of his congregation two or three times in Gray's Inn Fields 'which fields behind Gray's Inn is a place where seminarians and Catholics do resort sometimes to have conference together'. There was a special significance in the execution in Gray's Inn Fields in 1591 of Edmund Genings, condemned for his priesthood, and Swithin Wells, a gentleman who had harboured him. Father Genings had been arrested in the act of saying Mass in the house of his host in Gray's Inn Lane. The place of execution, about where Verulan Buildings now stands, was opposite that house. The

Benchers about this time and for long afterwards manifested much concern over the presence of strangers lodging in the Inn, while the maze of irregular buildings lent itself to such a desperate game of hide and seek.

One incident of these divided days well illustrates the tragic undercurrents which disturbed the flow of life in Gray's Inn, when by the statute 23 Eliz. c. 1 it was itself treason to be reconciled to the Romish religion. Henry Walpole was a member of the Society, a young man of promise, the heir to great estates in Norfolk and nephew to Serjeant John Walpole, an eminent leader of the Bar. Sensitive and intelligent, a wit and a poet, in sympathy with the Catholic view, he yet accepted the general pattern of the life of his time, till he encountered the influence of Father Edmund Campion, the most brilliant and gallant of the missionary priests then pouring in from overseas to minister to the Catholics. When the Jesuit was captured and executed in 1581 Walpole stood close to the scaffold and during the butchery his clothes were splashed with blood. He took this as a call to follow the same road as a Jesuit priest. Fresh from the dreadful scene, he composed a poem of great beauty, 'An epitaph of the life and death of the most famous clerk and virtuous priest Edmund Campion', which was secretly printed and widely circulated. Then he slipped out of England, was himself ordained priest and at last returned on the mission. Captured immediately after landing in Yorkshire, he was shut up for a year in the Tower of London and there in the Salt Tower his name may still be seen cut in the stone of his cell. It must have been done early in his captivity, for later he was so savagely tortured by the notorious priest hunter Richard Topliffe, also a member of Gray's Inn, the man who had arrested Father Genings that at the end his handwriting was like the first scrawling attempts of a child. Certain 'confessions' alleged to have been extracted from him are palpable forgeries; his crippled hands could not have produced the well formed script. He defended himself on his trial at York with an ability worthy of one who had mooted in Gray's Inn and died bravely on April 7th, 1595, refusing to the end to conform to the Established Church as the price of pardon. Aske, the Earl of Northumberland, Walpole, their tradition lived on, and a full century after Campion's blood splashed Walpole standing by the scaffold there were still Catholic barristers in Gray's Inn.

But Gray's Inn reflected other religious contradictions. Magnates of the Established Church stood on its rolls as members, Richard Bancroft, John Whitgift and William Laud, Archbishops of Canterbury, John Williams, Lord Keeper of the Great Seal, Bishop of Lincoln and afterwards Archbishop of York, these and others also. But there were other Protestant elements, not subservient to their authority, present in the Society, even among the Preachers. Doctor Cherke, the very first Preacher, had not long before his appointment been banished from Peterhouse and Cambridge University for asserting in a sermon '1, That those states of Bishops, Archbishops, Metropolitans (Patriarchs) and lastly of Popes were introduced into the Church by Satan; 2. That among the Ministers of the Church one ought not to be superior to another'.

Vigilant to enforce obedience to the Established Church, the Court of High Commission, set up under Elizabeth in 1583, exercised inquisitorial powers over both clergy and laity, Catholic Recusants and Protestant Nonconformists, and the profession of the law was no shield against its arm, the length and strength of which may be judged from the sad end of Nicholas Fuller, an eminent Bencher of Gray's Inn and a former Treasurer. Thomas Lad, a merchant of Yarmouth, and Richard Mansel, a preacher, having been long imprisoned by this Court, procured a writ of habeas corpus and Fuller appeared on their behalf, pleading so boldly that Archbishop Bancroft committed him to prison like his clients as a champion of Nonconformists, and there, despite the petitions of his friends for his release, in less than six months he died, in 1620.

But there were figures too powerful to be touched. In Warwick House next door to Gray's Inn lived Robert Rich, the second Earl of Warwick, a member of the Society, as had been his father the first Earl. Estranged from the royal court by his attitude in religious matters, he devoted much energy to fostering those ventures which bore fruit in the New England settlements, and his opposition to forced loans, the exaction of Ship Money and the Church policy of Archbishop Laud carried him to the front rank

of the Puritan party. He was a strong supporter of Dr. Richard
Sibbes, an ardent Puritan, Master of St. Catherine's Hall,
Cambridge, who at one time was deprived of a lectureship by the
High Commission Court and who as Preacher of Gray's Inn
attracted to the Chapel a remarkable auditory. 'He sometimes
had a little stammering in the time of his preaching but then his
judicious hearers always expected some rare and excellent notion
from him.' During his time, the Earl obtained from the Benchers
leave to build a special gallery for himself and his friends at the
east end of the Chapel 'for their better hearing the sermon.'
Sibbes died at his chambers in the Inn in 1635 but his patron
lived to see his enemies in Church and State go down before
the triumph of Puritanism in arms.

5

Civil Strife

WHEN the Great Rebellion sundered the loyalty of England, Gray's Inn stood a house divided against itself. If it gave the insurgent Parliament generals to command its armies in the field and a judge to doom the King to death, it gave the Royalist cause no less in courage and devotion, in council and in the field, and to Charles it gave the friend who stood beside him in Whitehall in the very shadow of the axe.

To trace the fortunes of the members of the Society in the epics and the betrayals of those revolutionary and iconoclastic years would be to weave a tapestry disproportionately vast, nor is it relevant to dig down to the roots of the conflict and its course, for its complex causes lay deep in history and its course ranged over the length and breadth of England and beyond.

The contest over the imposition of Ship Money marks the first perceptible steepening of the gradient in the descent of the nation into the abyss of civil strife. Gray's Inn stands at the top of that incline, for it was there in February, 1637, that the judges held their fateful meeting to discuss the case submitted to them by the King, first, whether in national danger and emergency he might command all his subjects to contribute towards providing ships of war for the defence of the Realm and secondly, whether he was the sole judge both of the danger and of the measures to be adopted to meet it. Four of the judges had received their legal education at Gray's Inn: Chief Baron Davenport, 'a studied lawyer and upright person'; Mr. Justice Hutton, senior puisne of the Common Pleas, called by the King himself 'the honest judge'; Mr. Justice Crawley of the same court, and, most important of all, Sir John Finch, lately appointed Chief

Justice of the Common Pleas. His father, Sir Henry Finch, a Bencher of Gray's Inn and later a Serjeant, had been a lifelong friend of Bacon and had, like him, experienced the difficulties of chronic financial embarrassment, but, for all his deep erudition and many natural gifts, had never been crowned by a corresponding professional success. Late in life he had obtained from Bacon as Lord Chancellor relief by way of injunction against his pressing creditors and he has had the posthumous consolation of ranking with him as one of the candidates for the authorship of Shakespeare's works. His son 'led a free life in a restrained fortune' with 'a good wit and natural parts' and an unusually persuasive tongue, which he placed at the service of the King as Speaker of the Commons, Chief Justice and, finally, Lord Keeper.

At the meeting at Gray's Inn there was much 'discourse and great debate' upon the question of Ship Money but in the end Finch brought his brethren round to a view favourable to the Crown and, though Hutton and another judge did not agree that it rested solely with the King to determine the state of emergency justifying the tax, they were persuaded that they were bound to conformity with the opinion of the majority. When, however, the matter came up for judicial decision in Hampden's case, Hutton was one of the dissenting minority who delivered opinions against the Crown, and so was Davenport, though on a technical point only. Hutton died before the final breach between King and Parliament but his son, Sir Richard Hutton, also of the Society, fell fighting for the royal cause. Davenport, whose technical dissent had not mollified the Commons, lived to see articles of impeachment against him carried up to the House of Lords in July, 1641. Crawley, who on the outbreak of hostilities went to Oxford to join the King, died in 1649 within a fortnight of his master's execution, having meanwhile been degraded from judicial status by the Commons. Finch alone survived to witness the Restoration. As Lord Keeper and a peer he became one of the men best hated by the Parliamentary party and just before Christmas, 1640, when the Commons carried a motion for his impeachment, he slipped off abroad away from the perils which were deepening over the King's friends and the fate which overtook the Earl of Strafford a few months later. About fifteen years afterwards, Cromwell's régime allowed him to return. In private retirement he lived just long enough to hail the advent of Charles II in 1660, emerging to sit on the commission that tried the Regicides, before death claimed him in November of the same year.

If Finch had been zealous to serve the King, other members of Gray's Inn were bold against the Government. When, as Speaker of the intransigent Parliament of 1628—the last before Charles made the fatal experiment of ruling for twelve years without Parliaments—Finch would have adjourned the Commons by royal command, three members of the Society were among the recalcitrants who held him down in the chair while the Grand Remonstrance was read, his kinsman Sir Peter Hayman, Denzil Holles and Walter Long. Finch entered the House of Commons no more until on December 21st, 1640, he came to its Bar from the House of Lords to make a speech in his own exculpation before the members considered whether to proceed with his impeachment. He spoke ingratiatingly and persuasively and then withdrew and for some little time silence ensued, broken eventually by Alexander Rigby, a Lancashire man and a barrister of Gray's Inn, who told the House that 'had not this siren so sweet a tongue surely he could never have effected so much mischief'. He turned the scales against Finch, whose friends were barely able to delay the impeachment by debating tactics till he could escape over the Channel out of reach of his enemies.

From beyond the seas he saw the whole succeeding tragedy played out and in every great scene members of Gray's Inn. Most of the chief commanders on both sides were members of the Society or became so afterwards. For the King were the Duke of Richmond, his kinsman, Commissioner for Oxford, the Earl of Lindsay, his Commander-in-Chief at the outbreak of war, killed at Edgehill, the Earl of Derby, who held Lancashire for his cause, Spencer Compton, Earl of Northampton, 'a man of great courage, honour and fidelity', killed at Hopton Heath. On the side of the Parliament, the Earl of Warwick, assured it the adherence of the Navy; Ferdinand Lord Fairfax commanded in Yorkshire and his son Thomas was Commander in Chief throughout the war, while Sir William Waller's early successes earned him the title of 'William the Conqueror'. Serving the same cause were Sir William Brereton, Sir Arthur Hesilrige, Denzil Holles and Colonel Ingleby. Even the practising lawyers threw off their gowns and took the sword. Christopher Fulwood, son of Sir George Fulwood, left Gray's Inn, where he had been Treasurer only a few years before, to raise a regiment of miners for the King in the neighbourhood of his Derbyshire estate but was mortally wounded and taken prisoner in 1643. Ten years later his impoverished son petitioned the Society 'for relief to buy clothes to cover his nakedness'. Alexander Rigby on the other side abandoned politics and the law to serve as a colonel in the Parliamentary army, won some striking successes but failed in his siege of Lathom House, gallantly defended by the Countess of Derby, till her husband fought his way to her relief. He survived the war to return to his profession and serve as a Baron of the Exchequer. David Jenkins, a choleric and indomitable Welshman, who in 1625 was fined for refusing to act as Reader and disqualified from ever being made an Bencher because of the 'peremptory answer' he had returned; who in 1631 had been again in disgrace 'for abusing Mr. Holt one of the Readers'; who had opposed Ship Money and monopolies and found himself in trouble with the High Commission Court, was a judge in South Wales at the start of the war. He took arms for the King, was captured by the Parliament, courted death by his bold and reiterated denunciations, written and spoken, of the illegalities of the rebels and was barely saved from execution by Henry Marten, a fellow member of Gray's Inn, a wild, whimsical, irresponsible figure, a determined republican, restless and aggressive as Jenkins himself. He sat in Parliament for Berkshire and told his fellow members that to make a martyr of the old gentleman would be to do just what he wanted and that the best thing was to keep him in prison in spite of himself. In 1657, after long years of captivity, Jenkins was released under surveillance and allowed to return to Gray's Inn. On the Restoration he was called to the Bench and might have been one of the judges at Westminister if he would have consented to make certain official gratituities.

If Jenkins escaped martyrdom other members of the Society did not. In January, 1645, Archbishop Laud fell a victim to

Parliamentarian vengeance four years before his master the King followed him to the block. The head of the first Charles fell and the second Charles became in right, though not yet in fact, King of England. His premature attempt to seize his Crown ended with the catastrophe of the battle of Worcester. He escaped abroad again, but the faithful Earl of Derby who aided his flight was taken and executed.

From the trial of King Charles himself all the judges as well as most of the responsible men in the State drew back and when a court was created for the purpose Algernon Sidney, nephew of Sir Philip Sidney, and like him a member of Gray's Inn, voiced their conviction when he declared that 'the King can be tried by no court and no man can be tried by this court'. To preside over it the triumphant faction had to resort to a lawyer of the second rank, John Bradshaw of Gray's Inn, who had already played an active part as prosecutor during several trials since the start of the war, including that of Judge Jenkins. Both the Attorney-General, Sir William Steele, afterwards Chief Baron of the Exchequer and Lord Chancellor of Ireland, and the Solicitor-General, John Cook, were also members of the Society. By an opportune illness Steele escaped the odious duty of conducting the prosecution, which his colleague, an extreme Roundhead of little eminence at the Bar, gladly performed with overbearing zeal. The faithful Duke of Richmond stood by Charles in his last hours and on the scaffold the King was supported by William Juxon, Bishop of London, who lived to see the Restoration of the monarchy and serve his sovereign's son as Archbishop of Canterbury.

The war dislocated the whole administration of justice. Some of the judges joined the King at Oxford, among them Chief Justice Bankes of the Common Pleas, whose wife nobly defended Corfe Castle against a desperate siege, Mr. Justice Crawley of the same court and Mr. Baron Leeke. All had been members of Gray's Inn. Others like Mr. Justice Bacon of the King's Bench, a kinsman of the great Lord Chancellor, and Mr. Justice Reeve of the Common Pleas, likewise former members of the Society, elected to stay in Parliamentarian London and administer justice in the almost empty courts at Westminster.

Other circumstances contributed to the confusion; the

impeachment of the Ship Money judges, like Davenport and Crawley; arbitrary action like the assessment of Mr. Baron Henden, another Gray's Inn judge, for the payment of a compulsory capital levy of a twentieth part of his estate towards the maintenance of the Parliament's army, because he had failed to contribute voluntarily; the appointment by Parliament's authority of new judges such as Serjeant Peter Pheasant, also a former member of the Society and himself the son of another distinguished lawyer who had been a Bencher.

In Gray's Inn, as in other Inns of Court, the war put completely out of gear the whole system of legal education. Readings and moots ceased and when the fighting ended in 1646 the buildings and gardens, after years of neglect badly needed restoration and repair. The members were dispersed and half of them politically excommunicated by their allegiance to a lost cause. The government of the Inn lay in the hands of those Benchers who had thrown in their lot with the now victorious rebels or at least refrained from breaking with them, men like Sir Thomas Bedingfield, whom the Parliament made a Judge of the Common Pleas in October, 1648, but who, after the King's execution in the following January, declined to act under usurped authority and retired into private life; Sir Thomas Widdrington, a willow of a man who on the same ground refused to continue to act as Commissioner of the Great Seal but later resigned himself to Cromwell's régime sufficiently to resume that office and afterwards to serve as Speaker in the Commons and Chief Baron of the Exchequer; Francis Thorpe, who has served as a colonel in the war and was afterwards a Baron of the Exchequer. There had been some calls to the Grand Company of Ancients and to the Bar during the war. Just before it ended a batch of twenty-six were called to the Bar with the provision that if it should thereafter appear that any of them had been in any service against the Parliament his call should be void. Among these new barristers were Thomas Povey, that model of discretion, who made himself so satisfactory a career in the civil service in the time of Pepys, and Charles Fleetwood, who after a distinguished career as a soldier, married Cromwell's eldest daughter the widow of Ireton, served on the Council of State, sat in the

Protector's House of Lords and became Commander in Chief.

Life in the Inn was radically changed. Though the practice of mooting was gradually restored, Readings lapsed and newcomers were admitted to the Bench on their mere undertaking to read if called on. From the Library, books were unaccountably missing and a new lock and key had to be fitted. Revelling was forbidden by order of the Parliament. Political conformity to the new régime was ensured by a Parliamentary decree of 1649 that all Benchers should subscribe the Engagement 'to be true and faithful to the Commonwealth of England as the same is now established without a King or a House of Lords'. In matters of religion conformity was the rule. Dr. Hannibal Potter, the Royalist Preacher was ejected by the Parliamentary delegates but Isaac Reynolds, the more pliant chaplain held his place, Vicar of Bray fashion, from 1623 to 1670, throughout the periods of Laud, the Presbyterians, the Independents and the restored Anglican religion. In the Hall good manners had sadly decayed, and in 1656 the Benchers noted with disapproval the throwing of bread and knocking and breaking of pots, while members habitually rose to snatch food before the waiters had brought it to the tables, 'much more than in former times'. The Inn itself became dangerous by reason of the intrusion of undesirable outsiders and in 1651 Thomas Tisdale, the Under-Treasurer, was murdered in his chambers. In its public relations the Society stood well with the ruling powers. The Earl of Warwick was high in the councils of the Protector, whose son Henry was likewise a member. Moreover, the Earl's grandson and heir was the husband of Cromwell's daughter Frances. Pillars of the Commonwealth were not lacking on the roll of members but in every other respect the Benchers faced a formidable task in attempting 'to reduce this Society to its former happiness and honour'.

The one decided achievement of this period proved abortive. After a long and tiresome correspondence with the appropriate Government department the Society succeeded in negotiating the exchange of the yearly rent payable by it to the Crown and the equivalent stipend for a chaplain payable to it by the Crown. The effect of their cancellation was to make the Society master in its own house but at the Restoration the transaction was repudiated and the final settlement was deferred to the following century.

6

The Restoration

AT first the Restoration seemed to bring Gray's Inn back to its former normality along with the other Inns of Court. The Regulations laid down for them by the judges in 1664 suggests life cast in its ancient mould. The Inns of Chancery were to be strictly subordinate to the Inns of Court to which they belonged. No one not usually in commons in the Inns was to be allowed to lodge there and since 'by the neglect of commons in the vacations the gentlemen of the Inns of Court are often drawn to frequent ordinaries, gaming houses and other places of disorder, whereby the neglect of their studies, if not the corruption of their manners, is occasioned' commons were to be kept both in vacations and term time. Cloaks, swords and daggers were forbidden in Hall and Chapel. Students called to the Bar had to be 'of seven years continuance and have kept the exercises within the House and abroad in Inns of Chancery and have been frequently in commons'. Even after call the barrister could not practise in the Courts of Westminster for three years more unless he had acted as Reader in an Inn of Chancery, since 'over early and hasty practice' made them 'less grounded and sufficient, whereby the law may be disgraced and the client prejudiced'. As for the Benchers, they must be chosen for their learning, for their duly keeping the exercises of the House and for their honest behaviour and good disposition.

The Gray's Inn Benchers supplemented these rules from time to time. For example, no one must be called to the Bar till he was admitted to a chamber. Members must not keep women in their chambers, even their wives. Before eating in Hall, they must pay for their commons in advance. Gowns must be worn in Hall and members must 'behave themselves decently according to the ancient orders'. The seven years standing prerequisite to call might be reduced to five if the member had already spent two years in Staple Inn or Barnard's Inn. To qualify he must also have been in commons two weeks every term and four weeks every Long Vacation for five years and he must have performed six grand moots in the Library and four in an Inn of Chancery. (These Library moots held three times a week in moot weeks were presided over by barristers of three years' standing.)

The Restoration placed religion again on its former footing. Dr. Hannibal Potter, the Royalist Preacher, deposed during the rebellion, was reinstated. The Established Church soon reasserted itself, with the promulgation of the old regulations that members must receive the Sacrament regularly in the Chapel. In 1669, the year in which Dr. William Claget, a prominent anti-Catholic writer, became Preacher, the fabricated scare of the 'Popish Plot' was reflected within the Society in a drive to ensure that 'Papists or so reputed and Irishmen' did not evade the test of the oaths of allegiance and supremacy. In the panic, Charles Ingleby, a barrister of the Society, was charged with treason and brought to trial at York but honourably acquitted. He survived to serve as a Baron of the Exchequer under James II, whose reign witnessed a Roman Catholic revival in Gray's Inn. Several Catholics were called to the Bar by royal recommendation and one besides Ingleby attained a Judgeship, Richard Allibone who took his seat in the Court of the King's Bench. Both were displaced after the revolution which brought in William of Orange, whose reign closed the Bar to Catholics for nearly a century till the Roman Catholic Relief Act, 1791.

The flood tide of revival at the Restoration brought back in the Inn the old recreations. Before the Puritan interlude, Christmas, Candlemas and All Saints had been the occasions of Grand Weeks. Now Grand Weeks and Grand Days returned, the members contributing to defraying the expenses, while at Christmas the rules against gaming were suspended. As in the old days, the Christmas revels formed a link with the Royal House. The celebrations of the Christmas season in 1682-3 so pleased Charles II that he knighted Richard Gipps, the Master of the

Revels. The festivities started early in November and continued each Saturday for two terms, reaching their climax when Gipps, attended by his revellers and comptrollers, drove in state to Whitehall to invite the King and Queen, the Duke and Duchess of York and the rest of the Court to a masque and banquet in the Hall on Candlemas Day.

Distinguished public figures honoured the Society and were honoured by it in being admitted to membership, the Duke of Ormonde, who had held Ireland for the late King, George Monck, Duke of Albermarle, who had brought the new king into his own, Sir Edward Walker, Garter King-of-Arms, Sir William Dugdale, his successor, then Norroy King-of-Arms, equally distinguished as a faithful servant of the royal cause and as a legal historian and antiquarian. In the same spirit Lord John Seymour, son of the Duke of Somerset, was called to the Bench as an assistant within three months of being admitted to the Society. The two Kings-of-Arms continued a long traditional connection between the Society and the holders of heraldic office—Sir Thomas Wriothesley and Sir William Dethicke in Tudor times and, after them, William Camden, Sir Richard St. George, and Sir William Segar under James I. Segar, indeed, left more than a transitory mark on the Inn. His son Thomas became Steward (unfortunately not among the most successful in the Society's annals) while his grandson, Simon, as Librarian atoned for any paternal deficiencies by recording for posterity the contents of a great number of the Inn's ancient records the originals of which have since completely vanished.

Glimpses of Gray's Inn in the diary of Pepys confirm the impression of its variety, intimacy and charm. The gardens were a fashionable walk for the ladies and their gallants. Here and there, particularly in the gateways, were little shops. There was a barber's in the Steward's Court where Pepys was a customer. When he visited the chamber of his friend Hewer in the Inn he found it 'very pretty and little and neat'. Evelyn too has left a pleasant picture of the chambers of Dudley Palmer, an assistant to the Bench and a Fellow of the Royal Society. He dined with him there in 1661 and noted with delight his 'clocks and pendules, especially one that had innumerable motions and played nine or ten tunes on the bells very finely, some of them set in parts, which was very harmonious . . . he also had good telescopes and mathematical instruments, choice pictures and other curiosities'.

Within the little closed world of Gray's Inn problems and difficulties arose as they had always done and were settled. But sometimes there intruded tragedy final and irrevocable. The republican Algernon Sidney, charged with complicity in the Rye House Plot and executed in 1683 was, like so many of his family, a member. It was another Gray's Inn man, Richard Nelthorp, who was the unwilling cause of the death of Dame Alice Lisle, condemned for harbouring him after the failure of Monmouth's rising. He himself was executed in 1685 before the gate in Gray's Inn Lane, dying 'very composedly'. Pathetic and futile was the case of the student Bird, son of a rich north country attorney, who, having secretly married beneath him, was so terrified of his father's anger that he murdered his girl wife in a field near Kensington. He was hanged at Tyburn in 1691, Dr. Wake, the Preacher of the Society, later Archbishop of Canterbury, riding with him in the coach that carried him to the gallows.

Still, for the most part, the Inn could cope with its troubles easily enough. Laundresses had to be restrained from throwing dust and ashes out into the courts. Books disappeared from the Library and a catalogue was ordered to be made so as to render the librarian personally responsible. Tempers were hot and disturbances in Hall occurred too often. In 1669 George England, a barrister, came up to the Bench table in a violent manner creating a disturbance. Next year William Player, a barrister, and Samuel Starky, another member, 'in a very factious, riotous and seditious manner' came up to the Bench table and tried to drag away the waiter there so that the Benchers had to rise and rescue him. Another disturbance in June 1681 was political and arose out of an attempt to pass an address of thanks to the King for having dissolved Parliament. The ringleader was William Scroggs, son of the Chief Justice just resigned, who had himself been a member of the Society. With him some of the wilder spirits in the Inn (several of them in military employment and only nominally attached to it) came tumultuously into Hall without gowns and wearing swords and 'in an irregular way encompassed the Bench' standing on the tables with loud acclamations and flinging up of hats. At this time Scroggs was a knight, a King's Counsel and himself a newly elected Bencher. That fact alone would suggest that an extraordinary change had occurred in the constitution and discipline of the legal profession.

There had in fact been a fundamental change. The heart and centre of the old educational system had been the Readings. The Civil War and the interregnum broke their continuity and the breach proved irreparable. Too long uprooted, they withered and it was useless to try to replant them. At first the attempt started bravely enough, although interrupted by the Great Plague of 1665 and the Great Fire of London in the following year. During the Commonwealth Benchers had been elected on their undertaking to read when called on. The Restoration soon witnessed a vigorous attempt to enforce the obligation. Refusal to read was visited by fines varying from £10 to £150. Failure to pay the fine was punished by seizure of the defaulter's chamber. But all was useless. In 1675 the Society sent Readers to Staple Inn and Barnard's Inn for the last time and in 1667 Sir Robert Baldock, afterwards a Judge of the King's Bench, held the last Reading at Gray's Inn itself. For a dozen more years the ghost of the old practice still lingered on. In 1686 nineteen members were summoned to attend pension 'to accept their call to the Bench in order to read in their turns' and till 1688 the lists of Benchers present at pensions continued to bear the affix 'Armigeris et lectoribus'. Money payments were accepted in lieu of reading. The grand company of Ancients survived a little longer but after 1709 no more were called to that degree. With the decay of the old system of studies, the old revels and relaxations decayed and by 1682 the head cook was being granted increased wages to compensate him for the loss of his profits for the discontinuance of Readings and Grand Days. Only occasionally, as in 1689 when the newly created Serjeants held their feast at Gray's Inn, was there an echo of the old life.

Many reasons for this breakdown in formal legal education may be suggested—the increasing availability of printed textbooks, the initiation and growth of the practice of calling to the degree of Serjeant-at-Law men who had performed no Reading, the heavy expenditure on incidental hospitality imposed and demanded by custom and, not least important, just ordinary human indolence. But above all it was a change of spirit; the changes initiated in the 16th century were working themselves out. The social readjustment after the old public charities of the Middle Ages were transformed into the private property of the new rich had its counterpart in the realm of the mind and the mediaeval idea of a communis sententia yielded to the notion of private judgment. So in the Inns of Court the democracy of disputation in the Readings and moots in which the principles of the common law were hammered out term after term by a whole professional hierarchy of men combining at once the functions of schoolmaster and scholar withered in the new atmosphere, as the moots followed the Readings in decline. Learning in the law could be and was attained by other means, but legal education gradually went underground into the private study where personal contact in chambers transformed the law into an esoteric art secretly acquired. Several results ensued. In the first place the fact that a man was called to the Bar and turned loose on the public as a practitioner was no guarantee of even minimum attainments or competence and the profession became overcrowded, standards being relaxed all along the line from admission to call. Next, the legal profession itself, hitherto bound together in the common interdependence of the Serjeants' Inns, the Inns of Court and the Inns of Chancery was irretrievably split. When the Inns of Chancery lost contact with the Inns of Court the attorneys and solicitors, whose status in the hierarchy of the law they had formerly secured, drifted into professional isolation. For the Bar, the dissolution of the ancient public obligations to learn and to teach meant that, in the absence of ascertainable standards professional advancement became unpredictable. If the Benchers were no longer to be Readers how were they to be appointed? In 1690 an Ancient of Gray's Inn, passed over in two calls to the Bench, claimed the promotion as of right on the ground of seniority but the Judges held that there was no such right and that call to the Bench was purely discretionary. The common bond had given place to private judgment just at the time when in a wider sphere the man of taste had supplanted the artist in giving outward form to the social scene—the master of artists rather than the master of arts, the connoisseur rather than the maker, fastidious, sophisticated and refined, averting life's cruder contacts and smoothing away their evidences from his immediate surroundings. Poetry was hardening into literature and, in the arts, classical regularity was ousting the riotous spontaneity of a fresher and less self-conscious epoch. At the time when Molière, in a very modern-sounding phrase, expressed the fashionable opinion of

> ' Le fade goût des monuments gothiques
> Ces monstres odieux des siècles ignorants '

the face of Gray's Inn began to be transformed. This was achieved partly by pulling down and planned rebuilding. Thus in 1676 part of Stanhope's Buildings and Christopher's Buildings in the north west corner of Coney Court were ordered to be pulled down and rebuilt. In 1685 Howland's, Cage's, Gooderick's and Downes' Buildings, comprising the south-west corner of Holborn Court, were the subject of a similar order and with them vanished the passage into Bentley's Rents behind the west side of the Court. Three years later the old Gray's Inn Lane gateway, under which Jacob Tonson, the bookseller, had a shop, went the same way and was replaced. At the west end of the Inn Warwick House was pulled down and Warwick Court built on the site. Its garden was the property of the Society, which in 1694 granted a building lease of it to Dame Barbara, widow of Mr. Justice Allibone. The six charming brick houses erected by her were at first simply a continuation of Warwick Court shut off from the Inn by a pair of iron gates at the north end.

The transfiguration of Gray's Inn was hastened by three disastrous fires which impoverished the Society for half a century to come—impoverished it so decisively that in 1690 it was ordered 'that no wine be brought into Hall at the charge of the Society till the debts of the same are paid'. The first fire in February 1680 started in a set of chambers in the passage between Chapel Court and Coney Court and burning northwards devastated nearly the whole of what afterwards became the garden side of Gray's Inn Square. In January 1684 there was another conflagration, starting on the floor above the library in the building opposite the Gray's Inn Lane gate, then still called Bacon's Buildings. 'It burnt very furiously being so dry a season that no water was to be had in a long while; it consumed two or three whole staircases but at last by blowing up and the engines it was happily extinguished.' But the library was lost and three people were killed. Finally one night in January 1687, while the members were in the midst of their revels, a neglected candle set fire to some first floor chambers in Osbaldestone's Buildings. The Hall doorkeeper saw the flames in the northeast corner of Holborn Court but when the porter and he broke in the fire 'burst out upon them'. Osbaldstone's Buildings and the houses on the east side of the Court were consumed.

These catastrophes alone would have occasioned substantial rebuilding even had they not overlapped other schemes of reconstruction, sometimes with confusing results. Thus, after the fire of 1684, which destroyed the old Bacon's Buildings, their name passed to their southern neighbour which happened at the time to be in process of demolition and reconstruction by members of the Bacon family. This new block on the south side of the passage into Field Court had till then been occupied by a house called, after an Elizabethan Bencher, Grimstone's Buildings. Before the end of the seventeenth century Coney Court and Chapel Court had been rebuilt on a uniform plan.

One great change, which was a turning point in the architectural development of the Inn, occurred in 1685 when the ancient buildings dividing Coney Court from Chapel Court were found to have become so ruinous that there was nothing for it but demolition. At first it was suggested that a new and bigger Chapel might be erected on the site but finally in 1699 extensive reconditioning of the old Chapel was begun in the course of which the last of the chambers built above it vanished. The two courts were thus merged into one and gradually the whole came to be known under the name of Coney Court, though the northern portion, on a slightly higher level than the southern, remained partitioned off and laid out, grave and treeless, with squares of grass and cross walks and a sundial, while the remainder was open to carriages and wheeled vehicles. The two parts were railed off from each other and at each end of the railings two or three broad stone steps ascended from the lower to the higher level. The name Chapel Court was still in use in 1722. In 1693 it was ordered that a ball be set over every door in Coney Court 'with figures thereon for distinction'.

The abortive scheme for the transfer of the Chapel from its old site represented one of those hopeful incursions into the lives of the Inns of Court which were a special feature of the career of Dr. Nicholas Barbon. Over the world of the man of taste his shadow falls like a portent of the future, the world of the man of business, the man whose concern is with things not directly for their own sake but as trading assets only, as abstractions in a profit and loss account. The type is no novelty. Chaucer's merchant suggests his counterpart in the fourteenth century but it was only later that the social scene came to be framed in his image.

Barbon was the most successful of the speculators who pushed out the built-up area of London in the time of Charles II till it resembled in shape some sea monster lying along the north bank of the Thames with its jaws enclosing St. James' Park and the tip of its tail at Limehouse. Roger North of the Middle Temple, who knew Barbon well, has left a lively portrait of him. The son of 'Praise God' Barbon of the Commonwealth days, he was bred a doctor of physic but after the Great Fire went into business as a builder. 'His talent lay more in economising ground for advantage and the little conveniences of a family than the more noble aims of architecture and all his aim was profit.' He was 'an exquisite mob master and knew all the arts of winding or driving mankind in herds'. In persuading people he always assumed 'that however adverse at first . . . they would come down to profit' and so 'all other arguments he esteemed . . . vain loss of time'. He would either give or accept insults as business expediency demanded. In negotiation he always satisfied everyone but disappointment invariably followed in performance, for he deliberately overtraded his stock because, as he said, 'It was not worth his while to deal little; that a bricklayer could do. The gain he expected was out of great undertakings'. Rather than borrow capital at high rates of interest he kept perpetually in debt, staving off his creditors by every device known to the law. He found that even paying their ultimate litigation costs was cheaper than interest. An exceedingly ingenious spinner of schemes, he advocated a plan for debasing the currency which he called 'raising the value of money'. His supporters, says Macaulay, were partly dull men who believed what he told them and partly shrewd men who were perfectly willing to be authorised by law to pay a hundred pounds with eighty'. He was also the father of fire insurance in England.

There had been many vicissitudes in Barbon's dealings with the Middle Temple. With Gray's Inn his relations were wholly unfortunate. The Society found his terms for the building of a new Chapel unsatisfactory but worse befell about this time. Barbon was developing a building estate by very questionable means in Red Lion Fields just west of Gray's Inn and one day in June 1684 the members sallied forth and fought a pitched battle with his workmen. Soon afterwards there was further trouble when Barbon marched two hundred of his men about the fields shouting and waving their hats as a challenge. The Crown was also concerned with his proceedings and took legal action, for what is now Theobald's Road was then the King's private way to Newmarket and there had been several encroachments on it by Barbon. So far as the quarrel with Gray's Inn was concerned, Chief Justice Jeffreys offered to act as arbitrator. He had already, on the occasion of the riots, 'rattled away at the Benchers about it, saying that if they cannot govern the House he will send somebody who shall do it for them'. In 1685 the Society expended £1 14s. 0d. on 'a treat pro the Lord Chief Justice' in the chambers of Sir William Williams in Coney Court. Meanwhile Barbon built on vigorously and the Benchers had their hands tied by Jeffreys' intervention. Their case was probably not assisted by the fact that Williams was an old rival of Jeffreys and had once, as Speaker of the House of Commons, administered a reprimand, making him kneel at the Bar of the House. Barbon was not the only speculative builder who was annoying the Society and in 1687 Jeffreys, now Lord Chancellor, was arbitrating in this matter also, for in that year the Benchers appointed a committee 'to attend Sir Christopher Wren from time to time concerning the last order by the Lord Chancellor in the matter of difference between the Society and Mr. Skipwith, Mr. Rich, Mr. Metcalfe and others'. Six months later they humbly accepted the Chancellor's proposals touching Skipwith's building in Gravel Pit Field.

So Gray's Inn was almost hemmed in with buildings on the west, and far beyond, on both sides of the road to Tyburn, houses stretched continuously, well beyond St. Giles' in the Fields. South of Holborn Court too buildings and alleys were thickening. Parellel to Gray's Inn Lane the Court behind the Bishop's Head ran down towards the Inn. Parallel with the passage to the Holborn Gate and a little east of it was George Yard with its old timbered houses built round two airy courts. The Society had to be very watchful of these near neighbours to prevent nuisances such as drainage abuses, tavern disorders or the keeping of a noisy school. On the north, however, the Inn still touched the fringe of a countryside of lonely fields and lanes and as yet no houses lay between it and Highgate Hill.

In this period men trained at Gray's Inn were still playing a distinguished part in the Courts as judges and advocates, men like Sir William Gregory, Sir Thomas Powell or Sir Cresswell Levinz on the Bench at Westminster, Sir Constantine Phipps, Lord Chancellor of Ireland, or Sir William Jones, Attorney-General. To this period in the history of the Society belongs Sir Salathiel Lovell, called to the Bar in 1656, Serjeant at Law in 1688, Recorder of London in 1692, who achieved the final distinction of becoming a Baron of the Court of Exchequer in 1708 when verging on his 90th year.

One figure, however, overshadows all the others, that of Sir John Holt, Lord Chief Justice of England from 1689 to 1710. He compensates the Society for its connection with his much hated predecessor Scroggs. Holt had a hereditary link with Gray's Inn through his father, who was a Bencher before him, and his chambers were in Osbaldestone's Buildings beside the Chapel. He stands at a turning point in English legal history looking both back to the old and forward to the new. He maintained unflinchingly the independence of the judges and the integrity of the law in the face of Parliament, which he was still close enough to mediaeval conceptions to regard as not itself independent of the control of ethics and philosophy, holding in the case of *City of London* v. *Wood* (1701), 12 Mod. 669, that a statute involving a contradiction might be void. 'It is a thing against all laws', he said, 'that the same person should be party and judge in the same cause, for it is a manifest contradiction, for the party is he that is to complain to the judge and the judge is to hear the party; the party endeavours to have his will, the judge determines against the will of the party . . . if an Act of Parliament should ordain that the same person should be party and judge, or, which is the same thing, judge in his own cause, it would be a void Act of Parliament'. Yet, holding to the past, he looked forward too, grasped the changes coming over commercial conditions and framed solutions harmonious to the rules of the common law. In legal administration his example set new standards and his decisions are enshrined in the reports but, even more than they, his monument is in the living tradition of the law of England and of her judges, in which across the centuries and on the very ground of Gray's Inn he stands for his successors as more than a good judge, as the mirror and model of good judges.

7

Eighteenth-Century Calm

IN the 18th century much that had been fluid in English life set in a mould, the mould of the classical ideal. The age was marked by the steady advance of elegance and refinement. Poised and collected, the man of taste by his patronage set the tone of society, most of all in London. At the accession of Queen Anne the town extended little beyond Soho Square. The City, risen again after the Great Fire, its approaches still guarded by its ancient gateways, was still visibly the core of the capital. But in the next hundred years that compactness was lost. The gates demolished, all but the outwork of Temple Bar, no longer made traffic bottle-necks. The planned and orderly dignity of new streets and squares reached out further and further through the former farm lands westward to touch Hyde Park and north of Oxford Street towards the village of Marylebone and the fatal cross-roads at Tyburn. But no age is all of a piece; each displays, like a cross-section of geological strata, the relics and the influences of what has gone before. In the older quarters sinking into slums, Drury Lane for instance, and the streets clustered round St. Giles's, no longer in the fields, the raw crudities of a Hogarthian underworld stank to heaven. West of Gray's Inn on the land of the manor of Bloomsbury straight streets and regular squares of symmetrical houses were being laid out. Towards the City the pestilential waters of the Fleet River were arched over to run henceforth underground. But Holborn, Chancery Lane, Fetter Lane, little changed save for a slowly growing appreciation of the need for better paving and lighting, still displayed on every side the picturesque, irregular gables of the age before the Great Fire. There life was a world removed from the elegance of

Cavendish Square or Berkeley Square. Take one point as an example. In Holborn in the middle of the century one house in every five was a licensed house.

It was in the 18th century, that Gray's Inn definitely assumed that shape which it retained almost unmodified until the great bombardments of 1940-1. Now was a period of recovery. Impoverished by the devastating fires of the sixteen-eighties, wrestling with laxity and waste on the part of its officers and servants and negligence in the collection of its revenues, it was not until 1740 that the Society, which twenty years earlier was in 'great decay and ruinous condition', could record that by good management it had become 'more wealthy and in good condition'. Henceforth that prosperity was reflected in terms of the finances of a new age in investments in East India annuities and Consolidated Bank annuities.

The century witnessed gradual but steadily accumulating changes in its appearance, some of them improvements, others fashionable errors of judgment. In 1722 the separation between Coney Court and the former Chapel Court, was modified by the substitution of a row of posts for the dividing railings, and in 1793, the union between the two was finally consummated by the adoption of the name Gray's Inn Square. In 1745, the prevalent taste for order and regularity found offence in the 16th century porch at the north doorway of the Hall and destroyed it, not without a solitary protest from Mr. Andrew Wither, the senior Bencher, who pointed out that 'the well designed porch and three very convenient and useful rooms originally built with and making part of the Hall, together with a chamber of two pair of stairs adjoining thereto will be all pulled down and utterly destroyed, which rooms must be some otherways supplied at the expense of the Society'. To this the surveyor replied: 'Mr. Wither's protest I humbly conceive to be answered by the taking down of a ruinous irregular building and constructing a sound, uniform and regular structure in lieu thereof'.

From 1738 to 1752 the re-building of the south side of Holborn Court was proceeding in a leisurely fashion, some houses in the rear having been purchased to enlarge the site. Now disappeared the last remnants of the lath and plaster Elizabethan chambers, the 'Paper Buildings' as they had come to be called in contrast to the solid masonry of early Tudor. In digging the foundation of No. 1 Holborn Court a spring was found and a pump erected to preserve the benefit of it. There still remained in the north-east corner of the Court the cluster of buildings enclosing the little passage or yard by the south side of the Chapel, leading to the Duchy of Lancaster Office next to the Hall. This alley-way was closed by a wall with a door and in it was another pump.

In the north-west corner of Holborn Court another irregular group of houses adjoining the Hall gave also onto Coney Court on the north and Field Court — as the former Steward's Court was now called — on the west. The year 1789 saw a major structural change when this old group of buildings was pierced to make a carriage-way along the west end of the Hall joining Coney Court and Holborn Court. Till then the sole connection had been the narrow passage-way east of the Chapel.

Field Court too underwent some changes. Till 1722 the garden wall had run along its northern side pierced by a small ornamental door-way. Now the Treasurer, William Gilby, was authorised to set up in its place a stately and beautiful iron gateway and 'iron pallisadoes on a parapet wall'. The building at the eastern end of the Court with the passage down into Holborn Court was adorned with a colonnade of round pillars rather like those in the old Cloisters in the Temple. Till 1766 the lower level of Holborn Court was here reached by steps, instead of a slope later contrived. The paving of the Court, laid at different times, was varied and irregular. In 1725 a pavement of flat stones six feet wide was laid from the garden gate to the gate of Fulwood's Rents and another across the Court from the passage into Coney Court. In 1774 another part was 'new paved with Purbeck squares'.

Beyond Page's Buildings — from 1731 known as Nos. 1 and 2 Field Court — lay the miscellaneous collection of houses which from 1793 was named Gray's Inn Place. For long the buildings erected here on the Society's property in the late 17th century remained a mere continuation of Warwick Court shut off by a gate from the Inn proper, till in 1749 other gates and boundary stones were set up to enclose them. Meanwhile in 1714 there were erected the pleasant low-built stuccoed houses afterwards known as Nos. 1 and 2 Gray's Inn Place, north of Warwick Court and at right angles to it. A similar block corresponding to it and subsequently numbered 3 to 5 was built shortly afterwards on the same line eastwards up to the rear of Page's Buildings. Between these two new buildings was a broad space giving a view into the gardens on which they both backed. As one came up Warwick Court into the Inn from Holborn this gap lay straight ahead. If one turned left in front of the first block of buildings one came to a gate since replaced by a blank wall leading out of the Inn on the west; or turning right along the front of the second block one passed into Field Court by way of the passage running through Page's Buildings.

As with the Tudor porch of the Hall, so with the elaborations of Bacon's design for the Walks, the 18th century demanded and effected a simplification. His mount was levelled and his summer house destroyed and the work carried out in 1755-6 converted the gardens into a place of lawns and grassy slopes, gravelled paths and vistas of trees, with a long terrace looking out northward approached by steps and later on, in 1769, adorned with two alcoves facing each other at either end. Earlier in the century the Walks had narrowly escaped far greater transformations. In 1715 and for about a dozen years afterwards a scheme was in the air for building on their western part a new Serjeants' Inn but in the end it came to nothing.

It was from the gardens that the encroachments of the builder were most regrettably apparent. At the start of the century the west side of Bedford Row, where Chief Justice Holt had a house, was already up, but the long rectangular enclosure of Jockeys' Field still lay between it and Gray's Inn. In 1715 the Society had a mind to purchase it but the matter was dropped and soon afterwards the east side of Bedford Row was erected there. Only the northern prospect towards Highgate Hill now remained unimpaired but half a century later this too was obstructed by the advancing city. The way along the garden had hitherto been a country road, the boundary itself a ditch with, from 1717, a low mud wall and before that a broken fence. Now a row of houses was built opposite the gardens and in 1759 a solid new wall was put up, leaving only a gap opposite the end of John Street down which the open country could still be glimpsed 'just enough of the prospect to make the loss of the rest more sensible'. Two years later the Society shut itself in by planting a double row of elms along the terrace. Still, as late as December, 1780, Samuel Romilly could write from his chambers in the north-west corner of Coney Court: 'The moment the sun peeps I am in the country. A cold country it is for, having only one row of houses between me and Hampstead and Highgate, the north-west wind blows full against the chambers'.

Such was the general aspect of the Inn but even the 18th century did not so rationalise it as to exclude all incongruities. In several odd and unexpected corners little shops still carried on business. Thomas Osborne, Richardson's publisher, had premises in Page's Buildings. It was here that Dr. Johnson once felled him with a folio Septuagint of 1594. ('Sir, he was impertinent and I beat him.') Richard Tonson, the bookseller, and his brother Jacob had an establishment in the Gray's Inn Lane gateway and Jacob afterwards had another in the Holborn gate, where there were shops on both sides of the way as late as 1770, when the Society demolished those on the west and had the site paved. A book-binder, a stationer, a barber, a breeches maker all found nooks and corners for their trades.

The Society itself almost went into business in 1777, purchasing two houses east of the Holborn gate to build the Gray's Inn Coffee House, communicating internally with the Inn. This it let to a succession of tenants. In 1784 the chambers over the Holborn gateway having been left long uninhabited by the tenant Richard Kendall, a Fellow of Peterhouse, his furniture was removed from them by order of the Benchers and in the following year they were included in the letting to the coffee house tenant.

Public offices too established themselves within the Inn, the Nisi Prius Office and the Pipe Office in Page's Buildings and the Hawkers' and Pedlars' Office in Warwick Court. The Duchy of Lancaster Office had, of course, long occupied the chambers between the Hall and the Chapel. When it moved out in 1788 the premises were taken over by the Benchers; the ground floor became the Pension Room and the upper floor the Library, a new staircase being built to give access to it. Railings erected in front, continuing those set up in 1742 before the Hall, were carried along to enclose the Chapel too.

Until the removal, the Library had been in the north set of chambers on the first floor of No. 1 Coney Court, on the site of the old Bacon's Buildings of before the fire of 1684. Since 1771 the Pension Room had been in the south set and after 1781 the linen and plate had been kept in the room adjoining it. Earlier in the century the Benchers had held their meetings in the Library. The Library itself was still small, despite a great effort made to improve it in 1725. A legacy might give an occasional opportunity for a few purchases. Not only legal literature, like *Viner's Abridgement,* was added to it. Such works as the *Universal History, Hurd's Dialogues* or *Postlethwaite's Dictionary,* found their way into its shelves and *Johnson's Dictionary* was acquired within two months of publication. But the whole collection was still adequately housed in a single room.

Amid all the changes of the first half of the 18th century the often repaired but never thoroughly reconstructed Chapel remained, as it was described in 1773, 'a gothic structure that has marks of much greater antiquity than any other of the buildings'. Contemporary engravings give a clear idea of its external facade about this time. Above the three great windows were four little oval ones regularly spaced. Between the two westernmost of them, rather in the situation of a nose to a pair of eyes, was a small square window. There were three doors, two rounded ones on ground floor level and a square one at the western extremity approached by railed steps and evidently giving access to the gallery at the lower end of the Chapel. Above was a little clock-tower and cupola. Stuccoed without and white-washed within the Chapel had put on a truly Protestant simplicity. Its Communion plate was modest and an inventory of 1704 enumerates only 'two flaggons, two challices, one patten'.

The Church of England, still dominant, though not unchallenged, set the standard of the religious life of the average man. To receive Communion according to its rites was a prerequisite of call to the Bar and in 1786 it was ordered that a book be provided for the members to sign on doing so, the

Preacher and the Clerk of the Chapel subscribing their names as witnesses. At service the congregation occupied their places in strictly regulated seniority. The gallery in the south-east angle, the pews on either side of the Communion Table and in the body of the Chapel, the gallery at the lower end, each had its allotted occupants, Judges, King's Counsel, Serjeants, Benchers, gentlemen of distinction, barristers, students, tenants, and servants. In this setting the religious life of the Society moved with simplicity and decorum. The purchase of a velvet pulpit cloth and cushions and a handsome velvet cloth for the Communion Table, all fringed, the publication of the Preacher's sermons, occasional repairs and white-washings for the fabric, these mark the even tenor of its way.

As for the Hall, it altered but little. Outside, the sundial on the south wall still recalled a simpler age. Within, the changes were none of them radical. There were repairs from time to time. The floor might be relaid, the roof retiled. In 1706, the walls were repanelled with Norwegian oak. There was the unfortunate order in 1765 'that the wainscote be varnished and the screen painted and the north and south windows glazed with crown glass in lead', an operation which most fortunately the great bay window escaped. In 1736 twelve leather-seated walnut chairs for the high table were ordered at 16s. each. For the rest plain oak benches were the order of the day. New tables were acquired in 1745.

The Hall was still the heart of the Society, warmed by the charcoal fire on the hearth, brightened by the painted portraits and the armorial bearings of those who had made it illustrious, but the pulse of life was now beating more slowly than in the vivid tumultuous days that had gone before. The students must still keep their terms by dining but the Readings had ceased and nothing had taken their place; the sole trace of any substitute was a series of lectures delivered in Hall between 1753 and 1769 by Danby Pickering, a barrister of the Society. On his becoming a Bencher they were discontinued. It was pure personal initiative if some students like Samuel Romilly organised little meetings in their chambers to argue out doubtful points of law.

As a qualification for call the moots lingered on in a shadowy sort of way throughout the century in the form of exercises presided over by barristers but by 1795 they had so far become simply excuses for convivial extravagance that the Benchers expressly emphasised that there was no order requiring any entertainment to be given on the performance of an exercise or on call to the Bar. Students having started by inviting those who had assisted them at the exercises and a few special friends, the practice quickly grew till a general invitation to all and sundry became a moral and social obligation. The exercises can have been little more than a formality. The other conditions for call, as settled in 1765, prescribed a period of five years from admission (reduced to three for university graduates) and the keeping of twelve terms in Hall.

The fare at table was substantial but not luxurious. From 1751, when the catering in Hall was improved and the price of the commons was raised from 8s. to 9s. a week, the bill of fare included beef, mutton, veal, pork, tongue, brawn, rabbit, pigeon, fish, with apple pie, gooseberry pie or plum pudding. In 1757, Colchester oysters made their appearance on Fridays in Michaelmas Term. Even in a hard-drinking age the wine allowance was moderate, two bottles to a mess in 1797. Port was the most favoured drink, brought by the pipe and bottled in the cellars, but claret, burgundy and sherry, madeira, moselle and a little champagne were all available. During the century the dinner hour advanced from 1.0, till in 1782 it was fixed at 4.0.

The plate with which the board was garnished still remained modest; the inventory of 1756 enumerates only two tankards, four sauce boats, four candlesticks, two large bowls with covers, a goblet, a ewer, eighteen table-spoons, one soup-spoon, two marrow-spoons, six salts, three castors, an orange strainer, two salvers, a monteth, and a large dish. By the end of the century this was but little augmented. There were now thirty-six table-spoons, twelve silver forks, and four castors. Among the additions was a silver tea-pot, but pewter still seems to have been in ordinary use for most purposes.

During the 18th century a new use was found for the Hall as a court of justice. Through *Bleak House* every one knows that the sittings out of term of the Court of Chancery were held in

Lincoln's Inn Hall. In 1789, on the request of Lord Chief Baron Eyre, a former Bencher, Gray's Inn afforded similar accommodation for the Court of Exchequer. The arrangement lasted far into the 19th century long after Eyre had removed to the place of Chief Justice of the Common Pleas.

In all respects the Inn was remarkably self-contained. There were no paupers within its gates, although it contributed regularly to the support of the neighbouring poor. What it required it contracted for without the intervention of any local authorities. New River water came in and was paid for. There was a link with the Brooke Street sewer and that was paid for. In 1730 a regular contract was made for the lighting of the courts and squares with globular oil lamps. In 1739 there were nine maintained in summer and thirty-one in winter. All through the century the lighting was progressively improved. From 1777 there was a lamp on each landing. Though fires had lost their former frequency, since the only serious outbreak was at No. 3 Coney Court in 1717, the Inn maintained its own fire engine and hose. In this state of autonomy it remained independent of the demands of parish authorities. In 1771 an attempt was made to assess it for rates 'for 4,151 yards for paving, cleansing, and lighting the squares, streets, lanes and other places within the city and liberty of Westminster and parts adjacent, . . . at the rate of sixpence per yard amounting to the sum of £203 15s. 6d. per annum'. The Benchers, however, resisted and in 1774 a favourable decision was obtained from Lord Chief Justice Mansfield.

In another important respect, that of self protection, the Inn looked after itself. In 1730 and 1742, regulations were laid down governing the night watch. By night the porters guarded the gates and there was a shelter for a watchman in each court. One of the watchmen's duties was to enter each staircase and with a loud voice cry the hour of the night and the weather. They were to light the gentlemen to their chambers and once the watch was set only members were admitted to the Inn. In 1762 it was found necessary to post a watchman outside the gate in Gray's Inn Lane to see that no filth was laid against the buildings. The watchmen were paid a shilling a night and from 1784 the head porter had to keep a book to record their names and the times of their going on duty and leaving. In 1793 an armed watchman was stationed in the gardens.

These precautions were not superfluous. Thus in November 1785, about nine in the evening, two men with pistols raided the chambers of Mr. Alan Chambre, a member of the Society, afterwards a Justice of the Common Pleas, and held up and robbed his clerk, his pupil and a client delivering a brief, leaving them all tied up with their own handkerchiefs. About a week later there was a similar attempt at the offices of an attorney at No. 8 Holborn Court. He however, sitting in an inner room, heard the exclamation of his clerk, slipped out by another way, locked the outer doors and gave the alarm. The sequel was two executions at Newgate and a reward of two guineas voted by the grateful Benchers to each of the two constables who assisted in the arrests.

Early in the century there was another curious criminal episode in the Inn. A mysterious series of robberies occurred over a long period and went unsolved until the death in 1737 in a madhouse in Red Lion Square of a gentleman called Rudkins who had chambers at the top of No. 14 Holborn Court. Only then were his rooms broken open, revealing a hoard of missing property and a complete house-breaking outfit. When he had been planning a raid on one of his neighbours he had been in the habit of ostentatiously mounting his horse as if he were going into the country, subsequently slipping quietly back unobserved. It was remembered that every execution day, but at no other time, he would go to the Coffee House by the Holborn Gate to sit in the window and watch the condemned go by on their way to Tyburn.

As to the government of the Society, now that the Readings had fallen into disuse, the Benchers were recruited simply by a system of co-option. A call to the Bench was obligatory on those chosen and refusal to accept was visited with a fine. Eight sets of chambers were reserved for Benchers who held them on condition of giving certain stated attendances at Pension meetings and keeping terms in Hall, while the holding of the Resident Bencher's chamber at No. 2 Coney Court from 1737 onwards entailed a certain period of actual residence.

The Benchers' jurisdiction still extended to the superintendence of Staple Inn and Barnard's Inn, but, as the educational system of the Inns decayed and fell to pieces, their dominion became more and more shadowy. Meanwhile the gentlemen of these subordinate Inns of Chancery, under their Principal and Ancients, were well content to limit their activities to keeping terms by dining in their charming little Halls and finding pretexts to fine one another in terms of bottles of claret.

In 1734 an event occurred, little noticed but important as marking the Benchers finally becoming masters in their own house; this was the purchase on February 5th for £100 of the fee farm rent payable to the Crown. Henceforth the Society was nobody's tenant.

Early in the century the Benchers had a good deal of servant trouble and in 1721 a committee appointed to investigate the affairs of the Society found the Steward's accounts very erroneous and his fees, salary and perquisites excessive. The butler's claims were likewise found unreasonable. The workmen were charging occupants of chambers double what the work they did was worth. The sequel was a general reorganisation of the staff from the Head Porter downwards. He was to receive a salary of £18 a year plus certain fees and perquisites. The under porter, who took over the duties of the office of scavenger, now abolished, got £9, also with fees and perquisites in addition. Their duties as to cleaning and lighting the lamps, cleaning 'the bogghouse', and taking care of the fire engine, were strictly specified. Salaries rose as the century proceeded. The cook, who in 1739 was getting £20 a year 'for himself, scullion and turnspits' was allowed £50 in 1782.

Long service was the general rule. Thus Gorham was the Society's bricklayer from 1726 to 1797. Thomas Adams, the Chief Butler and Steward, who died in 1781 owing the Society over £400, had served it in various capacities since 1735. His predecessor John Beaver, whom he succeeded as Steward in 1752, had held office since 1700 and had already then been sixteen years in the Society's service.

Despite some untoward incidents, the whole trend of 18th century Gray's Inn was towards gentlemanly reasonableness and order consolidating itself in a life of quiet leisure, good taste and security. Life flowed on embanked and no longer in a turbulent tide. The regular squares and gardens were symbolic of the change. New inventions were welcomed—a 'machine fire stove' for a set of chambers in 1760, a new iron range for the kitchen in 1766, a water closet in 1788. Disturbances were rare, though occupants occasionally made nuisances of themselves. One might try to encroach on the gardens; another might keep pigeons; another might cause a disturbance by locking up a child; another might make several kinds of noise at very early and improper hours. Tragic incidents, like the fatal duel in the Walks in 1701, which had its sequel in the conviction of Captain Greenwood for manslaughter, were few and far between. Women were still forbidden residence in the Inn and tenants had occasionally to be restrained from attempted evasions of the ban. Laundresses, relics of a cruder age, had to be dissuaded from emptying chamber pots out of the windows, carrying buckets of filth about at unseasonable hours of the day and doing washing in the chambers.

But amid the advance of refinement there was still room for some exponents of good old English eccentricity. The places where Dr. Johnson lodged are almost as numerous as the beds in which Queen Elizabeth slept and Gray's Inn is, of course, among them; in Staple Inn he wrote *Rasselas* in a week to pay for his mother's funeral. From Gray's Inn his friend Arthur Murphy, dramatist, actor, wit and eventually barrister and commissioner in bankruptcy, issued for a short time the lively periodical called the *Gray's Inn Journal.*

William Cobbett, Johnson's equal in sturdy individuality, spent a few unhappy months in 1783 as an 'understrapping quill driver' to an attorney at No. 12 Coney Court. 'No part of my life', he afterwards wrote, 'has been totally unattended by pleasure except the eight or nine months I spent at Gray's Inn. The office—for so the dugeon where I worked was called—was so dark that on cloudy days we were obliged to burn candle. I worked like a galley slave from five in the morning till eight or nine at night and sometimes all night long. . . . When I think of the saids and so forths and the counts of tautology that I scribbled over, when I think of those sheets of seventy-two words and those lines two inches apart my brain turns.' No wonder he left in such a hurry to join the Marines that he joined the 54th Regiment by mistake and before he knew where he was found himself on foreign service.

A gentler shade, little remembered now, is the Reverend Adam Buddle, who was Chapel Reader or assistant to the Preacher from 1702 until his death at Gray's Inn in 1714. Poor Mr. Buddle, very hospitable and fond of his friends, was, in a quiet way, one of the most accomplished botanists of his day. Botany, he said, in one of his sermons, is 'the most innocent, most primitive study designed at first even in Paradise as a diversion for the busy inquisitive mind of man'. But there was no fortune in botany and Mr. Buddle died poor. The Benchers in 1705 had already made him a grant 'to supply his extraordinary occasions' and after his death they helped his widow. There is no clue to his resting place in St. Andrew's, Holborn, but the buddleia, named after him, is his memorial.

An erudite oddity and enthusiastic collector who lived in Gray's Inn was the antiquarian Thomas Rawlinson, called to the Bar by the Middle Temple in 1705. At his chambers he accumulated books and manuscripts in such uncontrolled quantities that in the end there was nowhere for him to sleep except in the passage. Joseph Ritson, another eminent antiquarian, a barrister of the Society, lived on the first floor of No. 8 Holborn Court, from 1780 till his death in 1803. Towards the end of his life he suffered a nervous breakdown, barricaded his door against all comers and started a bonfire of manuscripts which nearly set the building alight, so that the Steward had to break in to intervene.

Even in its oddities Gray's Inn was a little realm apart. The echoes of the great outside world of public affairs sounded within its gates, now loud, now faintly, but effected no radical change in the tempo of the life of the Society. In 1723 Christopher Layer, a Jacobite barrister of the Society, was executed at Tyburn for high treason in conspiring against the newly established Hanoverian dynasty. He died bravely and betrayed no one. The Jacobite rebellion of 1745 evoked a declaration of loyalty to King George from Gray's Inn. In 1777 a donation of a hundred guineas voted by the Benchers 'for the relief of our troops at Boston employed in suppressing the American rebellion' aroused a protest from some of the Bar that they had no power so to dispose of the Society's funds. The protest was rejected. In June 1780, the Gordon Riots, with flames springing up all along Holborn and the mob breathing threats of destruction against the Inn, specially obnoxious to them because of the number of Catholics living there, found the members standing to arms at their gates to defend the Society. (A few years earlier, in the last penal prosecutions of priests for saying Mass, it had been the firm of Dyneley & Ashmall, attorneys, with offices in Gray's Inn, which had defended over twenty of them, generally gratuitously.) That same month of June saw the drafting of a detailed code of 'Rules and Orders to be observed by the Gentlemen, Members and Inhabitants of Gray's Inn associated for the purpose of learning military discipline', designed to put training on a permanent footing; but the closing century was to see the capital and the nation in far greater peril. In 1798, as the lengthening shadow of the great French war and the threat of invasion darkening over England turned almost every able-bodied citizen into a part-time soldier, the Volunteers of the Holborn parishes marched and drilled in the once quiet gardens.

Still, these were but echoes of another world. Throughout the century the Inn had been sinking ever deeper into peace and somnolence. After the colourful restless days of Elizabeth and the Tudors, the turbulent times of the Stuarts, the tide was receding, leaving it a back-water. No longer did it number on its rolls, as a matter of course, leaders in the law and in the state. It is true that at the start of the century it bred Lord Chief Justice Raymond, himself the son of a former member and Justice of the King's Bench, and later there was Lord Chief Justice Eyre. Again Charles Wolfran Cornwall, Speaker of the Commons from 1780 to 1789, was a Bencher. But it was becoming clear that the type of man predestined to success was gravitating more and more to the other Societies, less and less to Gray's Inn, though, of course, the start is not everything. There were other members like Sir Thomas Clarke, who was Master of the Rolls from 1754 to 1764 and who sprang from the most uncertain origins, while Samuel Romilly, whose lasting glory it is to have been the first to undermine the granite structure of a merciless and implacable criminal code, came from a family of Huguenot refugees.

Nevertheless, though life flowed quietly within the Inn the Benchers of that age, working, building, deliberating, fixed its form to reflect their underlying conceptions of society—formal, orderly, with the turbulence of cruder existences shut well away without the gates. The rough, clamorous life that once filled the Hall with riot and contrast was tamed. The rich, creative exuberance of Readings and masques had subsided. The age had shaped Gray's Inn to its own image and likeness.

8

Nineteenth-Century Vicissitudes

FROM May 1827, to November 1828, a bright clever-looking
lad of about fifteen or sixteen worked at No. 1 Holborn Court,
Gray's Inn—it became South Square in 1829—as clerk to Mr.
Edward Blackmore, attorney. In that period his pay rose from
13s. 6d. to 15s. a week, but not content with such promising
prospects, he abandoned his office stool to fling himself
imprudently into journalism. His name was Charles Dickens.
Twenty-two years later, viewing the scene of his former labours
with an eye no more nostalgic than Cobbett's remembering the
same employment in the same surroundings, this is what he
wrote: 'When my uncommercial travels tend to this dismal spot,
my comfort is its rickety state. Imagination gloats over the full-
ness of time when the staircases shall have quite tumbled down—
they are daily wearing into an ill-savoured powder, but have not
quite tumbled down yet—when the last prolix old Bencher, all of
the olden time, shall have been got out of an upper window by
means of a fire ladder and carried off to the Holborn Union;
when the last clerk shall have engrossed the last parchment
behind the last splash on the last of the mud-stained windows
which all through the miry year are pilloried out of recognition
in Gray's Inn Lane'.

The office where Dickens worked looked out at the back onto
the space separating the south side of Holborn Court from the
shops in the Holborn highway, a squalid little trench, as he saw it,
with rank grass and a pump, its empire divided between rats and
cats 'and a few briefless bipeds surely called to the Bar by voices
of deceiving spirits seeing that they are wanted there by no
mortal'. Hereabouts, you remember, poor Mr. Phunkey, the

97

junior counsel in Mr. Pickwick's case, had his chambers, while Mr. Perker, that intelligent attorney, had his office in Gray's Inn Square. No, there is no doubt that by the turn of the 18th century Gray's Inn had become unfashionable and for several decades continued to decline into further depths of unpopularity.

The Society had not, of course, ceased to breed successful lawyers. There was a period during the eighteen-twenties when all three of the puisne judges in the Court of King's Bench—Bayley, Holroyd and Littledale—were men trained at Gray's Inn. So was their contemporary Mr. Baron Hullock, who served in the Court of Exchequer when it was still holding its out of term sittings in Gray's Inn Hall. Another was Mr. Justice Gaselee, appointed to the Court of Common Pleas in 1824, who is supposed to be the original of Mr. Justice Stareleigh of 'Pickwick'. There were others too besides judges. Edward Gibbon Wakefield, who in the end turned out so much more of a credit than appeared at first sight, was admitted to the Society in 1813. He prefaced his career as an Empire builder and chief founder of New Zealand by two speculations in matrimonial fortune hunting. The first, an elopement with a ward in Chancery, proved eminently successful. The second, after he had been left a widower, the abduction of fifteen year old Emily Turner from boarding school, brought him into the dock at the Lancaster Assizes in March, 1827, strangely enough before Mr. Baron Hullock, and earned him a three years prison sentence. In gaol he turned his interests into other channels and became one of the pioneers of a new enlightened colonial policy.

Basil Montague, K.C., one of Lamb's circle and editor of Bacon's works, was a member of Gray's Inn and so was another of his friends Bryan Walker Procter, author, dramatist and poet under the name of Barry Cornwall, a solicitor before he was called to the Bar in 1831.

Lamb himself, though so true a child of the Temple, found it in his heart to praise Gray's Inn. He saw it not as the headstrong Cobbett nor yet as the hostile Dickens, to whose unfriendly eye even the Walks—turf, trees and gravel—wore only a legal livery of black. For Lamb in 1822 'they are still the best gardens of any of the Inns of Court, my beloved Temple not forgotten, have the gravest character, being altogether reverend and law breathing'. Yet even for him they had been finer five and twenty years before. Then 'the accursed Verulam Buildings had not encroached upon all the east side of them, cutting out delicate green crankles and shouldering away one of two of the stately alcoves of the terrace – the survivor stands gaping and relationless as if it remembered its brother'.

Verulam Buildings, commenced when Samuel Romilly was Treasurer, were put up in 1803-11 and Raymond Buildings, matching them on the west and faithfully reflecting all their least attractive characteristics, rose in 1825. They marked a lapse into uglification that was to be characteristic of the new century. Their dark repellent brickwork and grey slates, harsh and forbidding beside the mellow rosy tones of the older squares, form an appropriate start for an age which was coming to treat airier rooms and broader staircases as an end in themselves to which aesthetic considerations were wholly irrelevant. So early they could not altogether escape a suggestion of Georgian proportions and in date, of course, they were Georgian, though the spirit they breathed was that of the Industrial Revolution.

At the start of the century London was still in a sense a large country town. A stag hunted from Uxbridge by the Duke of Clarence's hounds could run through open country north-east to Highgate and south to Bloomsbury, where, clearing a gate, it turned into the Duke of Bedford's private road at the end of Tavistock Square, fled down Woburn Place through Russell Square, finally making for refuge in an open doorway in Montague Place. But if on one side Gray's Inn lay so close to fields and to the fashionable sequence of streets and squares spreading in planned regularity over the acres of the old manor of Bloomsbury, on the other side the ancient irregular gables of the older London, picturesque and full of character, but often crumbling into dilapidated and unwholesome slums, presented an unchanged face to a changing world.

By the end of the century London was stretching continuously out beyond Stoke Newington in the north and Brixton in the south, beyond Notting Hill and Kensington in the west and Bow and Blackwall in the east. Nor was the change merely one of scale. The whole character of the town and indeed of the entire nation had undergone a fundamental alteration. The man of business was now in charge, his ascendancy recognised and secured by the Parliamentary reform of 1832, and the old aristocracy of the man of taste was henceforth in retreat, stubbornly, but in the long run unsuccessfully, fighting a rear-guard action. Happy the nobleman who had a coal seam under his estate or a piece of land that could be developed as a seaport or a fashionable building estate or who could join the commercial men in the railway building mania.

The face of a town reflects the soul of its inhabitants and, as the century advanced, the face of London clearly reflected the dominant influences at work, the urge for commercial expansion, the primary preoccupation with profit as an end in itself and as a standard of judgment, the belief in the unlimited possibilities for progress and universal felicity inherent in enterprise and invention freely fostered by business men.

From the City of London family life retreated, as homes and churches fell to the house-breaker to make way for offices. Architecture, which at any rate till after the Regency displayed the qualities of either a discreet good taste or a pompous magnificence, lapsed either into the mere ostentation of self-advertisement or the unrelieved dullness of the totally utilitarian. From George IV and the classical grace of the old Regent Street the century moved confidently on to Shaftesbury Avenue, Charing Cross Road, Hungerford Bridge, the tram-clanging Victoria Embankment, the Metropolitan Board of Works, the London County Council, the metropolitan boroughs with mayors and aldermen to replace the old vestries, and all the demonstrable advantages of good pavements, improved road surfaces and planned drainage. In the rising tide of improvement Gray's Inn lost its local extraterritoriality to the new Holborn Borough Council. In 1830 it had defeated in the King's Bench an attempt to levy a poor rate on the occupants of chambers but in 1899 the current was too strong and the Local Government Act brought it within the Council's jurisdiction.

Measure the changes of the century in Holborn. A stag hunt in Bloomsbury at its start and in 1900 the 'Twopenny Tube', the

Central London Railway, running beneath its pavements. The road that went westwards from Newgate past Gray's Inn changed indeed with the times. No longer did the procession of the condemned go by to the hangings at Tyburn—that had ceased before the end of the 18th century—though public executions before the gaol itself continued till 1868. In the eighteen-sixties Holborn Viaduct, ponderously ornate, bridging the ravine where the River Fleet had flowed, saved the labouring horses of buses and drays the heaviest of the pull up to High Holborn. In 1868 Middle Row, the island group of ancient buildings projecting into the highway just west of Staple Inn, made way for a great five globe gas standard elaborately ornamented with flowers and leaves rather like the one that stands just opposite the Law Courts to-day.

Street lighting was a growing preoccupation. The smoke of the coal on which the new industrial England was built lay heavy over the town, sometimes thickening to fogs of legendary opacity. The horse-drawn traffic clattered past the gates of the Inn, rattling carriages and carts and rumbling drays. Yet their day was shortening. Starved out by the new railways, the stage coach was at its last gasp by the middle of the century. The old coaching inns of Holborn went down—the George and Blue Boar in High Holborn, demolished in the sixties, and the great White Horse in Fetter Lane in the nineties—and all through those years the old buildings about the Inn crashed one by one.

A world was crashing with them. The tide of inventive progress and commercial profit stayed for no man and by the forties and long after, huddled on the floors of the squalid overcrowded lodging houses of slums never far off, the dispossessed, the human wreckage of the old discarded order, sank to rot—coachmen, guards, ostlers, horse-keepers, harness-makers, farriers, coach-builders, inn servants, watermen put out of work by the new steam boats, and then and later, artisans whose painfully acquired skills had been superseded by new processes of manufacture. These fell while others rose. And for those who did not fall, from the artisan class upwards, there was warmth and comfort and sentiment and security by the hearth side in the cosy over-furnished interiors of an age of plenty and limitless possibilities.

And what was happening within Gray's Inn's gates during those years of transformation? In 1826, as a reaction perhaps from the utilitarian intrusion of Verulam and Raymond Buildings, the Hall, the Pension Room and Library, the Chapel and its porch and the archway into Holborn Court were romantically swamped by a tidal wave of false gothic, uniformly covered with stucco and battlemented in the then fashionable style. The warm red Tudor brick vanished from sight; grey slates replaced the former tiles and a new lantern, deemed more appropriate, crowned the roof instead of the ancient louver which is said to have inspired Andrew Hamilton, a member of the Inn, when he drew the plans for the cupola of the State House at Philadelphia in 1722. Within, the Hall was little changed. Beyond the middle of the 19th century it was still being put to a dual purpose, for after the Court of Exchequer ceased to sit there it was for a while used by the Insolvent Debtors Court.

The Holborn gate succumbed to stucco in 1867 and was never uncovered again. The Hall was happily scraped clean in the nineties and its red brick restored, but not the Chapel. Nor were the Pension Room and Library next door. The redecoration of 1826 had given them a step gable. Subsequently this had been removed in favour of crenellations to correspond with the Hall and Chapel. Their lighting had also been improved by substituting a single broad mullioned window on each floor for the three plain windows above and below. All these features remained at the end of the century.

But already by the eighteen-thirties the Library was outgrowing the simple room in the old Duchy of Lancaster Office and the obvious direction in which to expand it was south of the Chapel. Finch's Buildings next to the Hall and Denny's Buildings beside them, now numbered respectively 10 and 9 South Square, were old and dilapidated and it was decided to demolish them. By 1842 a new building, faced with grey stone, designed in a style generally reminiscent of the Tudor had risen on the site, blocking up the south windows of the Chapel and touching 8 South Square. A flight of steps with a broad canopied porch led into an entrance hall dominated by a great curving staircase with polished banisters. The old Pension Room on the ground floor with the library room above looking onto Gray's Inn Square were preserved with the addition of a long and spacious new room on the ground floor facing South Square for the use of the Benchers and a corresponding library room above it, as well as a smaller library room above the porch. Still the Society's collection of books grew and in 1884, when it numbered about 15,000, a further extension eastwards was contrived behind the east end of the Chapel, with five windows overlooking Gray's Inn Road.

The nineties saw great changes. The 'Sahara' desolation of Gray's Inn Square, which had filled young Dickens with raging depression, was relieved by the planting of plane trees all round it in 1890. (For over a hundred years it had been utterly bare without either grass or greenery.) The last little shop in the Holborn gateway was shut up in 1892. Once a bookseller's, it had for many years fulfilled the lowlier functions of a newsagent's.

In 1862 the three north windows of the Chapel were filled with glass representing Christ with the Doctors in the Temple, the Sermon on the Mount and the Ascension. In 1893 the Chapel underwent a complete transformation, with carved stalls and benches, a marble floor, an organ in the south-east corner and a wooden gallery within the entrance at the west end. It was not a very happy period of church decoration and, with the best will in the world, the effect achieved was to wipe out any atmosphere of antiquity in favour of the sort of stereotyped gothic standardised all over the country. To the credit side was the retention of the fine Jacobean pulpit cleaned of paint, the rediscovery and preservation of an old holy water stoup and the substitution of an oak ceiling for the 18th century plaster one. In 1899 new glass was added, an east window representing five Archbishops of Canterbury; Saint Thomas à Becket—whose earlier image had been destroyed by order of Henry VIII—Whitgift, Laud and Juxon, all members of the Society, and Wake who had been Preacher from 1688 to 1694.

It was chiefly in the south-west part of the Inn that the closing century saw the most drastic alterations. At the bottom of Gray's Inn Place, you remember, there were two little low cottage-like buildings backing on the gardens. Early in the nineties the eastward one adjoining Page's Buildings was pulled down and replaced by the only piece of pure and unadulterated Victorianism that the Society ever permitted itself. (The Temple has far more.) With its mixture of stone and brick, its mansard roof, its great ornate pillared entrance, it was obviously a product of 'the best contemporary thought' in commercial architecture. At once ostentatious and undistinguished, it remained a standing warning to future Building Committees of how not to please posterity.

About the same time the old range of buildings adjoining, which closed the west end of Field Court, started giving anxiety of a rather peculiar sort. Doors would open and shut without visible human agency; clocks would stop as if an unseen hand had arrested the pendulum; cabinets were precipitated onto the floor. A climax was reached when a bed on the top storey moved in the night from one side of the room to the other while its occupant slept. Mysterious groanings and creakings added terror to these phenomena till the tenants became convinced that a supernatural cause was at work. A surveyor's report soon allayed their fears. The old buildings had long been a little out of plumb – so long that no one noticed a slight additional list which, though imperceptible, was quite enough to account for the movement of the furniture. In obedience to a dangerous structures notice the chambers were demolished and, curiously enough, never rebuilt. They left the ugly end wall of a house in Fulwood's Rents looming blindly over the Inn and in those days commercial enterprise was not slow to take advantage of a heaven-sent poster hoarding. 'Pin-up girls' of the naughty nineties with black stockinged legs and swirling 'can-can' petticoats were soon advertising 'Illustrated Bits' and 'Pick Me Up' – '32 pages, brightest stories, smartest pictures, fun, fact, fancy. 1d. weekly'. Aspinall's enamel praised itself alongside the India and Ceylon Exhibition at Earl's Court. The new world was looking into the Inn with a vengeance.

Not that the Inn had been previously insensible to modern improvements. Gas appeared experimentally on the staircase of No. 2 Raymond Buildings in December, 1857, and within a year it had replaced oil illumination throughout the Inn, though it was another forty years before the bare jets gave place to incandescent lighting in the Hall – four gasoliers of five lights each. Since 1815 the Hall had no longer been heated by an open fire on a central hearth. A large three-sided cast-iron stove about 3 feet 6 inches high with a barred grate at each side had been installed. It was only removed in 1897 when less obtrusive heating arrangements were adopted. Similarly in 1828 it had been decided to heat the Chapel 'on a new principle'.

And what of life in the chambers of the Inn? Mostly the residents were a bachelor community but women, though few, were no longer barred. Benchers, judges, barristers, students, Bohemians might be found in the rooms up the old staircases or perhaps a struggling young solicitor with his pretty wife and family. Early in the century the two charming little buildings at the end of Gray's Inn Place, backing onto the gardens were each inhabited by a barrister, his young wife and three or four lovely children. Thus old ways were relaxed. Just as women could now dwell in the once semi-monastic community, so serjeants, who formerly died to the Society when they were admitted to Serjeants' Inn, and solicitors, who had not had any place in an Inn of Court, could enjoy limited membership for the purpose of holding chambers. The old outlines were becoming blurred.

Rents were low in those days, so low that even if you were poor, so poor that dining out at a chop-house or an evening at the theatre in the pit was a matter for calculation and reflection, six rooms at the top of one of the old buildings perhaps on two floors connected by a little private staircase, was not beyond your reach. In those days too there was a little shop conveniently round the corner where slices of cold boiled beef, very red and sometimes tasting strongly of salt-petre, could be had on very reasonable terms.

If you were more prosperous there was the Gray's Inn Coffee House, with its imposing canopied portal flanked by tall bay windows, next to the Holborn gate, which was in all essentials an outpost of the Inn. There, of course, David Copperfield dined, on his return to England, in the solid substantial room with its shining mahogany tables boxed in by partitions crowned with comfortable green curtains on brass rods. The sanded floor, the perfectly trimmed lamps, the two large coal fires and the rows of decanters, completed the picture. There he slept in a vast wainscoted apartment over the gateway in the sedate immensity of a four-poster bed. There he was directed by the waiter to the chambers at No. 2 Holborn Court where his friend Tommy Traddles was living with his young wife, waiting for his chance at the Bar.

Thus directed, you remember, he found the name on the doorpost, climbed to the very top of a crazy staircase, 'feebly lighted on each landing by a club-headed little oil wick dying away in a little dungeon of dirty glass', till he knocked at the door and a sharp little lad, half footboy, half clerk, admitted him to the charming domestic scene where the young couple were living in cheerful gipsy simplicity, fitting home and profession into two rooms below and a little attic in the roof ('a very nice little room when you're up there'). 'Our domestic arrangements are, to say the truth, quite unprofessional altogether, my dear Copperfield. Even Sophy's being here is unprofessional. And we have no other place of abode'.

If you lived in Gray's Inn Square you might look out across the gardens of an evening at the setting sun and think how pleasant it was, forgetting perhaps the odour of cock-loft within. If you lived in Field Court, you looked one way through a stately wrought-iron gateway to a deserted tree garden, an exercise ground for children and nursemaids, one or two corps of volunteer riflemen and a score or more barristers who liked to smoke in the open air. The other way you looked to Fulwood's Rents, then a dirty narrow slummy blind-alley of fine houses decayed from which on Saturday evenings there floated language that made it advisable to close one's windows if there were ladies present.

But in the heart of the Inn a great quiet brooded over all. The sense of quiet was deepened rather than broken by the songs of finches, linnets, robins, wrens and even thrushes in the Walks, or the sound of a violin in one of the chambers playing a melody of Purcell perhaps or a sonata of Beethoven. 'Nothing else in London' wrote Natheniel Hawthorne, 'is so like the effect of a spell as to pass under one of these archways and find yourself transported from the jumble, rush, tumult and uproar into what seems an eternal Sabbath'.

Within the chambers themselves was an informal cosiness of fine dark panelling, varnished or painted, finely carved mantelpieces, solid mahogany furniture, deep armchairs and firelight flickering from deep fireplaces. But for the solitary man, of course, that quiet, even that cosiness, could be desperately lonely. The sole caller might be the old bonneted laundress who cleaned the rooms, her black bundling figure looking like a bulky, badly rolled family umbrella. His only salute might be from the porter at the gate. Such lonely men have died behind closed doors and no one been aware of it for weeks or months.

They were a varied company, the residents of Gray's Inn. For a short time the sophisticated Thackeray, sure of fame, had chambers there. So had simple old Sam Denton, of whom all we know is that he was admitted in 1792, that he was practising as an attorney in Gray's Inn Square in 1812, that he figures in the Law List till 1836 and that he left this ingenuous record pasted inside a little satinwood tea caddy: '5 Commandment, Honour thy father and thy mother that thy days may be long in the land which the Lord thy God giveth thee. My mother gave this tea caddy in the year 1790 or 91 when I went to reside in my chambers 2 Field Court, Gray's Inn, of which I was admitted a member. I never will part from it. Oh how I admire my tea caddy and my silver cream jug. I am 76 next birthday, Sam Denton'.

There was Sir Charles Lyall, who abandoned practice at the Bar to devote himself to geology and lived in Raymond Buildings. So did William Broderip, a Bencher of the Society and a Metropolitan Magistrate, but by taste a naturalist and a collector in the tradition of those other collectors and scholars who made the Inn more than an ordinary dwelling place. He was a Fellow of the Linnean Society and the Royal Society and the conchological cabinet at his chambers acquired international fame, being ultimately purchased by the British Museum.

In contrast call at No. 8 Gray's Inn Place during the years 1896-8. A refugee from China, whose head the Empress-Dowager would have had if she could, was living there reading in the British Museum and studying European constitutions. Behind its placid 17th century facade he evolved the Three Principles of the People which were to become the gospel of a new China. His name was Sun Yat-sen.

And as London grew vaster and more impersonal and more unwieldy, the simple charm of life in the little enchanted island of Gray's Inn became more palpable so that at the very end of the century a lady who loved it wrote: 'I would rather, for my part, have a dinner of herbs in Gray's Inn in a low-roofed panelled parlour with windows open on the green enclosure below, than enjoy all the dainties of the clubs in a Palace Mansion with all the newest electric appliances. I would rather hear the dim echoes of the past in the rustle of the Gray's Inn elm trees . . . than boast of a theatre agency next door or live in a West End street of ever so desirable people'.

But how was Gray's Inn adapting itself in the exercise of its purely professional functions to the great transforming changes of the century? How were the demands of a new age being met in the vacuum created by the decay of the old structure of the Inns? In the middle of the century the forms still survived without much substance to justify them. Thus when a member of Gray's Inn became a Serjeant he still gave a breakfast to his fellows in Hall. The great bell tolled for his departure from 8.30 to 9.0 in the morning when he would drive in wearing his new purple robes and full-bottomed wig. He himself breakfasted in the Pension Room with the Benchers while the barristers and students sat down to the meal in Hall. The Ancients of Staple Inn and of Barnard's Inn who had already arrived in procession, attended by their Head Porters and other officers, had their own table. After an ample repast the cloths were removed and bowls of spiced wine were brought in. Finally, when the complimentary speeches were finished, the Steward of the Inn would present the new Serjeant with a silver purse containing forty guineas. Such, for instance, was the ceremony in honour of Mr. Serjeant Allen in 1845.

The outward show was pleasant enough but what was the inward reality? At Barnard's Inn and Staple Inn it was vaguely remembered that once upon a time Gray's Inn used to send them Readers but what they read about or why no one could recall. Solicitors and attorneys no longer looked to the Inns of Chancery for their professional training and organisation and in 1825 they took the decision that led to the formation of the Law Society. One by one the Inns of Chancery cut their connection with the law and dissolved their Societies. Already in the 19th century some were demolished but Staple Inn, purchased in 1884 by the Prudential Assurance Company, was not destroyed. On the contrary the plaster which had covered up the beauty of its fine timbered facade was scraped off and its Hall, quadrangle and garden were most happily preserved. Barnard's Inn eventually came into the hands of the Mercers' School when it removed from Dowgate in the City.

The Serjeants too had fallen from their high estate. In 1846 they received their death blow in the abolition of their exclusive right of audience in the Court of Common Pleas. In 1873 their last remaining privilege, the requirement that the Common Law Judges must all be of their Order was abrogated by statute. In 1876 the Serjeants dissolved their Society, sold their Inn in Chancery Lane and returned each one to the Inn of Court whence he had originally come.

In the administration of justice modern methods were now all the rage. The establishment of the County Courts in the eighteen-forties revolutionised practice in minor litigation. But that was not enough. The spirit of the age was tending towards centralisation, simplification, the tearing up of old boundaries, the levelling of old distinctions, the rationalising of old anomalies. In 1857 Doctors' Commons, a quaint little first cousin of the Inns of Court under the shadow of St. Paul's Cathedral, was swept away. In the courts which sat there a little family party of Doctors of the Civil Law enjoyed their monopoly in suits about people's wills and people's marriages and disputes about ships and boats, as readers of *David Copperfield* will remember. Incidentally, Sir Herbert Jenner Fust who was Judge of the Court of Arches there from 1834 till his death in 1852 was also a Bencher of Gray's Inn. So was Dr. John Lee, a learned, distinguished and versatile member of Doctors' Commons. He founded the Lee Prize at Gray's Inn.

Then in the seventies came the great Judicature Act which completely transformed the administration of justice in the

Superior Courts and in the sequel those courts themselves migrated from Westminster Hall where they had sat from time immemorial. There had been much dispute about where to put them; Lincoln's Inn Fields narrowly escaped being fixed on and a site in the neighbourhood of Gray's Inn was also canvassed but the spot eventually chosen was a warren of ancient and picturesque slums lying between Lincoln's Inn and the Strand. In the reorganisation Chancery retained its identity. The composite jurisdiction of the Probate, Divorce and Admiralty Division kept alive the memory of its ancestor Doctors' Commons. But the King's Bench Division eventually swallowed the old Courts of Common Pleas and Exchequer which thereafter were only a memory. Sir John Huddleston, a former member of Gray's Inn, who became Baron of the Exchequer in 1875, was the last judge ever so appointed and afterwards he used to call himself 'The Last of the Barons'.

The new age saw an enormous increase in the number of barristers. At the start of the century there were fewer than 900 in England. By the time it was half way through there were over 3,000, an increase which incidentally revolutionised the whole background of practice and spelt death to the system under which men lived in their working chambers. Henceforth there was not accommodation enough for that in the Inns of Court and under the new dispensation the normal thing was for several men to share a set of chambers for professional purposes only. This development indirectly produced the result that Gray's Inn, remotest of all the Societies from the Law Courts, was resorted to less and less by barristers setting up in practice.

The spirit of the age in its demand for change and improvement was well aware of the shortcomings of legal education, long a matter (this is Dickens again, but perhaps he was particularly unlucky) of 'having a frayed old gown put on in a pantry by an old woman with St. Anthony's fire and dropsy and, so decorated, bolting a bad dinner in a party of four, whereof each individual mistrusts the other three'. Anyhow the professional training for call to the Bar was virtually non-existent, little, if anything, more than eating the prescribed number of dinners in Hall and being proposed by a Bencher. In the eighteen-forties the governing regulations had changed little since 1762, save that taking the

Sacrament according to the rites of the Church of England had ceased to be one of the conditions. Gray's Inn, fighting its declining popularity, admitted students for the purpose of being certified as special pleaders and conveyancers, an indulgence frowned on by the other Inns, for special pleaders, while allowed to do the same chamber work as barristers, could undercut them in the matter of fees, since, not being called to the Bar, they were not subject to the same professional conventions.

In 1846 it was felt that students ought to be encouraged to sit for examinations though these were not yet made compulsory. The four Inns decided to institute lectureships and require candidates for call to produce certificates that they had followed two of the four courses provided. The scheme started successfully but by 1849 only the real property lectures at Gray's Inn (thanks to the qualities of the lecturer, 'a pleasing manner and an oratorical delivery') were being really well attended. Gray's Inn, besides lectures twice a week in term, was organising moots on alternate Thursdays. In 1852 the training of the Bar was placed on a regular basis by the establishment of the Council of Legal Education, though compulsory examinations did not start till 1872.

In the second half of the 19th century Gray's Inn was well and truly in decline. Even some of those whom it had called to the Bar abandoned it in the days of their success. Frederick Thesiger, sailor turned lawyer, who has been a midshipman and was present at the second bombardment of Copenhagen in 1807, became Lord Chancellor Chelmsford. Soon after his call at Gray's Inn he had migrated to the Inner Temple. So too Vice-Chancellor Bacon went off to Lincoln's Inn. Then there was the sad case of Dr. Edward Kenealy, Q.C., the brilliant and erratic Irishman elected a Bencher in 1868. His blind and violent advocacy in the case of the Tichborne claimant in court and in public agitation led him to such heights of indiscretion that in 1874 he was disbenched and disbarred. Yet, even so, these years were not wholly dark. Some stars glimmered in the obscurity. There were Lord Fitzgerald, Lord Watson and Lord Shand, Lords of Appeal in Ordinary, Lord O'Hagen and Lord Ashbourne, Lord Chancellors of Ireland. Lord Romilly, Master of the Rolls, son of Sir Samuel Romilly, and after him the second Lord Romilly, Clerk of Enrolments in Chancery, carried forward a family tradition. The Society could also claim Lord Justice Lush and Lord Justice Holker, Mr. Baron Huddleston and Mr. Justice Manisty, while in 1881 H.R.H. the Duke of Connaught brought to its Bench the lustre of the Royal House.

Nevertheless the Inn seemed to be stricken with a wasting disease. New men were no longer becoming members. The Hall was almost empty at dinner time and where the other Inns called a score or more of students to the Bar each Call Day, Gray's Inn was fortunate if it could muster half a dozen. In the three years from 1870 to 1872 the average call was one a term and in 1873 not a single man was called to the Bar by the Society. Out of these depths it might well have been that Gray's Inn would rise no more, but at the darkest a ray of light shone through. With courageous resilience the Benchers set themselves to find a remedy and, mustering resources far from abundant, they established the Bacon and Holt Scholarships in 1873. About the same time Joseph Arden, 'an old and attached member of the Society', afterwards a Bencher, made a gesture of generosity and faith in the future and founded the Arden Scholarship, emulating John Lee later a Bencher, who had founded the Lee Essay Prize ten years before. Thus they cast their bread upon the waters and in time it did return. Young men who felt a true vocation for the Bar but whose ability might well have been thwarted by lack of means, became conscious that at Gray's Inn they could find encouragement and the offer of a helping hand. These in the future produced a vigorous and loyal generation.

But other domestic troubles still lay ahead and it was a long time before the ravages of the lean years could be repaired. By 1891 the number of Benchers had shrunk to a bare sixteen and several of them had not attained even moderate professional distinction. Worse still, the affairs of the Society had fallen into the gravest disorder. The Steward gambled on horse races and was interested in little else. A large overdraft was annually augmented by a chronic deficit. Apathy, neglect and inefficiency were carrying the Inn rapidly down the steep road to insolvency. It was through the initiative of a group of new Benchers, particularly Miles Mattinson and Lewis Coward, that it was rescued from extinction. A committee was appointed in which they were the leading spirits and, by indefatigable analysis of innumerable small figures in the accounts, there were laid bare the magnitude and extent of the neglience that had allowed anybody and everybody to victimise the Society. Milk, for instance, cost it half as much again as the market price and under cross-examination the dairyman explained: 'Well, you see, it's like this, Mr. Coward. The Benchers of Gray's Inn they like a special kind of milk; it's neither cream nor milk and that's why we charge a bit more'. Another instance. Since time out of mind a colony of rooks had made their home in the garden trees. In the seventies, after some fellings, they had disappeared for a while but they soon returned and the gardener was accustomed to draw five shillings a week for food for them. Disturbed again, perhaps by the erection of some corrugated iron buildings in the Walks for classrooms, they departed again but fifteen months later the gardener was still indenting for the money for the food. Cross-examined and driven into a corner, his last line of defence was: 'Well, I put it down but the starlings ate it'. That sort of thing indefinitely multiplied was firmly checked and by 1897 the financial crisis was surmounted and the Inn saved.

As for the prospects of the younger students, this is the sort of advice that someone contemplating membership of an Inn of Court would have been given towards the end of the century: 'Then there is Gray's Inn. It is perhaps the least popular of the Inns. Too many Irishmen go there. But it has produced Lush, Manisty, Holker and Huddleston and what was good enough for them should be good enough for you. You would probably not find yourself in the same mess as a future Lord Chancellor but there is little in that. When he reached the Woolsack he would probably pass you in the street'. But the future was as usual to cheat the prophets.

As for the life of the members they could meet by day in the Common Room established in 1890—luncheons were not yet served in Hall—up a twisting staircase in the ancient building beside the passage from Gray's Inn Square to South Square. It was a convenient innovation but the real heart of the Inn was, as always, the Hall for all occasions. There the moots, placed on a

113

regular footing in 1875, were argued after dinner before distinguished lawyers from all the Inns. There in 1894, to celebrate the tercentenary of its first performance, *The Comedy of Errors* was presented by the Elizabethan Stage Society. There, in honour of Queen Victoria's Jubliee in 1887, a very ladylike and unmistakably Victorian revival of the Masque of Flowers was presented by the members. Great Grand Night in that year saw the Duke of Connaught as Treasurer dining at the high table with Cardinal Manning, the Prime Minister, Lord Salisbury, the Lord Chancellor and the Lord Chief Justice as his guests. The rejoicings of that year echoed the spontaneous loyalty the Inn had always demonstrated to the Crown, as in 1842, for instance, when the failure of the attempt of John Francis to shoot the young Queen on Constitution Hill was celebrated in Hall with champagne all round, in which her health was drunk with the most moving enthusiasm.

But it was on ordinary dining nights that the Hall was at its most characteristic. The dinner hour was six and for the members the robing room was beneath the great carved screen. Bench, Bar and students, all gowned, sat in messes of four in strict order of seniority, a sociable practice which defeated the formation of cliques. Men of every walk of life, not only lawyers but journalists and economists, soldiers and sailors and civil servants enlarged one another's knowledge of life and the ways of the world. The Preacher sat fourth in the Senior Mess with the Benchers, whose table was lit by candelabra. The Chapel Reader sat fourth in the Senior Bar Mess. One or other had to be present to say grace and indeed there was ample for which to thank Providence in those solid, satisfying Victorian dinners and that generous wine allowance which made for lingering at table far into the evening. When any man left, the next in seniority would move up into his place. The senior Bar table was furnished with hot water stands for the plates and each mess had its own substantial joint and other dishes.

On Call Nights call to the Bar was in the Pension Room where each man shook hands with all the Benchers present. The speeches which the newly called were required to make in Hall after dinner were listened to with critical gravity but no want of conviviality and on occasion wine glass casualties were high. There would be songs, perhaps 'Cockles and Mussels' from Laurence Counsell, often senior in Hall, a handsome old gentleman with long silky white hair and beard, or an Irish rebel song from Tim Healy, then the spearhead of the Irish Nationalist Party in Parliament, baiting Ministers and Members with his irrepressible and devastating wit. The great stove in the centre of Hall radiated a warmth of generous intensity which joined with the food and the wine and the talk, with the gleam of the silver and plate, so lavishly bestowed on the Society in the first part of the century, and above all with the ancient spell of the great Hall itself, to fuse all spirits in a glow of contentment and good will. Once again the Benchers could look down, not on empty and deserted tables but on a great room filling with young men of promise and determination, junior barristers and students. On the rolls were men like Henry Duke, massive of form and impressive in diction, who had graduated to the Bar from the press gallery of the House of Commons. There was a dry young civil servant and brilliant economist called Sidney Webb. There was J. R. Atkin, pale and ascetic looking, somewhat aloof but not unfriendly. There was that sturdy, pugnacious, versatile genius, Hilaire Belloc, though his road to fame did not lie through the Law Courts. There was F. E. Smith, his contemporary at Oxford, dark and dashing, bold, scintillating and sardonic. It was a great day when Smith was called to the Bar in Trinity Term, 1899, with about thirty other students. Two other future Benchers were called with him, Shadi Lal, the first Indian to become permanent Chief Justice of a Province and afterwards a member of the Judicial Committee of the Privy Council, and Bernard Campion, long a leading member of the Metropolitan Bench. One did not need second sight to foretell success for such men. Nor were they alone of their kind. The corn was green on the land that had lain fallow for so long. Soon would be the harvest.

9

Twentieth-Century Revival

IN 1901 Gray's Inn reviving stood on the threshold of a century rich with the illimitable promise of inconceivable progress. The Edwardian decade, the gorgeous sunset of the Victorian era, seemed to hold out the certainty of an even more glorious morrow. Overseas the Boer War was ending in the pacification of South Africa. At home never before had living been so cheap, so affluent and so lavish. It was the apotheosis of the commercial civilisation of free enterprise for the man of business whose sense of quality, if not his taste, in furniture, clothes and building gave its character to an age which, with all its vitality, was fundamentally money-minded. The over-blown opulence of the time was enjoyed in varying degrees by all classes. If the scale of living for the wealthy was fantastically profuse, even the poor man could have his solid meal of steak, chips and tomatoes for sixpence; his beer was 1½d. a pint and last thing on Saturday night when the butchers sold off their stocks by auction he could buy for a shilling as much meat as he could carry home. The common creed was the optimism of progress certain and inevitable through ever more delightful vistas of material well-being illuminated by the sun of a beneficent science. Social reform was in the air and the Liberal administration of the decade following 1905 entered into enthusiastically with the introduction of old-age pensions and insurance schemes for the relief of the less fortunate and heavier taxation for the better off, raising income tax to the unheard height of 1s. 2d. in the pound.

The London of that day was a capital which, in marked contrast with Paris, was framed in the image and likeness of man, not woman. In the City and the legal quarter the lady clerk had

117

barely set her foot. In the Bank of England there were some few and if one of them had to go from one room to another she was expected to put on her hat. Professional dress was formal and severe. No barrister ever went to his chambers attired otherwise than in top hat and frock coat.

In 1901 the pageant of horse-drawn traffic still gave a picturesque vitality to the street scene. Along Holborn past Gray's Inn Gate it clattered all day, smart carriages, prosaic four-wheeled cabs, trim trade vans, lumbering drays, the fantastic, dashing two-wheeled hansoms, with the drivers perched behind their high roofs, omnibuses with the outside passengers sitting two and two facing forwards, their knees protected in wet weather with oil-skin covers. All this was passing and by 1914 the internal combustion engine was king of the road—squat taxi-cabs, fast open motor-cars and tall, narrow, vibrating motor-buses with uncovered top decks. Holborn was fast losing what remained of its old-world character. Steadily the old houses were being replaced by elaborate offices and in 1905 a grandiose piece of town planning drove the broad new boulevard of Kingsway through a quarter of dilapidated slums. Next to the Holborn gate of Gray's Inn, where the old coffee house used formerly to dispense its impeccable hospitality, a warren of little offices now displayed to the world a most disconcertingly over-decorated facade.

Gray's Inn with its 250 inhabitants was still an island of quiet but it was not immune from the intrusions of the outside world. To the disgust of those who disliked the idea of seeing it 'municipalised', the local authority took over its lighting and paving in 1902 and persuaded the Benchers to replace the wall at the north end of the garden by an open railing, in return for undertaking to lay Theobald's Road with wood blocks. This was duly performed in 1903 but soon the tenants were complaining that the Society had had the worst of the bargain, for hardly was the wooden surface complete when the centre of the street was torn up again and relaid with granite blocks for the purpose of a new horse-drawn tramway system. The clatter of the hooves on the stone and the ring of iron-bound wheels echoing through the Walks was shattering, nor did the day-long moan of the electric trams soon afterwards introduced leave much to choose between one discomfort and another. In 1906 a tenant, lamenting the destruction of the wall and the subsequent innovations, complained of the street dirt blown into the chambers by north winds and the vibrations making ornaments on the mantelpiece do a St. Vitus's dance. There was nothing rural left in the surroundings of the Inn. By 1914 the rooks, which had returned to the Walks after their earlier migration, had given the locality up in despair and left, this time for good.

Changes, of course, occurred within the Inn. In 1905 electric light made its appearance rather tardily in the Hall. In the same year the rambling irregular block of buildings next to it with the colonnade towards Field Court and the Steward's office towards South Square was demolished amidst loud protests from the traditionalists and replaced by a new structure in which the kitchens remained as they had formerly been in the basement, while a new robing room occupied the ground floor, classrooms the first floor and the Common Rooms the top. Externally the new building harmonised very well with its Georgian neighbours, though the interior with its ugly stone stairs and 'County Court green' dado on the walls was forbiddingly institutional. In 1912 a lawn was laid in South Square and a handsome statue of Francis Bacon was set up there, the work of Frederick Pomeroy, who also made the statue of Justice on the Central Criminal Court.

So life flowed confidently on. In 1907 Prince Arthur of Connaught joined his father as a Bencher. The membership grew in numbers and distinction and the Inn steadily regained its influence. On July 2nd, 1914, in the Treasureship of Sir Richard Atkin, then a Judge of the King's Bench Division, the Society entertained 500 guests at a great ball in the Hall decorated with pink and red roses, while music played in the illuminated Walks. The summer was still unclouded but in little more than a month the Long Vacation opened to the bugles of war. Germany, invading Belgium to attack France, had set Europe ablaze. The conflagration, it was feared, might not subside till after Christmas.

The Society immediately threw itself heart and soul into the war effort nor did it flag as the struggle dragged on and on with ever more exhausting casualties, bitterness and privations through the four years during which the powers of evil seemed to have taken possession of the soul of Europe. The 15th battalion of the Royal Welch Fusiliers set up its headquarters at No. 6 Gray's Inn Place. Ivor Bowen, K.C., one of the Benchers, promoted from Captain to Major and afterwards to Lieutenant-Colonel in charge of the Headquarters Depot, was one of its leading spirits. All the officers were made honorary members of the Bar Mess at luncheon. The refugee members of the Belgian Bar were likewise made free of the Hall.

Half the students had joined the forces within four months of the declaration of war. At the same time the Benchers took the initiative in forming the Holborn Volunteer Training Corps for the older men with headquarters in Verulam Buildings. Ultimately it became the 6th City of London Volunteer Regiment with a definite part in the scheme of London's defence. The squares and the garden, where marching feet quite wore away the grass, were transformed into parade grounds and sometimes there would be as many as 900 men drilling there at once.

But amidst the clash of arms the law was not quite silent and the life of the Inn went on. Dining terms continued to be kept in a Hall from which the stained glass was removed for safety, but from Hilary Term, 1917, the dinner hour was put back from 7.0 to 1.15. The dinners and also the luncheons, maintained daily throughout the war, took on a strange frugality as the food shortage and the rationing system grew more and more severe. The library remained open, though the librarian Mr. M. D. Severn, joined the Forces early in 1915. Services in the Chapel continued under the sole charge of the Preacher the Rev. Reginald Fletcher, the Chapel Reader, the Rev. John Phillips, having volunteered for the army.

In autumn, 1915, the air raids on London began, to the incredulous horror of a generation who still clung to belief in the old civilised restraints of warfare. On September 8th an incendiary bomb fell on the garden terrace while an explosive bomb in Jockeys Fields shattered every window in Raymond Buildings. On October 13th at about 9.0 at night an explosive bomb and a shower of incendiaries dropped on the Inn. The bomb landed in the garden near the back of No. 4 Gray's Inn

Square, breaching the ground floor wall and doing extensive blast damage to the two adjoining buildings. Some of the incendiaries failed to ignite but two burnt themselves out in great mounds of fire in the middle of South Square. The most perilous fell through the roof of the Benchers' robing room next to the Hall, setting the whole interior ablaze, but the staff, pouring water down through the hole it had made, eventually put out the flames. On December 18th, 1917, an aerial torpedo weighing 110lbs fell through No. 6 Gray's Inn Square penetrating from roof to cellar, but failed to explode.

By the time the war was ended over 300 members of Gray's Inn had seen service in the Forces; forty-four of them gave their lives. Among these last was Lieutenant Cosmo Romilly, a great-grandson of Sir Samuel Romilly, called to the Bar in 1913. A tablet and a window in the Chapel commemorated their service and their victory. The living who returned found, not empty protestations of gratitude, but understanding and encouragement and were granted the privilege of being called to the Bar without further examinations. One of those who availed himself of the concession was Captain Frederic Sellers, M.C., of the King's Liverpool Regiment, who in the ripeness of time justified the confidence of the Society by becoming a Lord Justice of the Court of Appeal.

In 1915 and 1916 the Treasurer of the Inn had been the distinguished civil servant Sir William Byrne, a Bencher since 1905. From 1917 to 1919 the Treasurership was in the keeping of the brilliant and unforgettable F. E. Smith—Sir Frederick Smith, Attorney-General, when he took it up, Lord Birkenhead and Lord Chancellor when he laid it down. The first great event in the Inn after the end of hostilities was a House Dinner in his honour on May 9th, 1919, a unique occasion in that besides the English Lord Chancellor there was also present as a Bencher the Lord Chancellor of Ireland, Sir James Campbell, afterwards Lord Glenavy.

After the declaration of peace the English continued to celebrate the anniversary of the Armistice of November 11th, 1918. It was as if they felt instinctively that this was not really peace but only a truce. The old Europe and the old world were shattered beyond repair and the end of the fighting had not exorcised the evil spirit which seemed to brood over the world waiting for a second chance to strike. Crisis succeeded crisis at home and abroad. The miseries of unemployment became a running sore on the body politic. The man of business was still dominant but he was now a business imperialist. The times were marked by rationalisation in the factories, mass production making creative artistry and personal craftsmanship less and less an economic possibility; by the swallowiing up of small independences in the supposed greater efficiency of larger and larger units, combines, chainstores and monopolies; by an increasing anonymity and remoteness veiling personal responsibility for public and private actions. 'Safety First' and a somewhat elderly emphasis on the cult of physical comfort and labour-saving devices imperceptibly increased the complexity of the social machine as self-help and the domestic arts lost ground in an almost universal demand for ready-organised services and switch-run gadgets. Individuality lost ground as more and more abandoned the burdens of family home life for the termite collectivism of 'luxury' flat blocks or jettisoned personal responsibility for their own careers to seek safe jobs in the great business organisations. In this general decline of independence the warning sounded from the Bench of the growing despotism over the individual of departmental government, less and less controlled by Parliament or the Courts, aroused but little alarm. The face of the town reflected the trends of life. The fussily conspicuous Palace Mansions now gave place to the stark functional lines of Tiptoff Court. The great new flat blocks and office blocks and factory works changed and dehumanised the face of London, as the mechanisation of transport and the advent of the saloon car, and the covered-top omnibus had transformed the traffic from the spectacular cavalcade it used to be to what looked, for all the world, like an endless stream of monstrous insects crawling or scurrying by. The obsession with locomotion reflected a rootless restlessness which grew ever more pronounced, as the bonds of social conventions and traditional morality were alike relaxed.

The remains of 18th-century London languished. Mayfair was penetrated by business enterprise and as for Bloomsbury, its 'good old Tory brick-built streets' had become the territory of an intellectual Bohemia which stood to the world of the mind rather as Soho to the world of the gastronome. The graceful Foundling Hospital which for nearly 200 years had given it a focal point, had been demolished and its sky line was dominated by the London University's new functional sky-scraper, the technician's conception of a Temple of Learning. Here and there, unaccountably surviving, isolated relics of an older world could be found by the curious. Staple Inn still stood, a treasured museum piece with its little 18th-century quadrangle, and beyond its charming little Hall a garden and a fountain. It is true that from 1937 its famous timbered front was a mere facade hung, by a miracle of engineering, on to the face of a newer building erected behind it. The tourist was unaware of this and concentrated delightedly on the old painted board which announced: 'The porter has orders to prevent old clothes men and others from calling articles for sale. Also rude children from playing. No horses allowed with this Inn'. Further down Holborn the explorer might find hidden away among newer structures the tiny Hall of Barnard's Inn, restored with its timbered roof by the Mercers' School, and incorporated in their buildings. Down Fetter Lane was narrow Neville's Court where a forgotten row of 17th century houses with front gardens and a golden laburnum survived under constant threats of destruction at the hands of the house-breaker.

Solid in the midst of this changing scene, Gray's Inn retained its ancient collegiate character and pursued its way in learning and good gellowship, breeding up and binding together men of integrity trained to play their part in the administration of justice honourably and as friends. And now it was not only men, but women too since the Sex Disqualification Removal Act, 1919, had opened the Bar to them. In 1903 a committee of judges had dismissed an appeal by Miss Bertha Cave, a young lady whose application for admission to Gray's Inn had been refused by the Benchers. On January 28th 1920, Mrs. M. E. Share-Jones, the first woman student, joined the Inn. But the distinction of being the first woman barrister of the Society was not to be hers. That was to be achieved by Miss Edith Hesling, admitted in

October, 1920, and called on June 13th, 1923. She became Mrs. Bradbury and her daughter Anne was herself admitted in 1948 and called on June 6th, 1951. At Gray's Inn, more than any other Inn, women established themselves as part of the community on a footing of unembarrassed equality and a day came in Trinity Term, 1937, when the Treasurer, Lord Atkin, called to the Bar his daughter Mrs. Rosaline Youard.

Strangely, in the unstable years after the war Gray's Inn ripened into a period of prosperity and renewed vitality. In part it was the harvesting of the wise sowing of the late Victorian Benchers. In part it was the faithful, efficient and unobtrusive administration of Mr. D. W. Douthwaite, son of a former Librarian, whose Under-Treasurership stretched from the start of the century almost to the second world war. Much also was due to the impetus given by the dynamic personality of Lord Birkenhead.

Then there was the Holker bequest, that strange fairy god-mother inheritance from a time already half forgotten. John Holker, the plain, heavy Lancashire man, had made a great name for himself on the Northern Circuit partly by his outstanding ability and partly by his mastery of the art of never seeming to be cleverer than the people he was addressing. He sat in Parliament for Preston and as Attorney-General in Disraeli's Government he literally worked himself to death with the combined strain of politics and practice. In January, 1882, he was appointed a Lord Justice in the Court of Appeal but he was worn out. Four months later he died aged fifty-four. He left no children but Gray's Inn and its members became his heirs. Through his widow, who survived him for many years, his estate, according to his wishes, came to the Society, with the addition of her own, for educational purposes and for the assistance of the members.

The inheritance, amounting to about £100,000 fell into the possession of the Society in 1926 and bore its first fruits in the erection of the Holker Library. At that time the Society's 26,000 books far exceeded the accommodation available for them, and it was decided to build an extension on the site of the East Library put up in 1884 and of the adjoining building No. 7 in the north-east corner of South Square. This new structure, designed by Sir Edwin Cooper, was opened in 1929. To the extent that it was of red brick and continued the roof line of the adjoining chambers it matched the Georgian square. The irrelevant green shutters on the ground floor, where the Under-Treasurer's new offices were accommodated, were a less happy feature. So were the round lamps in iron standards, for all the world like petrol pumps, that flanked the main entrance steps. Above the ground floor was a single lofty oak-panelled chamber with a white barrel ceiling from which hung cut-glass lustres. Round three sides of it ran a gallery half way up the tall Renaissance windows. At the far end where the new library joined, at a right angle, the old Middle Library erected in the eighteen-forties was an octagon with a domed ceiling. Here from above the fireplace the portrait of Lord Justice Holker in his robes looked down the full length of the room towards the door leading out onto the staircase landing where Lady Holker in all the finery of a Victorian ball dress was painted leaning pensively against a pillar.

Though impressive to look at, the new building was something less than a success as a library. The air of spaciousness was produced at the expense of shelf room, and though in the octagon the decorative effect of row upon row of books soaring upwards to the cornice was considerable, the loftiest were totally inaccessible save to those who could scale the longest and dizziest ladders. Further, the appointments were of such surpassing magnificence that no ink-pots were allowed in the room for fear of accidents.

It is hard to stand aside from the architectural fashions of an age, whether they be good or bad, and it is at least fortunate that no one ever tried to graft onto the Inn any examples of the current theories of 'functionalism', for the functions of the Society happen to be very different from any within the apparent scope of the functionalists with their inflexible subordination of human values to technical considerations. Nevertheless the Inn's inter-war building was, on the whole, unmemorable. In 1930 and 1931 the reroofing of the Hall with tiles to replace slates went with the removal of the gothic stucco from the face of the North Library and the Pension Room and from the Chapel, the porch of which was at the same time demolished. The new retaining wall of red brick continuous with that of the Hall matched its Tudor and 17th-century neighbours in material, but in design and in inspiration bore little relation to either.

In 1932 the old 'Sahara' of Gray's Inn Square, was laid with grass divided north and south by a gravel walk. The improvement was undeniable and undoubtedly saved the centre of the Inn from becoming a car park, but the execution was somewhat heavy handed and failed to exploit the decorative possibilities of the fact that the level of the ground rose quite decidedly from south to north.

In Field Court, between the house beside the Fulwood Rents gate and a rambling old building by the passage to South Square, there used to be a short wall beside which there was a shady tree. In 1934 the wall and the tree disappeared to make way for a new building. Externally this matched the Georgian Inn very well, though internally the rooms missed the Georgian felicity of proportion. Perhaps this was partly because by current standards it was felt unreasonable to ask any one to walk up to the top of a four storied house and a lift had somehow to be fitted in. The consequent restriction of space made the staircase a good deal steeper than it might otherwise have been. At the back of the building glazed brick made its first appearance in the Inn.

In 1935 it was with some apprehension that the sensitive saw the demolition of the charming little 18th-century cottage building Nos. 1 and 2 Gray's Inn Place which had fallen into sad decay. In fact its reconstruction turned out to be a masterpiece and model for work of that kind. The new house reproduced all the most attractive features of the old and a second floor was added so harmoniously that afterwards it would have taken an unusually penetrating eye to detect that there had been any rebuilding at all.

Of the Benchers in the years between the wars Lord Birkenhead undoubtedly exercised the most potent influence of any. His inexhaustible vitality, his youthful zest for life in all its aspects preserved unimpaired in the young Lord Chancellor—he was only forty-six when he attained the Woolsack—the same qualities that had marked the brilliant and self-confident undergraduate. He died before he was old, passing like a meteor through the generation which he startled and enlivened. In battle, whether in court or in Parliament, his powers of sarcasm and invective made him a deadly and ruthless opponent, but in friendship and affection he was most faithful and generous and Gray's Inn had a large place in his heart. His brother, Sir Harold Smith, K.C., was his fellow Bencher. His son, who succeeded him as the second Earl of Birkenhead was admitted to the Inn in 1920 as Viscount Furneaux. The coming of age of that son was celebrated by a dinner in Hall at which the father spoke movingly of his great love for the House. 'A Gray's Inn man', Lord Birkenhead once said, 'is better than any other man, and no damned nonsense about other things being equal'. His infectious confidence raised and sustained the morale of all, from Benchers to students, who came within its influence, and long survived him in its effects.

If Lord Birkenhead was the well-omened meteor of the thirties, Sir Dunbar Plunket Barton was its pole star. He had been a judge in Ireland from 1900 to 1918 and after his retirement he lived for several years in the Resident Bencher's chambers on the ground floor of No. 2 Gray's Inn Square. Never was there a more youthful octogenarian. His slim upright figure and brisk jaunty walk became as much a feature of the Inn as its buildings and its trees. Everyone welcomed his lean, whimsical, distinguished face with the neat white moustache, his rapid, rather stumbling, utterance and resonant voice. (He did not shout but his speech had a characteristic pitch which made it audible quite a long way off.) His unselfconsciousness, his sensibility, his guilelessness, which could believe ill of no one, made him singularly lovable. His genius for friendship, his humour, his quick, agile, interested mind were not blunted by the advancing years. His little ground floor flat with the french windows leading out onto the Walks became the focal point of the personal life of the Inn where everyone from Bencher to student was sure of a welcome and past and present met, for he was indefatigable in his researches into the long story of the Society, and made himself its historian and its chronicler.

His neighbour in Gray's Inn Square was Lord Merrivale, President of the Probate, Divorce and Admiralty Division, and he too became an integral part of the familiar scene. Like Thomas Coventry, who led the Inner Temple Benchers of Lamb's remembered childhood, 'his step was massy and elephantine, his face square as the lion's, his gait peremptory and path keeping, indivertible from his way as a moving column'. None who saw him as he crossed the Square ever lost the vision of his solid figure, deliberate and majestic as a great ship of the line in the old sailing days, or forgot the sound of his voice booming like a well-directed broadside. Divested of their robes many judges shrink to the stature of a common litigant. Not so Lord Merrivale. Wherever he walked the majesty of the Courts of Justice went with him. Yet as one saluted him one caught on those massive features the light of the innate kindliness which was a very part of his great soul.

While he was reading for the Bar and eating his dinners in Gray's Inn Hall Lord Merrivale—he was then plain Henry Duke—worked in the press gallery of the House of Commons. After he had established himself in the law and taken silk he sat in the House himself in the first years of the 20th century and he was Chief Secretary for Ireland in the troubled times following the 1916 rising. He and old Tim Healy could share many memories—Tim the intransigent Parliamentary rebel in the fight for Ireland's independence and the mellow, bearded elder statesman of the years of its early liberation. Tim Healy was a mass of contradictions, a mixture of bitterness and charm, emotional sentiment and utter ruthlessness, tenacity and irresponsibility, savage wit and invective and tender kindliness, intellectual force and agility and sincere simple devotion to the Catholic faith. He was supreme at the Bar as surely as in Parliamentary warfare and in 1929, the year after he ceased to be Governor-General of the Irish Free State, he was Treasurer of Gray's Inn to which he had come half a century before as a humble student.

Lord Atkin lived in the Inn and he exercised a most potent influence on its affairs. His figure slight and erect, his manner modest and charming, his face firm and keenly intelligent, yet gentle and reposeful, its clear-cut outline emphasised by the dome of his bald head—everything about him suggested the quiet strength and immovable integrity that was his being.

Succeeding his father Lord Watson both as an honorary Bencher of Gray's Inn and a Lord of Appeal in Ordinary was Lord Atkin's colleague in the House of Lords, Lord Thankerton, a keen, vigorous, hard-working Scot, whose thick dark hair parted in the middle and brushed back from his long strongly marked features suggested a man little touched by the passage of years.

Lord Fairfield, who retired into the quasi-anonymity of an unfamiliar title in 1939 at the end of his judicial career, is remembered rather as Sir Frederick Greer for his long service as a judge of the King's Bench Division and a Lord Justice of the Court of Appeal. He too played a leading part as a Bencher of the Society. In his exterior there was a suggestion of granite but the warm humanity that struck all who came in contact with him remained a final and lasting impression.

The keen features and short iron-grey beard of Sir Montagu Sharpe made him a noticeable figure among his fellow Benchers. As Chairman of the Middlesex Quarter Sessions he had a reputation for a Draconian administration of justic but his softer moments, if they can be so called, were given to archaeology and ornithology, to the antiquities of Middlesex and the preservation of wild birds. He it was who in the early nineteen-twenties presented the Society with a pair of young ravens from the Grampians, who, before they finally joined their relatives in the Tower of London, lived happily in the gardens for about five years in a remarkable house fitted with an ingenious arrangement of shutters adjustable to ensure their comfort in any state of the wind.

By contrast there was Sir William Clarke Hall, the white-haired idealist of Old Street Magistrates Court—a practical idealist despite the exaggerated lengths to which some others have carried his principles. His zeal for the effective reformation of young offenders and for an understanding approach to their problems revolutionised the whole administration of justice in the case of delinquent children and the whole practice of probation. Gray's Inn was indeed strongly represented on the Metropolitan Bench. Sir Robert Dummett—he was knighted when he became Chief Magistrate in 1940 shortly before his death—and Bernard Campion, K.C., were potent influences in the important sphere of Magistrates' Court work and as Benchers of Gray's Inn rendered it good service.

Among the old men were Sire Lewis Coward, dominant by his extraordinary height, and Sir Miles Mattinson, short and business-like, veterans of the old crisis days of the nineties. With them Herbert Manisty, K.C., who has been Treasurer as long ago as 1910, carried on the tradition of his father the judge.

Younger than they was Sir Albion Richardson, K.C., white-haired, vigorous, genial and knowledgeable, who had come to the Bar later than most men, after some years as a practising solicitor. He had been several years in Parliament and his lively mind had absorbed a rich store of reminiscence and anecdote gathered in many fields. He seemed to know the inside story of every curious or notable incident or scandal in the past half century or more.

Younger again than he, Sir Walter Greaves-Lord, short and rubicund, and Sir Malcolm Hilbery, tall, elegant and discrimin-ating, simultaneously promoted judges of the King's Bench Division in 1935, bore a useful part in the affairs of the Society. And there was another, not yet a judge, still, indeed, a member of the junior Bar, whose influence in every sphere was profound, Augustus Andrewes Uthwatt. There were no inhibitions or diffidences about his approach to life. His lined features were full of character and mobility. The rapidity of his speech made his utterances somewhat jerky. So were his movements, for there was nothing prim or deliberate about the way he would stretch his arms and legs, his changing attitudes expressing the restless energy of his mind; he had perhaps the most rapid brain in the legal world. In personal relations he remained wholly unself-conscious and no respector of persons, his speech unstudied, colloquial, direct and forceful. Later he was a judge of the Chancery Division from 1941 to 1946, when he went to the House of Lords as a Lord of Appeal in Ordinary with the title of Lord Uthwatt of Lathbury.

These, in the years between the wars, were to the young student the gods, 'the old men covered with a mantle', the same in quality as those remote 18th century Benchers who so awed the child Lamb long ago in the Inner Temple gardens. Wherever he looked, past and present fused and mingled inextricably.

Coming in by the Holborn entrance he might glance to the right at the neglected strip of grass behind South Square. By some ancestral memory it was still known as 'the paddock', though many a long year had passed since any member turned his horse in there. If he strolled in the gardens they still breathed the air of the 18th century, though the elm trees had given place to planes, more resistent to the corrosive atmosphere of London, and on the teak benches was the name of Lord Birkenhead. If he cared to plunge into legend he could dream that the ancient catalpa tree had indeed been brought from America by Raleigh, as tradition had it. If he entered the new Holker Library, where Mr. Severn presided vast and benevolent, in a moment he might step back a hundred years into the eighteen-forties, passing through into the long simply furnished Middle Library, with its ornamented wooden ceiling in which the golden griffin on a sable escutcheon formed the motif of the decorations. At the far end he could step further into the past, the North Library that was part of the old Duchy of Lancaster building, and here, among the oldest and heaviest folios in the collection, he might gaze with curiosity at a large glass case containing the charred and battered remains of the fire bomb that had set the Benchers' Robing Room alight during that terrible war to end all wars. Here too on an iron stand was preserved, bright and polished, the aerial torpedo that had failed to explode in No. 6 Gray's Inn Square. Outside, the Benchers' staircase was dominated by an enormous full-length portrait of the great Chief Justice Holt which had once hung in the Hall of Barnard's Inn.

Even in the rather drab interior of the Lecture Room and Common Room block there was the same unpremeditated mingling of past and present, the same sense of continuity. It was not invariably agreeable. For example, at the head of the staircase was an atrocious painting of Queen Elizabeth in the Walks preserved as a memento of the Victorian production of the Masque of Flowers. The two Common Rooms, beige and rather nondescript, like a not very prosperous club room, were for writing, gossiping, reading old volumes of Punch, having boiled egg teas and, since cards were forbidden, playing interminable games of dominoes or 'bones'. (Angry shouts of 'You've cut off my bone' would startle the unsuspecting stranger.) The Common Room also provided a venue for the deliberations of this committee or that and the meetings of the Debating Society. Originally adorned with photogravure reproductions of such masterpieces as *The Angelus,* with a stuffed peacock, once unaccountably shot by a member in some remote place, and with a couple of dingy unmeritorious paintings of departed barristers now sunk in oblivion, its whole aspect was completely transformed when Sir Dunbar Plunket Barton covered the walls with a magnificent collection of over a hundred fine engravings of famous figures in legal history from Chief Justice Gascoigne to the worthies of the immediate past.

For the cheerfulness of a convivial atmosphere the younger members tended to migrate to the great wine bar at Henekey's next door to the Holborn gate, beamed and spacious, over-shadowed by enormous vats and warmed by the great threesided iron stove that had stood in the middle of Gray's Inn Hall during the previous century.

The sense of continuity was never lost and because it was alive and spontaneous it had always a personal significance. That stream of continuity watered all sorts of enterprises and activities. The Gray's Inn Masonic Lodge was founded and flourished. The magazine *Graya* established itself as the chronicle of the passing pageant of life in the Inn. There was the Debating Society, the Field Club, the Golfing Society. Every set of chambers in the Inn had its own memories and its own surprises. There was the cheerful Christmas garland that was always hung on the door-knocker of one of the old houses in Gray's Inn Place. If you climbed to the top of No. 2 South Square you could recognise the very chambers where Dickens fixed the abode of Tommy Traddles. There they were still, complete with the little attic in the roof which his Sophy had papered herself. It was now used as a studio by Edna Clarke Hall, the artist wife of the magistrate, and here above the safes and the deed boxes and the drab drudgery of the lower floors you emerged unexpectedly in warm lamp light or in open-windowed day into the delicious disorder of a large low room, a sort of roof-top cottage, full of colour in the flowers, in the spontaneous haphazard furnishings and in her own light, delicate, elusive water colours, fresh and unstudied —an impression of her son making cider or of the chance medley on her kitchen table in the country.

The byways of life in the Inn were as varied as its residents. On the formal corporate side time had brought about certain relaxations. In an age when religion no longer constituted the framework on which society hung, the Chapel and its services played a less conspicuous part than formerly as a common bond among the members. Sometimes there was a marriage to celebrate, sometimes a memorial service to hold, but they no longer gathered there together Sunday after Sunday for a single united act of worship. The office of Chapel Reader did not survive the first war. At first it was merged with the Preachership under the style of 'Chaplain'; then in 1928 the title of 'Preacher' was restored but the Chapel Readership was not revived. It must always have required rather a brave man to undertake to become the regular instructor of a congregation of lawyers. Dr. Walter Matthews, afterwards called to be Dean of St. Paul's, was a man fully equal to the task and when he vacated his pulpit, on his translation to the Deanery, he was invited to return to the Inn as an honorary Bencher. Canon Ottley of Canterbury stepped into his place and fulfilled his trust faithfully and well. If the lamp of religious observance in the Society burnt lower than formerly it yet burnt clearly and steadily.

And still every night the voice of the Chapel bell spoke to the Inn when the curfew rang at 9.0, as it had rung time out of mind. It was then that the Inn was at its most reassuring and its most serene, when the shadows gathered, when the daily working life had ebbed away and the old dark outlines gave the past even greater solidity than in the light of day. When the clanging bell at the gate had summoned the night porter and he had shut one safe within, there came upon one amid those enclosing walls the sharp sense of what Lamb meant by 'the sweet security of streets'. Over the roof lines and the chimney tops the great bulk of the Hall loomed, solid, friendly and it seemed immovable. Perhaps the lights shone jewelled through the emblazoned windows, for here as always beat the heart of the Society, the fountain of its life blood.

Here were held the House Dinners, the high days of celebration or congratulation when the Bar, not usually orators among themselves on their domestic occasions, for once in a while spoke their hearts. Here was the dancing when a ball was held, when flowers were piled high even in the deep embrasures of the windows, turning the whole place into a garden, and music sounded again from the great carved gallery. Here before dinner four times a year in Hilary, Easter, Trinity and Michaelmas Terms, were called those who were to be admitted to the Bar. The 'Call' was literal. As each name was read out by the Under-Treasurer the candidate, wearing a Bar gown for the first time over evening dress, stepped up to the middle of the dais where the Treasurer shook his hand pronouncing the words: 'I hereby call you to the Bar and do publish you barrister'. In Easter Term, 1926, H.R.H. Prince Henry, afterwards created Duke of Gloucester, stood at the head of the group of students to be called, being co-opted a Bencher later the same evening.

The normal call night started in gravity and formality and ended in uproar. Before the Benchers left the Hall to return to the Pension Room for their port, their madeira and their dessert they drank the health of the newly called proposed in a speech by the Treasurer. Later in the evening the senior barrister in Hall, 'Mr. Senior' for the night, again proposed their health and afterwards each had to rise individually to make a speech in acknowledgment. Most of them, too shy or too lazy to wish to attempt a flight of eloquence, had made collusive arrangements with their friends to be shouted down and counted out almost the moment they rose to their feet. The self-confident and the ostentatious who wanted their carefully prepared felicities to take full effect were shouted down just the same. The pandemonium was indescribable but never did the heights of riot and commotion reach such a level as at the annual smoking concert in Hilary Term when, after the usual dinner with the usual wine allowance, the whole Society settled down, with churchwarden pipes and cigars, to an evening of unlimited whisky and beer. (This was the only entertainment to which the women never penetrated.)

Then there were the Grand Nights, when the Benchers' table

was filled with guests of distinction from every calling and from every nation. Each entered from the lower end of the Hall, passing up to the dais preceded by Mr. Ivey the Head Porter, rubicund, moustachioed and imposing, with his purple gown and his great staff surmounted by a silver griffin. No matter how complicated or exotic the name and title of the visitor, Mr. Ivey mastered it with military precision, and in the voice which in his years with the Colours had stiffened a thousand Guardsmen, he would intone as he passed through the assembled ranks of barristers and students, followed, say, by a bearded and turbaned potentate: 'By your leave, gentlemen. His Royal Highness the Maharaja of Patiala'. Each Grand Night was a masterpiece for Mr. George Barker, lean and vigilant in his black gown, the Society's butler and a genius in his calling, with all the personality of an Irish ancestry and the impeccable correctness and authority characteristic of a training in the Brigade of Guards.

Before the Benchers and the guests went to their places they descended to the body of the Hall and took, by immemorial custom, a sip from a great loving-cup and a minute square of toast and during the meal the loving-cup passed from hand to hand, spiced, potent, but deceptive in its seeming innocuousness, each member drinking, while his neighbours stood with him, to 'the pious, glorious and immortal memory of good Queen Bess'. On this night, after the Benchers and their guests had retired, the senior in Hall proposed the loyal toasts which were drunk standing. (In the Pension Room these were honoured every night but, by ancient custom, sitting.) And after the loyal toasts there was always another, gathering into a single word the rooted growth of centuries, the deep-founded building of successive generations, the loyalties, the common memories and traditions, the collective expression of a family at home, 'Domus' – The House.

On moot nights the Benchers would return early to the high table and, presided over most likely by some distinguished lawyer from another Inn, would hear four students or newly called barristers argue a case according to the procedure of the Court of Appeal or the House of Lords, on which the President would finally deliver a judgement.

But it was on ordinary nights that the great Hall was most itself. The Bar took their places in strict order of seniority but with the students now the custom had lapsed and they sorted themselves out into messes of four as they assembled in Hall. When the butler knocked for silence and the Benchers made their entrance preceded by the Head Porter, perhaps there might be fewer than four and then barristers of students would be invited to join them to make up their mess, for here there was never any tradition of inaccessibility between one generation and another. They shook hands with the members of the senior Bar Mess and then, since the Preacher no longer attended as a matter of course, the senior Bencher present recited the trad-itional Latin grace; 'Benedic, Domine, nos et haec tua dona quae de bonitate tau sumpturi sumus. Per Jesum Christum Dominum nostrum. Amen'.

The tables shone with the accumulation of silver and plate, each piece some member's tribute of affection and devotion. Conspicuous there stood in place after place the silver beer mugs growing in number year by year since 1918 when Sir Frederick Smith gave three and Sir Warden Chilcott six. By 1939 the number had grown to 58, each engraved with the name of the donor, Healy, Mattinson, Coward, Merrivale, Clarke Hall, Uthwatt, Hilbery, Furneaux, all these and many more, remembered, as it is best to be remembered, in good fellowship and conviviality. So in the very act of eating and drinking, cheer-fully and happily, the younger recalled the older and the living those who had gone before. So too they saluted their fellows, each member of each mess toasting the other three by name, each mess toasting by name the members of the one above and the one below, making new acquaintances, confirming links already forged. Dining and wining together, they mixed and learnt to know one another, as they could never have done in a mere lecture-room association. They absorbed unconsciously the atmosphere, the restraints and the public opinion of the profession, a thing impossible at a mere technical institute. They mixed and talked as equals, young undergraduates and older men from every profession, with every variety of experience of the world, doctors, architects, schoolmasters, soldiers and sailors, politicians and civil servants. There were old people too, still active at an age when others are sinking into a routine of golf and somnolence; Harold Cox with his thick white hair and moustache and rosy complexion, who had been editor of the *Edinburgh Review* and now lived in Raymond Buildings, content to remain a student simply because he liked the company in Hall; Ernest Butcher, bald and forceful, a veteran Fleet Street man who had come to the Bar late in life and left his mark on the Inn in the conception and inception of its magazine *Graya*—the last silver tankard presented in 1939 was in his memory; Mrs. Florence Coxon, a gracious old lady who had been Mayor of King's Lynn and was called to the Bar when she was over seventy —her husband, Major Coxon, studied with her but did not reach his call before his death. There were men and women of every race and colour, from within the British Dominions and from without them, for since the Promissory Oaths Act, 1868, dispensing with the oath of allegiance, foreigners could be admitted to the Bar. The accents of Lancashire and Yorkshire and London, of Ireland, Scotland and Wales, mingled with those of France, America, Arabia, India and Africa. These years of keeping terms, even had there been nothing else, would have been by themselves a liberal education. At the end of each meal the cook in tall white cap was ceremonially conducted by the Head Porter to the high table to receive the comments of the senior Bencher present and submit the next menu.

Dinner is over and grace is said: 'Agimus tibi gratias, omnipotens Deus, pro donis tuis. Per Jesum Christum Dominum nostrum. Amen'. The Benchers withdraw, the junior walking first. The waiters busy themselves removing the cloths from the great refectory tables, serving coffee and bringing chairs from the Benchers' table for the use of the senior Bar table. (Paradoxically everyone in Hall sits on benches except the Benchers.) Now pandemonium breaks out. 'Up, Junior! Up, Junior!' The junior in Hall rises nerviously if he is new. 'Down, Junior! Down, Junior!'. The game of baiting the junior never palls. Somehow through the din he must get across to the far end of the Hall the petition 'Mr. Senior, Sir, may we have your permission to smoke?' When the Senior decides to hear him permission is granted. Then come the charges for breaches of the customs of Hall. Someone has dined in a coat which is not black. Someone in toasting has addressed the next mess as 'Members of the Upper Mess' when he should have said 'Gentlemen', or conversely someone has addressed another mess as 'Gentlemen' when, a lady being among them, the form of address should have been 'Members'. The junior in a mess is perhaps aggrieved because he has not been allowed, according to custom, to be the first to help himself to the cheese. The charges are pressed and defended. Mr. Senior adjudicates. The standard penalty is a fine of a bottle of port (5s. in those happy days when the dinner was 3s. 6d. for soup, fish, entrée, sweet, cheese and coffee, besides a liberal allowance of wine and beer).

So the evening lengthens out in mock indictments, in discussion and exchange, perhaps in song. The port circulates with the round wooden snuff box more than a century old, inset with a silver coin of Elizabeth. The lights are turned out, all but those illuminating the canvases of the portraits looking down from the walls and, amid the dimness of the high black beams of the roof, the dark emblazoned panelling, the strange half-guessed carvings of the great screen, shines the glow of the past reflected from scarlet robes and rich embroideries. In this light of other days the present sits and talks and drinks and draws new strength for whatever is to come.

10

Destruction

ON September 1, 1939, the German armies invaded Poland. On
September 3 Britain and France declared war on Germany. This
time there was no easy calculation that the operations might end
with a few months' campaigning. The twenty years' truce was
over and everyone was well aware that if the Great War of 1914
had been the war to end war, the greater war of 1939 might well
turn out to be the war to end civilisation. Pacifist propaganda had
left no one in any doubt of its potential horrors and from the
first premature wailing of the air raid sirens a few minutes after
the initial emergency announcements on the wireless, anticipation
was always ahead of reality. Yet in the first months the doom
seemed suspended. Poland had been battered down in the east
but in the west, along the French border, there was only an
uneasy sparring – reconnaissance, skirmishes and affairs of out-
posts. German planes appearing periodically on the East Coast
were quickly driven off. Life in London, if not normal, went on
quietly enough.

In those first months Gray's Inn was little changed, though it
seemed a very far cry from the garden party only five weeks
before the outbreak of war when the guests moved across the
dappled sunshine on the lawns to the music of the band of
the Welsh Guards and in the Hall, transformed with flowers,
there was dancing to 'The Blue Danube' or 'Jeepers Creepers'
from the string band of the Royal Artillery. The rigours of the
precautionary black-out of all lighting suspended dining in Hall
and the students fulfilled their obligations to tradition at
luncheon times, eating gowned at a special table of their own
parallel to the high table, while the other members sat informally

where they would, choosing their meal as usual from the day's bill of fare. The ceremony of call to the Bar was transferred to the privacy of the Pension Room, though the Treasurer and Benchers still toasted the newly called in Hall according to custom. Over sixty members of the Society were already with the Forces and news of the early casualties was coming through – the first Gray's Inn barrister lost, Paymaster Commander Lawrey, who went down with the Courageous in September, 1939, and the first student Major Thomas Todd, R.A.M.C., killed in a motor-car accident in France.

The stained glass remained in the Hall, but set in fittings which would enable them to be removed at very short notice. The lustres were taken down in the Holker Library and in the basement, its windows blocked with solid baulks of timber and its ceiling strengthened by solid supports, a shelter and a small first-aid post were established.

Suddenly to the inadequately prepared armies of the West came the stunning experience of the lightning stroke of fully mechanised warfare. In April, 1940, Norway was invaded and overrun. In May it was the turn of France. The Germans struck through Holland and Belgium round the end of the massive frontier fortifications in which the French had put all their trust. By the end of June the Continental catastrophe was complete. An heroic effort of improvisation had withdrawn the British forces across the Channel moat into the island that was now a fortress and the German armies lined the opposite shore eager for the word to invade. The preliminary air assault was not long delayed and constantly increased in intensity so that by September London was a battlefield. Day and night bombs fell on every quarter, yet still, heavy though the damage was, the number of buildings hit was small compared with those untouched. The nights were noisy and alarming with the drone of aircraft engines, the whistle of bombs and the bark of gunfire. The damage was scattered and unpredictable and till the end of the year Gray's Inn escaped very lightly, though in those months the legal quarter was badly hit. Lincoln's Inn and the Law Courts were damaged and both Temples devastated. The smell of burning became menacingly familiar. Life was lived from hour to hour and one Chancery judge, at the end of an afternoon when he had to adjourn before delivering judgment, gave the effect of his decision without reasons, explaining, with a smile, that the times were uncertain and, as he had made up his mind, it would be a pity if the parties never knew what his decision was.

Early in September a small bomb fell in the Walks, shattering windows in Gray's Inn Square, and towards the end of the month the menace came nearer when three great gaps were torn in the frontage of High Holborn—at Featherstone Buildings on the north side, at Great Turnstile opposite, which was blocked by rubble, and a little further east where a large office building backing onto Stone Buildings, Lincoln's Inn, was destroyed and over fifty people in the shelter beneath were killed. Early in the following month a little old fashioned Italian restaurant called Manzoni's between Gray's Inn Road and the Holborn gate of Gray's Inn (much resorted to by members of the Society) was destroyed in a morning raid, the bomb killing a full bus load of office workers. Soon afterwards a tenement block in Baldwin's Gardens just opposite the Gray's Inn Road gate was completely demolished.

On November 5th, a whole stick of small bombs fell on Gray's Inn straddling Verulam Buildings. A member who was in bed there at the time said that the sensation was as if some malignant giant were striding forward hurling down missile after missile with all his might. Next day the visible marks were several small craters in the Walks, the wall beside Gray's Inn Road hit and one of the houses in Gray's Inn Square damaged on the garden side; a glancing blow had bitten a piece out of its first and second floors leaving the ground floor and the top floor untouched. Still the damage was superficial and in the pure frosty moonlight of that winter the outlines of the Hall, the Chapel and the well-ordered squares, with the bare trees in the gardens beyond, had the remote perfection of a painting rather than of something in this world.

Just before the end of the year the fury of the attack on London intensified and in one fiery night almost half the City was burnt, the devastation stretching as far west as Fetter Lane. On the following morning all round St. Paul's Cathedral, where the Christmas tree in the porch stood decked with coloured lights, the flames were still flickering among the smoking ruins.

The night of January 1st, 1941, was particularly lovely with bright stars and a young crescent moon. Suddenly about twelve o'clock Gray's Inn was shaken by an explosion more violent than any it had previously felt and glass rattled down from almost every window. A parachute mine had fallen in Theobald's Road just outside the Walks. Several houses at the corner of John Street and a great length of the garden railings were down. The north end of Raymond Buildings and the little lodge by the gate where the gardener lived were blasted through and through. A water main had been burst open and a cascade flowed down the steps of the terrace, strewn with the broken branches of trees while on the street side a broad stream took its course eastwards before turning south to run down Gray's Inn Road. When the water was got under control flames from a broken gas main leapt high into the air. Everywhere in the Inn one walked on a carpet of broken glass.

Worse followed on January 11th, when South Square was hit by a high explosive bomb, small by comparison with some that were falling elsewhere, but big enough to do considerable damage. It landed just outside No. 3 on the south side tearing off the face of that building as well as that of No. 5 in the south-east angle facing west. Francis Bacon was hurled from his shattered plinth and lay with mud on his head. All the windows in the square were broken and a great part of the tiles stripped from the roofs. The Hall had its doors smashed but fortunately its heraldic glass had already been removed to safety and internally it suffered no damage. The Library and Common Room were thrown into complete disorder and in the Middle Library the ceiling showed signs of collapsing. But very soon the Inn had bound up its wounds and got on with its business.

Till the great fire raid on the City at the end of 1940 air raid precautions had been left to the Civil Defence Services. After that it was realised that if the whole of London was not to suffer the same fate every man, woman and child must take a hand in dealing with the incendiaries and gradually the Fire Guard service took shape.

The City had been helpless in the face of the disaster largely because by night it was a solitude of uninhabited offices with only a remnant of its old residential population and a scattered assortment of caretakers. Gray's Inn was faced with the corresponding difficulty that its members were dispersed, its residents few and most of the chambers let to solicitors or architects with no bond of personal loyalty to the Society.

Incredible as it may seem, it was about three weeks after the great fire raid before it was possible to collect the tenants and their staffs at a meeting in the Common Room to discuss the matter. They were united only in the anxiety to prevent the imposition of a compulsory scheme, which might have entailed onerous obligations strictly enforced, but the information available from the Air Raid Precautions authorities was of the vaguest on the crucial questions: What sort of a voluntary scheme would be acceptable? What sort of compulsory scheme would be the alternative? How many men would be needed? If a voluntary scheme were accepted would those participating be exempted from service elsewhere? A second meeting about ten days later made some progress with the formulation of a voluntary scheme but from the first it was evident that the bulk of the non-resident tenants experienced no feeling of obligation to protect the Society's property even though their own records, documents and furniture were equally in peril, and that, with honourable exceptions, they meant to undertake as little as they possibly could and pass on most of that little to their clerks. Mr. Ivey, the Head Porter, was in charge of the fire watching but it was more than even his experience as a Sergeant-Major in the Coldstream Guards could achieve to retain in the path of duty eminent solicitors filled with a dignified determination to be gone. He and Mr. H. W. Smith, the ever faithful robing room attendant, personally rendered unremitting service throughout the perils which ensued. The little Borough of Holborn was to prove the most dangerous part of London, with a civilian death rate of 6 in 1,000 as compared with 2 in 1,000 elsewhere.

So the fire watchers were installed in the south classroom with mattresses and blankets and hoped for the best. It was the worst that happened, though two months delayed, and meanwhile they learnt their way about the complicated roofs of the old squares with their steep pitch and central troughs, and the perpendicular ladders and labyrinthine beamed attics that led up to them.

The night of April 10th, was starry and moonless. A heavy noisy raid developed, with flares floating luridly down, non-stop gunfire and the sinister drone of aircraft, and soon the glow of great conflagrations was lighting up the sky-line. Quite suddenly watchers from a roof in Field Court saw the dome of St. Paul's brilliantly illuminated as an incendiary shower struck it to vanish again in a matter of minutes as the fire bombs were extinguished. Soon afterwards the patter of falling incendiaries was heard in and around the Inn itself. A furniture factory on the other side of Gray's Inn Road caught fire and blazed furiously, with such a fierce heat that No. 10 in the north-east corner of Gray's Inn Square caught alight across the full breadth of the street. Before the night was over it was destroyed and with it its two neighbours on either side. Somewhere beyond the blaze a high explosive fell blasting windows on all sides. Offices in Fulwood Place also caught fire and soon flames were spreading all along the west side of South Square. The Common Room was alight too, though since there was little wood in the structure the blaze did not spread to the lower floors. But the old houses with their timber framework and wooden panelling were hungrily devoured by the flames fanned by a strongish south wind. It was a spectacle of extraordinary and terrible beauty. With a dreadful crackling, the 'horrid, malicious, bloody flame' that Pepys had seen in the first Great Fire of London shone through an indistinct haze of red smoke drifting thickly across the foreground. It was as light as day and a cold night had become as hot as summer. On the other side of Gray's Inn Road between Theobald's Road and Baldwin's Gardens there was one solid mass of flames as the fire ate its way down the side streets. The tall church of St. Alban had been one of the first buildings to burn and on the other side of Holborn the great bulk of Wallis's department store was one enormous bonfire, against which the Prince Consort's equestrian statue at Holborn Circus was incongruously silhouetted.

The Hall was a grim sight, the red glare lighting up its darkness through the blown out windows. In the cellars beneath, at intervals during the night, cider was drawn from a cask to refresh the weary fire guards. When the 'All Clear' sounded at five the blue early morning sky was still heavy with night and the burning and in the light the fire fighters were surprised at their own smoke-blackened faces. Not all in vain they laboured with stirrup pumps, buckets and sandbags during the raid and its aftermath. Between their efforts and those of the firemen the flames that were catching Nos. 8 and 12 Gray's Inn Square were arrested and those which had spread from the Common Room across the passage into Field Court to catch the top floor of No. 1 Gray's Inn Square were extinguished. No. 3 Field Court was also saved after the fire which was destroying No. 4 beside the passage from South Square had begun to infiltrate through the party wall. Shortage of water had increased the difficulties of the night, for the great static water tanks, discreetly sunk into the terrace, were much too far away to be of immediate assistance at the real danger centre. Before the night was out the main water had failed and buckets could only be filled from the hot water taps in the Robing Room. All day long the ruins smouldered and to the sides of the buildings where the fires had been halted still clung a pattern of pipes from which the escaping gas burnt in great plumes of flame.

That was the first instalment of disaster. The next came on May 11th when the same dreadful scenes were repeated all over London. The Temple was devastated worse than before. St. Clement Danes was burnt. So was the north end of Stone Buildings, Lincoln's Inn. Pretty little Neville's Court in Fetter Lane, so long threatened by the indigenous housebreaker, was at last destroyed by a foreign enemy. But Gray's Inn suffered the heaviest blow of all. The Hall, the Chapel and the Library were burnt and in one great pyre four centuries and more of history went up in flame and smoke, leaving only empty shells. The pictures in the Hall and the escutcheons from the panelling had already followed the glass to a place of safety. The great carved screen had been taken to pieces ready for removal and, as the building caught alight, it was snatched from destruction at the very last moment. So too were most of the chairs made for the Benchers in the 18th century. With the Hall perished the whole of the east side of South Square along Gray's Inn Road and all the west side of Gray's Inn Square by the gardens, save No. 1 at the south end. Remnants of walls stood up jaggedly over piles of broken brick and rubble and more than a week later the ruins were still smoking.

After that there was a long respite of two and a half years. The assault on London slackened and died and the Inn picked itself out of the embers and set to work again with never a break in its continuity. During the raiding months patched and broken windows and roofs covered with tarpaulins had been an everyday commonplace for the remnant of the tenants, for blast travelled far and erratically. The gateway from Gray's Inn Road, for instance, constituted a perfect blast trap and again and again the effect of remote explosions was to tear out the glass and break the frames of the former book-shop window under the archway. Now at least it was possible to reglaze a window with a reasonable expectation of seeing it still intact in a month's time. There was no longer the recurring inconvenience of finding oneself suddenly cut off from water, gas or electricity. But all around in the chambers too badly damaged to be occupied the windows gaped with their smashed frames just as the blast had left them.

It was tragic that Mr. S. W. Bunning, the solid, sensible old Under-Treasurer, who as Chief Clerk had so faithfully seconded Mr. D. W. Douthwaite in the years of growth and development from the start of the century, should have come into such an inheritance of disaster when he succeeded to the office in 1937. Now all was to build up again from almost nothing. In the centre of the Inn only seven of the fourteen houses in Gray's Inn Square remained standing, four of them badly damaged with roofs partly open to wind and weather. In South Square only No. 1 east of the passage to the gate remained habitable.

The Under-Treasurer's office was transferred to No. 3 Field Court. Under the energetic direction of Mr. Barker, a temporary Hall was established in the classroom looking onto South Square. Most of the furniture, it is true, was improvised but by the end of June luncheons had been resumed and on December 5th it was possible for the Treasurer, Sir Malcolm Hilbery, and the Benchers to reinaugurate the formal public life of the Society, entertaining the Belgian Ambassador, Baron de Cartier de Marchienne, the Soviet Ambassador, M. Ivan Maisky, and the American Ambassador, Mr. John Winant, the Lord Mayor of London, Lieut.-Col. Sir John Laurie, and chiefs of the fighting services. Within the bounds of wartime austerity the Society's hospitality flowed again and it seemed a happy token that some of the wine drunk on this occasion had emerged unharmed from the cellars beneath the ruined Hall.

The north classroom was partitioned to provide accommodation for a Pension Room looking onto Field Court and a Library looking onto Gray's Inn Square. Virtually every book in the Library to the number of about 32,000 had been lost, save, of course, the most valuable which had been removed to safety. Apart from this the collection had to be built up again literally from nothing.

In December, 1941, Mr. M. D. Severn, the Librarian, retired after 46 years service. His second in command, Mr. Bernard Cocks, was with the Royal Air Force and the whole task of re-creating the Library as temporary accommodation fell on Mr. William Holden, hitherto the uniformed porter, who already had what looked like full time occupation as a Staff Captain in the Home Guard. Mr. Holden with his burly figure and heavy dark moustache, had shoulders broad enough to carry the responsibility and a lifetime of experience as an NCO in the Royal Artillery had left him with an intimate and thorough mastery of the art of finding his way about in all circumstances. At his touch shelves seemed to grow on the walls and books on the shelves. At a time when wood was virtually unobtainable he cut through the obstructions of red tape with energetic ingenuity to secure a handsome set of ornamental book cases from Cranford House in Middlesex, the seat of the Berkeley family, which the local authorities were proposing to demolish. Gifts and offers of presentations came from all over the world, including a set of statutes from H.M. The King through the Duchy of Lancaster Office, which formerly had been so long situated within the Inn.

The pause in the assault on London lasted till January, 1944. The fresh attack then mounted was rendered even more spectacular than the first by the greater variety of the resources at the

147

command of the defence, which often produced the effect of a colossal firework display. Again life and property became as chancy as a lottery but the Inn was spared further substantial damage, though in February a thick shower of fire bombs fell in the neighbourhood doing damage as far afield as Hatton Garden. Many burnt themselves out on the empty site by Baldwin's Gardens cleared after the destruction of the earlier raids, and only four fell within the precincts of the Inn, two on the roof of No. 12 Gray's Inn Square.

At this time one of the established defences against the raiders was the barrage of balloons, enormous silver whales riding the seas of the sky tethered by cables designed to obstruct hostile aircraft. One of these monsters lived in Gray's Inn Square. It had a concrete bed in the centre with a circle of concrete blocks sunk in the grass to secure it and a score of sturdy girls tended it by day and night, raising and lowering it as required, to the imminent peril of the surviving buildings when there happened to be a high wind and it plunged dangerously from side to side. This invasion finally completed the shattering of the collegiate atmosphere of the Inn. The girls had a hut at the north end of the Square where they kept a dog that barked incessantly all round the clock until at last, rushing too precipitately out into Gray's Inn Road, it was killed by a motor bus. The gates, of course, were never closed now, and often the incursions of wandering soldiers on personal reconnaissance were met by piercing defensive shrieks in the night.

After the new series of air raids came the ordeal of the flying bombs, the V1 weapon. Independent of the cover of darkness, they came over at all hours of the day and night bearing an enormous power of destruction. The monotonous roar of their engines and the sudden silence that preceded their earthward dive added a new feature of suspense to life in London. At night their fiery tails gave them the appearance of some mythological monster. All over London and the southern Home Counties they did tremendous damage but, though many fell near it, Gray's Inn was spared. The saddest blow in Holborn was the destruction one grey, dismal evening of the charming little Hall of Staple Inn. The pretty garden behind it was wrecked, its trees lopped, the pleasant Georgian houses overlooking it irreparably wrecked, while the

Hall itself collapsed, its fine timber roof heeling over like a stranded upturned ship.

The flying bombs were succeeded by the rockets, the V2 weapon, a man-made thunderbolt even more powerful than its predecessors, that arrived unseen and unheralded, shaking the earth and spreading desolation and ruin far and wide. In the face of them the only possible attitude was the stoical fatalism with which London had confronted the earlier perils. It was from a rocket that Gray's Inn suffered its last wound. Between Warwick Court and Brownlow Street there had stood before the war the ornate late Victorianism of the big First Avenue Hotel. Blasted in the early raids of 1940, it had stood a ruin ever since. On November 23rd it was hit by a rocket. The west side of Warwick Court and the pleasant red brick houses of Gray's Inn Place built in the 17th century were irreparably wrecked and eventually had to be pulled down, while the blast shifted tiles, brought down ceilings and broke glass in almost every quarter of the Inn.

For Gray's Inn it was the last blow. In the following year the fighting ended. There was no declaration of peace or even an armistice as it had formerly been understood. Rather the war subsided like a fire choked with its own ashes.

In the worst days of its desolation and the nation's peril, as the war was spreading to the ends of the earth, the Society had received comfort and support when the two leaders of the West, Winston Churchill and Franklin Roosevelt consented to become honorary Benchers. They had met for the first time in Gray's Inn Hall long ago in 1918 as guests of the future Lord Birkenhead, then Treasurer. Others too of this House held high responsibilities. There was Robert Menzies, Prime Minister of the Commonwealth of Australia, a distinguished lawyer and already before the outbreak of war a honorary Bencher of some years standing. There was Sir David Maxwell Fyfe, a Bencher, first Solicitor-General and then Attorney-General. There was Oliver Stanley who served both in the Government and in the Army. A son of the 17th Earl of Derby, when he was called to the Bar by Gray's Inn in 1919, he was carrying on a family association with the Society going back to the 17th century. There was Major Leonard Stone adapting his experiences in the first World War to hold command in the training establishment of the London Home Guard, where Mr. Barker, doubling his service at the Inn with a delighted return to his old profession of arms, served under him. Members of the Inn were to be found in every branch of public endeavour. By the end of the war over 400 had seen service in the Forces and more than 25 had given their lives.

Peril, as previously in history, had brought out all the stubborn, stolid, stoical, enduring, patient characteristics of the British. The break-down of normal life had also called into play their genius for individual improvisation and adaptability, still capable of asserting itself when opportunity offered and official rigidity left it scope. But the overriding necessities of war had produced a mental climate in which controls and restrictions flourished, the governors acquiring the habit of imposing them and the governed of submitting to them with little question. To those returning to the practice of the law or resuming its study this was to represent the most serious and fundamental problem of the coming age.

11

Resurrection

SOME cherished the belief that the end of the war would mean an automatic return to normality but the world that had been 'normal' in 1939 had gone for ever. Others hailed the conclusion of the most wasteful and destructive conflict of recorded history as just the very time to establish an earthly paradise in which drudgery and insecurity and frustration would vanish and crime would wither away because its economic causes had disappeared. The world, they assumed, was immensely rich, and nothing barred the way to perfect human felicity but muddled and inequitable distribution. Let distribution be economically planned and all would be well. An ever more intensive use of machinery would raise the material standard of living by multiplying wealth and relieving human beings of all the disagreeable kinds of work.

The change of Government towards the end of the war gave a powerful impetus towards political and economic planning which corresponded to a widespread popular impulse all over the world. For England the war in fact marked a turning point in history more decisive than any since the Reformation, yet the conditions for it had been long prepared and party politics had less to do with it than superficially appeared. The growth of combines and monopolies with their attendant satellites had, by restricting the field of personal enterprise, simultaneously prepared the way for full-scale nationalisation and State control of industry and effectively undermined the most powerful argument against them. On the other hand, the years between the wars had seen a notable increase of arbitrary interference by the Executive with the free ordering of life. The administration of the statutes under which this new despotism took shape was, almost as a matter of course, withdrawn from the daylight of the impartial jurisdiction of the ordinary courts of justice. In this atmosphere all political parties took for granted intervention in the affairs of the individual on a scale which fifty years earlier would have seemed like a fantasy from another world, as indeed it was. The differences between them were differences of emphasis and degree rather than of kind.

The fact was that the apostles of scientific progress with their belief in the universal competence of science in every field, including that of morals and ethics, had carried the world so far along their chosen road that more and more distinctly it was the image of the technician that was reflected in the social scene. This is not the place to discuss whether what has befallen us is our own fault for putting second things first, for trying, unsuccessfully as it is turning out, to buy the maximum physical comfort and mass-produced abundance with the minimum of effort, cost and responsibility. Be that as it may, government by technicians came well over the horizon in England. The dogma that 'the man in Whitehall knows best' is a long step on the road to the State in which officials govern and the police keep order. However, still to a large extent the technicians were kept in check by a public opinion, living on the accumulated capital of traditional respect for human personality, and by the Rule of Law guarded by men not yet forgetful of the concept of the 'free and lawful man' built up by the fathers of the Common Law, while the technician is concerned only with 'units of personnel'.

The development during the past three centuries of the doctrine of the absolute and limitless omnipotence of Parliament, uncontrolled either by philosophy, reason or religion (the modern equivalent of the 'Divine Right' of the Stuart Kings), enabled the Executive to cover with a mantle of technical legality a vast field of lawless and arbitrary action withdrawn from the salutary superintendence of the courts of law. The human person was left naked and unprotected to the adjudication of anonymous officials made judges in the actual causes to which they were parties, the very circumstance cited by Chief Justice Holt as an example of a thing beyond the power of Parliament to enact. Till some new Bill of Rights defines and limits the powers of mere

152

Parliamentary enactments one can only say, to borrow the words of an Edwardian judge, that Parliament cannot transform a wrong into a right; it can only make it non-actionable.

The exigencies of war gave further impetus to the growth of arbitrary legislation and to some extent weakened judicial vigilance when it was challenged. Nevertheless during those perplexing times there were still judges who could assert their true functions and in 1941 Lord Atkin, one of the greatest lawyers ever bred in the traditions of Gray's Inn, epitomised them in a noble declaration of principle: 'In this country amid the clash of arms the laws are not silent. They may be changed but they speak the same language in war as in peace. It has always been one of the pillars of freedom, one of the principles of liberty, for which, on recent authority, we are now fighting, that the judges are no respecters of persons and stand between the subject and any attempted encroachments on his liberty by the Executive, alert to see that any coercive action is justified in law'. It has been and remains the function of the Inns of Court to train up men filled with this spirit and the defence of the liberties of England depends on the continuity of that tradition.

In 1945 in what shape was Gray's Inn to face the problems of a new world? Physically it lay in ruins in the heart of ruined Holborn. Hall, Chapel and Library were empty shells. Half the other buildings had vanished and grass and young trees were growing in the foundations. To the materialist there could have appeared no reason why it should ever rise again. But the materialist is not in the deepest sense a realist and the Inn did rise. The first care of the Society was to kindle again to brightness the life that might so easily have been choked by the ashes.

Old Mr. Bunning died at the ending of the war, on Christmas Eve, 1945 just as his successor designate in the Under-Treasurership was returning from the Forces, and so Mr. Oswald Terry, tall, quiet, careful and correct, brought a younger spirit to the enormous task of reconstruction. The first urgent problem was the Library, already overflowing its provisional accommodation. A long, low, prefabricated building of concrete was immediately erected just within the garden gates and opened to the members on New Year's Eve, 1945, the north half as Library and the south half as

Common Room. The formal inauguration in the following June was the first social occasion organised by the Society since the end of the fighting. The enormous marquee accommodating the guests dwarfed the ugly little structure beside it, 'the architecture of the aftermath', in the phrase of Winston Churchill, who came as a Bencher to perform the ceremony. The artillery roll of a great thunderstorm and staccato rattle of pneumatic drills demolishing air raid shelters in Bedford Row provided a vividly reminiscent background of sound to the gathering but, by the time the company emerged after the speeches, peace was restored to heaven and earth.

Gradually, almost imperceptibly, the returning members and the new members refashioned the communal life of the Society. Sons stood where their fathers had stood, as Mr. Justice Barnard, whose father was a Bencher before him. The same names linked succeeding generations – Macaskie, Merrivale, Pollock, Terrell, Watson, Morison, Lush. The Masonic Lodge made good an achievement long dreamt of in the establishment of the Gray's Inn Chapter. The Debating Society and the Field Club resumed their normal functions and their periodic festivities. *Graya* after a long hibernation resumed its bi-annual publication. Senior and junior moots started again. As preparatory exercises for the full-dress affairs held in the Hall before the Benchers, the latter, presided over by less senior members of the Bar, had been an experiment, new just before the outbreak of war, and now they decisively established themselves as a success.

Amid the general dearth of a shattered capital physical reconstruction was naturally a slower matter but it never stood still. The great concrete blocks of the balloon site, so solid as to seem immovable, vanished in 1947 and once again the grass was tended in Gray's Inn Square, while in South Square Bacon's statue stood upright again on a plinth restored but still battle-scarred.

The burnt-out top floor of the Robing Room block was restored and a new Pension Room was established where the old North Common Room used to be. The entire space of the former north Lecture Room was thus left free for use as an annexe to the temporary Hall, it was in the other Lecture Room, transformed into a chapel with altar, pulpit, lectern and green hangings, that on Palm Sunday, 1949, the Preacher held the first service in the Inn since the war. From that starting point those services maintained continuity and were repeated four times a year.

The breaches torn in the boundaries of the Inn where buildings now vanished had formerly shut it off from the open street were closed by wire fences. The Walks, pitted with bomb holes, were smoothed again to lawns and the tennis court was marked out once more beside the old catalpa tree. The concrete water tanks sunk in the terrace were broken up and the ground levelled as before. Old planes were felled to let in more light and air and new ornamental trees planted. Thought could again be given to the flowers and in the springtime crocuses and daffodils bloomed on the banks by the steps.

The two great gaps in Gray's Inn Square could not yet be filled but the chambers damaged by the flames at the point where they had been halted were gradually restored. First No. 1 Gray's Inn Square was made sound again and in 1948 the entire ground floor north of the staircase was put into commission as a Common Room, leaving the whole of the temporary building in the Walks to the Library which was growing month by month and soon overflowed into the spare room opposite the Pension Room and even into the cellars of Mooney's public house, the Society's tenant a couple of doors east of the Holborn gate. Gradually the life of tenants and residents returned, as blasted chambers were repaired, and restoration was completed at No. 12, No. 8 and No. 6 in the great square. At No. 8, the eastern half of which had been particularly badly damaged, the discovery of a long forgotten vault sealed up beneath the cellar, yielded, besides the skeleton of a cat, a green glazed jug of the kind commonly used in the Inns of Court in the 17th century, another pot of similar design, charred, perhaps in an earlier conflagration, and three heavy glass bottles of the same period.

Strangely these relics linked two remotely separated ages in the history of the Society, living still after passing through unimagined changes and perils — living and growing. Take only the last fifty years. In 1901, when the Inn was just emerging from its period of eclipse, the admissions numbered 58 and the calls to the Bar 51. By 1938 the admissions had risen to 103 and the calls to

74. In 1946, with the Inn in ruins, the admissions were 243 and the calls 92. Trinity Term, 1949, saw 55 students called to the Bar, the largest number recorded in the annals of the Society. That year six of the new King's Counsel appointed were members of the Society, among them Miss Rose Heilbron, who after only ten years in practice was one of the two first women to attain that rank. Finally in 1950 with 265 admissions and 143 calls, Gray's Inn along with Lincoln's Inn led the Inns of Court in the training of the coming generation of barristers and judges. Its Bench was relatively small but that very smallness promoted the family spirit that was its strength.

The bravest and wisest decision of the Benchers placed the rebuilding of the Hall first among the tasks of reconstruction. The financially minded might have preferred priority for rent-yielding chambers; the practical might have voted for the re-establishment of the administrative offices. Mere practitioners might have demanded that a new Library should have paramount consideration. It was a deeper understanding that saw in the Hall the very heart of the Society's life and set about raising it up at the very first moment that the work could be undertaken. It was an instinctive assertion of the fact that wood and stone and glass gloriously worked are at once the fruit of the inner splendour of the human spirit and the food that nourishes it. To rebuild the Hall virtually as it had been was an undertaking that called for the highest skill and craftmanship. Steadily the work went on, underpinning the foundations, lowering the level of the cellar floor, strengthening the walls, adding a new servery where the old north-west door had been. Then as external completion approached, South Square became almost one vast carpenters' shop as the great timbers of 160 Kentish oak trees were formed into rafters for the new great hammer-beam roof and one by one the trusses were raised against the sky and the Hall took shape, once more dominating the Inn as it had dominated it throughout the changing centuries.

But the Society had not waited for the spaciousness and the glory of oak beams, of emblazoned panelling and windows, of the great carved screen snatched from the flames, which would link the old with the renewed. In Easter Term, 1946, Gray's Inn, first of all the other Inns to make the venture, resumed dining in Hall, simple dinners, fitting the plainness of daily life, but forging afresh for a new generation the old link of common cheerfulness and good fellowship in a united spirit. At first there were only three dinners a term, on Call Night and on the two nights when moots were held. In 1948 dining was extended to weekends, Friday to Sunday, so that men at the universities might have the opportunity to come down for them. Finally at Michaelmas, 1949, dining on every night of Term was resumed, again before it was resumed at any other Inn.

The setting was provisional, an old lecture room with green dado and makeshift benches and tables with inconvenient cracks and trestle supports hampering to the knees. Physically only the portraits rather incongruously adorning the drab walls with their brilliant colour and the silver tankards and cutlery gleaming surprisingly on such a board made a link with the splendid past. But the collegiate spirit was alive and caught up the new students across the gap of ten bitter years. Once again men and women of all ages and callings met to eat and drink and laugh and sing together and toast one another as their predecessors had done back through the long history of the Inn. Once again in a shattered world an ancient order was resumed and once again as before, half in earnest and half in jest, the customs were enforced by the arbitrament of 'Mr. Senior'. This was no technical college where mere skill and dexterity were sufficient. Here the members of a free and liberal profession reinforced for themselves and for one another that sense of human values which, in an age uniquely threatened by the inhumanity of the mere technician and specialist, stand in unprecedented peril. Despite the weakness or the self-seeking or the mere careerism of some, the free and independent adminis- tration of justice, resting on the ancient strongholds of the law, the Inns of Court, has stood for centuries on the invasion road by which the arbitrary power of the state has periodically advanced against the liberties of a free society—liberties sometimes too lightly held because too lightly taken for granted and now perhaps in danger of being too lightly bartered for the hope of a chimerical Utopia.

It was in Gray's Inn and her sister Societies that there took shape in friendship and good fellowship the concept of the free and lawful man, responsible for his own actions, free in a free society, the man whose house, however humble, was once proverbially his castle, just as Gray's Inn, through every change and in every generation, has been to all its children, home, the House —Domus.

12

Transformation Scenes

IF, at the end of the war, when Gray's Inn lay in ruins, those in charge of its destinies had followed the plausibly beguiling beckoning of unadulterated economics, they would have set to work instantly to erect luxurious rent-producing chambers, thereby ensuring the Society superabundant means to prosper at the corresponding cost of defeating its ends. The place of economics is to be the servant of the human will and its aspirations, not their dictatorial master. The function of economics is to say 'how' and 'how long', not 'what'.

But the first consideration of the post-war Benchers was to ensure the continuity of the spirit of the Inn, visibly recreating its living heart, just as the valiant Poles resurrected from the rubble of pulverised Warsaw its ancient image as they had known and loved it over the centuries.

Accordingly, with only the charred walls of its Hall still standing, housing a nesting owl high in an inner niche, Gray's Inn set about reclothing the skeleton with living tissues. Within those walls the former proportions of the Hall remained. The hammer-beam roof was reproduced exactly as it had been. The great 16th century gallery, snatched from the flames, was re-erected. The heraldic glass and the painted coats of arms of former Treasurers, providently stored in safety, returned to the windows and to the panelling. The portraits looked down again on the long refectory tables, the benches flanking them down the Hall, and the High Table with its red leather chairs on the dais. On December 5th, 1951, the resurrected Hall, re-planned by the future Sir Edward Maufe R.A., the Society's architect, was formally opened by H.R.H. the Duke of Gloucester, the Inn's royal Bencher, in the presence of the Treasurer, Sir William McNair, a Justice of the Queen's Bench. When the members resumed the use of their Hall for luncheons, there seemed scarcely to have been a break in continuity, for the only visible alteration was a bay window at the south end of the dais, while, outside it, a new servery had been built out from the lower end on the north side. In 1953 the east wall of the Hall was embellished with a Parliament clock.

On the first night of Hilary Term, January 16th, 1952, the Hall saw its first dinner since June 16th, 1939. Besides Benchers, almost thirty barristers and many students, all ritually gowned, dined as they had always done before, toasting one another in due form and observing the old-established customs. The evening ended convivially with songs around the tables. Two moots were argued that term, the first presided over by Lord Chief Justice Goddard. Call Night on February 5th was an occasion of loud and joyous celebration. Forty-nine students were called to the Bar, more than at any other Inn, all gowned and in formal evening dress, as of old. On February 1st, the uninhibited jollity of the annual pre-war smoking concerts was revived, its hilarity heightened by the presence among the performers of young Peter Ustinov, already emerging into theatrical fame. There were only two breaks with former dining customs. Table cloths were soon dispensed with, and silver tankards of beer no longer stood in all the places laid. The eagerness of the Benchers, barristers, students and staff to resume the life of the Inn ensured an auspicious launching on its post-war voyage.

In 1952 the Library walls were rising along the east side of South Square and by the end of the year the Pension Room block along its north side, red brick and Georgian in style, was externally completed, its entrance surmounted by the arms of the de Greys and the inscription, 'Surrexit Domus MCMLII'. The small Pension Room, corresponding exactly with the site of the old Duchy of Lancaster Office, adjoining the Hall on the east, was occupied by the Benchers. There was no attempt to reproduce the subdued elegance which had formerly harmonised with the fine moulded ceiling and linenfold panels of the old chamber. The plaster decorations were in bright primary colours, with the seal of the Duchy of Lancaster enormous in the middle of a ceiling adorned with red roses and, around the walls above the plain panelling, the arms of members of the Inn connected with the Duchy. Upstairs, where the old West Library had been, was the new Benchers' Library. The large Pension Room, soon completed, approximately filled the place of the old Middle Library. A room appropriated to the Treasurer was placed approximately where the old Benchers' Library formerly was.

Meanwhile, a start had been made in re-building the vanished chambers, Nos. 2 to 5 along the west side of Gray's Inn Sqaure and Nos. 9 to 11 along the east side. In South Square, only No. 1, east of the passage to Holborn, remained intact.

By 1953, Number 2 Gray's Inn Square had been completed, and by 1955 the whole of its west side was re-erected. By 1956 the rest of the square was finished. The external style was designed to match that of the surviving chambers, although the interiors were modern in plan. On the west side, three staircases were merged into two, and on the east, two merged into one. During this time, the burnt-out top of the Robing Room block had been restored and the Common Room re-installed there.

By 1957, most of the south side of South Square was complete and occupied. No attempt had been made to match No. 1, the sole survivor of the eighteenth century square, and, though the design has a 'Georgian' character, its topheavy mansards and heavy-handed ironwork balconies compared badly with that single relic of a more elegant age. Work on the new Library, which was to fill the whole east side of the square, was completed in 1958. The Under-Treasurer's offices and a large room suitable for arbitrations occupied the ground floor. Above was the Library itself, a single long room divided into bays on either side with partitioned galleries above them, a plain, workmanlike chamber. The opening ceremony was performed by the Prime Minister, Mr. Harold Macmillan. Externally, the building was conventionally Georgian in character, although somewhat lacking in authority and atmosphere. The Inn was now delivered from the prefabricated structure in the Walks which had done duty for a library since the end of the war.

By 1959 the damaged north end of Raymond Buildings had been restored, and by 1960 the west side of South Square was completed. In the south-west corner, No. 14, separated from No. 1 by the passage towards the Holborn Gate, was now joined to it at first floor level and above, and was designed to match it so that visually the two together formed a single harmonious unit. At the north end of the west side of the square, digging had disclosed a complete sixteenth century kiln, but most regrettably no pause to examine it was made in the work of excavation.

The next building to be completed was the Chapel. Before the war it had been rectangular, but in the restoration it was extended eastward by the addition of a chancel touching Gray's Inn Road. The former walls were still standing and the three windows on the north side retained their old proportions. Two windows on the south side, which had been deprived of their lights when the nine-teenth-century Library and Pension Room building had been erected against the wall, were retained but cut down to half their height, upsetting the visual balance of the Chapel's interior.

The Victorian Gothic style of the re-decoration of the Chapel in the 1890's was abandoned for a modern idiom with maple wood for the stalls, the benches and the western screen below the gallery. The altar, bearing along the front the inscription, 'Ad Majorem Dei Gloria', was presented by Mrs. Imogen Pilch in memory of her father, Professor Robert Warden Lee, a Bencher and an eminent scholar on Roman Law. The sole remaining visible relic of the mediaeval Chapel was the broken holy water stoup by the main door. At the re-dedication service on May 11th, 1960, by the Archbishop of Canterbury, the Duke and Duchess of Gloucester were present. Now professional singers replaced the choir of members and tenants which had done duty in the temporary Chapel since 1949. Regular services were resumed and in 1960 two weddings were celebrated, first that of the daughter of Sydney Thompson, the Society's housekeeper, and then that of Charlotte, the daughter of Master Henry Salt Q.C., a prominent Chancery practitioner. Once again in the Chapel the successors of the long line of distinguished Preachers to the Society, Canon Feilding Ottley, Canon Sydney Evans and later Canon Eric James, would deliver to the members of the Inn the spiritual message of the Church of England. Henceforth, too, the Chapel had its voice again, the bell sounding from its open turret, calling the Inn to prayer, tolling for deceased Benchers or marking the close of day and the passage of time in the nine o'clock curfew.

Since the destruction of the pleasant double row of seventeenth century houses in Gray's Inn Place by a V2 bomb, the site had been desolate. It was now decided to build on it the School of Law, headquarters of the Council of Legal Education, established to meet the new developments in training for the Bar. It was opened by Her Majesty the Queen Mother on June 10th, 1964. Modern in design, its scale was unexceptionable, but its style was not distinguished either by visual quality, authority or felicitous harmony with the rest of the Inn.

The Inn's next architectural adventure in 1964-65 unfortunately involved a serious historical and structural loss. East of the Elizabethan Holborn Gate, the Society still owned the building which had formerly been the late eighteenth century Gray's Inn Coffee House, now degraded and sub-divided for use as rather run-down offices with Mooney's public house embedded in the ground floor. A total re-building as chambers or offices was now planned. This put in peril the wood-framed gatehouse, the oldest surviving structure in the Inn, though externally the fact was disguised by an irrelevant but not unpleasing nineteenth century stucco facade. Unhappily the deep excavations necessary to lay the foundations of the ultra-modern building planned was so carried out as to cause the gatehouse to start slipping into the vacuum created, and spelt its doom. Someone had blundered. Now only a reproduction of the stucco facade masking a modern interior conceals what has happened.

Till this re-building, a squalid, neglected stretch of rank grass shut in by railings had lain behind South Square along its full length. Always known as, 'the paddock', it had no doubt once been used as a sort of pound for visitors' horses. It may well have been the last forgotten remnant of the original field or paddock on which what is now South Square was built when the Inn was being extended in the sixteenth century. Now it was turned into a passageway for vehicles leading to a gate into Gray's Inn Road.

In 1966 a minor but necessary and welcome piece of restoration was put in hand. Since early in the war, when railings everywhere were commandeered, supposedly as raw material for munitions, the low south wall of the Walks in Field Court had been first bare and then surmounted by pig wire. Now this was happily replaced with a new set of railings. Another step in the beautification of the Inn in that year was the placing of a sundial in the middle of Gray's Inn Square.

The last major piece of re-building was put in hand in 1970. The Edwardian structure west of the Hall housing the kitchens, the Robing Rooms, the Common Room, and the Head Porter's ground floor flat had long been felt to be inadequate, as had the Hall servery. In the planning of a replacement, the Inn had a narrow escape from having foisted on it a high-standing modernistic monstrosity with an awkward roadway running through it, but the scheme was killed by the protests of the members. Instead, a most satisfactory and ingenious design in elegant eighteenth century style by Raymond Erith and Quintin Terry was adopted, while an imaginatively decorative buttery was built out onto the end of the Hall. The plan involved moving westward the roadway joining Gray's Inn Square and South Square, and thereby the Inn unavoidably lost the pretty bridge which had joined the Hall gallery to the first floor of the demolished building. It was also necessary to obliterate the little sloping footway which had joined Field Court with South Square. The former building had not quite touched No. 1 Gray's Inn Square; the new one did, leaving a covered passageway at ground floor level. The new building comprised greatly increased accommodation, kitchens and a games room in the basement, robing rooms and the Head Porter's flat on the ground floor, a refectory for the students, a Common Room and two flats on the next two floors, while a spacious set of chambers for practising members of the Bar occupied the top floor.

Thus the Inn attained its present from and appearance. From a wilderness of broken walls and gaping cellars filled with weeds and willowherb, it had been transformed again into a home and working place for the lawyers who had inhabited it for six hundred years.

Just as the form of the Inn was restored, so the activities of the members among themselves gradually revived or new ones were initiated, binding them together: the Debating Society, the Golfing Society, the Masonic Lodge, the Field Club organising rugger and hockey matches, a chess club, a fencing club. In 1960 a tennis court was laid out in the south-west corner of the Walks and later croquet came much into favour. Gray's Inn Societies were formed at Oxford and Cambridge and other universities and also in several developing countries overseas. Finally one was established in North America. The Debating Society organised exchange visits with the King's Inns in Dublin. At bi-annual weekends at Cumberland Lodge in Windsor Park, Benchers, barristers and students mingled to enjoy informal talks and spontaneous entertainments. The Bar Musical Society would give concerts in the Hall. Benchers or men distinguished in the law delivered after-dinner talks, perhaps about the offices they held, perhaps on some legal topic of public interest. After dinner moots, presided over by some eminent lawyer, assisted by Benchers, were a regular feature of life in Hall. House Dinners were held to celebrate distinctions conferred on leading members of the Society. Each year the Treasurer would give a summer party in the Walks, just before the Long Vacation. There was no lack of events to be chronicled in *Graya* the revived magazine of the Inn.

In 1953, the year of the Coronation of Her Majesty Queen Elizabeth II, the Inn celebrated the occasion with a ball. In 1956 Her Majesty was present when an adaptation of the Masque of the Prince of Purpoole was presented in Hall. These occasions were the magnificent prelude to a regular chain of balls, dances and dinners, organised by the various societies, and dramatic entertainments, among them 'Twelfth Night' in 1961, 'Tartuffe' in 1963, 'A Penny for a Song' in 1967 and 'The Merchant of Venice' in 1975, all produced by the Bar Theatrical Society in Gray's Inn Hall, save for 'A Penny for a Song', which was played in the open air in Field Court.

Christmas was marked by a Carol Service in the Chapel at which representatives of the whole life of the Inn, Benchers, barristers, students, resident children and staff, read the lessons. Parties of carol singers went round the Inn, the choir of St. Alban's Church and children of the tenants. Christmas parties were held in the Common Room and later, more elaborately, in Hall, with music and seasonal readings delivered by the members.

Such was the life at many levels which Gray's Inn generated among its members, but, after all, the serious object of the Society is to promote the practice of advocacy. The essential usefulness of the brotherhood of the Bar fostered by the Inns is to facilitate the despatch of business in the Courts insofar as mutual trust is established between opposing counsel and between the judges and those who appear before them.

Since the end of the nineteenth century, the remoteness of Gray's Inn from the Law Courts had progressively inhibited the setting up of practising chambers there. Now, in the post-war resurgence of the Inn, the tide was reversed, and in 1965, in Gray's Inn Chambers, the newly-erected block at the Holborn Gate, practising chambers were at last established, the first for many decades save for the patent chambers, seeking refuge from the devastation in the Temple, temporarily set up at No. 1 Gray's Inn Square during the war. Master Douglas Frank Q.C. and the future Master Richard Yorke Q.C. were among the pioneers. But it was not till 1972-73 that the full flood of practising chambers really gained momentum. It was then that Master Stephen Terrell Q.C. set up his chambers on the top floor of the new Common Room block. Chambers were also established on the ground floor of No. 1 Gray's Inn Square under the superintendence of Master Rose Heilbron Q.C. (soon to be a High Court Judge), initially to launch young barristers whom the shortage of accommodation resulting from the unprecedented expansion of the Bar had left without a professional base. Largely owing to the energy and enthusiasm of Master Terrell, the start thus made was extended and eventually some twenty sets of practising chambers took root in different parts of the Inn.

The legal world into which the Inns of Court were inducting the young men and women coming forward as advocates was changing in the three decades between the 1950's and the 1980's more radically than during the whole of the century succeeding the great mid-Victorian law reforms. This is not the place to analyse the changes in detail, but they must be noted. In the field of the criminal law, the whole structure of the courts was transformed. In 1971 the Assizes and Quarter Sessions which had adapted themselves to changing circumstances from the mediaeval origins of our legal system were uprooted and replaced by a new structure of Crown Courts, partly administered by visiting High Court judges, partly by a new order of full-time Circuit Judges, and partly by a new species of part-time Recorders not attached, as Recorders had formally been, to one particular town. This involved a vast increase in the numbers of the second-rank judiciary, and solicitors were made eligible for appointment as Circuit Judges. This re-organisation was largely devised to cope with an enormous and ever-rising wave of crime washing over society, crimes more numerous, more complex and more ambitious in their scope than had previously been thought conceivable. Until after the war, four courts sitting at the Central Criminal Court had coped easily with the volume of London's major crime; by 1980, twenty-five courts were inadequate.

At the same time, a whole complex system of Legal Aid from public funds was established in civil litigation and criminal cases to assist the impecunious (or supposedly impecunious) litigants and defendants. The millions of pounds annually which this eventually absorbed raised the Bar from post-war depression to unexampled affluence, but there was more than that to the change. The Bar is not an adjunct to the Civil Service for adjusting the disputed rights of individuals. It is a body of independent men and women dedicated to the attainment of justice within the law, serving at once their clients and the common good. It may sometimes be their duty to their clients to fight the State stubbornly and bravely and there is a real danger that the maintenance of this independent spirit may be eroded or compromised when so large a proportion of the barrister's income is derived from payments by the State.

Further, Legal Aid has aroused in its beneficiaries a new spirit of irresponsible litigiousness, swamping the structure of the administration of justice and straining to the uttermost the financial resources which sustain it. The smooth working of the Courts has always rested on the assumption that not every dispute will lead to a writ and not every writ will lead to a trial. Till after the war, honest lawyers would do all they could to save their

167

clients from the time-wasting bitterness and botheration of quarrelling in public. Legal Aid created a situation in which the legally aided litigant might well calculate that, with everything to gain and nothing or little to lose by way of costs, it was the sensible thing to fight to the bitter end. Similarly, any domestic discord led easily to impulsive resort to divorce. Even some members of the Bar might find zeal to dissuade their clients from needless and unduly prolonged litigation somewhat diminished.

The increase in litigation and the lavish scale on which some cases were conducted, dragging out into hearings for many days and even weeks, demanded an unparalleled increase in the High Court judiciary. In 1951, there were ten judges in the Court of Appeal, seven in the Chancery Division, twenty-four in the Queen's Bench Division and nine in the Probate, Divorce and Admiralty Division. In 1983 there were nineteen judges in the Court of Appeal, thirteen in the Chancery Division, fifty in the Queen's Bench Division and seventeen in the newly-constituted Family Division, (The probate work of the former Probate, Divorce and Admiralty Divisions had gone to the Chancery Division and the Admiralty work to the Commercial Court in the Queen's Bench Division.)

The growth of the judiciary was paralleled by the increasing numbers of barristers and students. Until the early 1960's there were fewer than 2,000 practising barristers. By 1973 there were over 3,000, by 1977 over 4,000 and by 1983 over 5,000. About one-tenth of these were women. So steep an increase in so short a time posed a triple problem; first, how to give so many novices a proper grounding in the law and its practical techniques, and, equally important, how to induct them into the spirit of the profession without lowering the established standards of competence and instinctive integrity; secondly, how to find professional accommodation for them; thirdly, how to ensure that the profession should not be overloaded with barristers far in excess of the volume of work available for them. Litigation, like war (which in many respects it much resembles), is not a right but a misfortune. It is not a 'product' which should be promoted to provide employment. In the public interest it should never be regarded as a 'growth industry'.

In former times men came to the Bar with their eyes open, accepting that in so individualistic a profession as advocacy (acting is another) luck and personality play a decisive part, and those who lost in the lottery dropped out regretfully but uncomplaining. A generation nurtured in the Welfare State looked, not for a vocation, with all its risks, but for a career structure and quick returns.

The new-style student was also inclined to demand as of right 'facilities' and 'amenities' which his more robustly independent predecessors never expected. Calls to the Bar rose to a very high level. In the 1960's and after, there were never fewer than 500 a year and in 1971-72 and 1982-83 there were over 1,000. Gray's, with its high reputation for good fellowship and its generosity in scholarships and grants, attracted more students than any other Inn.

Not all those called to the Bar intended to practise in England. Many from overseas returned to their native homelands; many others went into government service or commercial employment, but the launching of those who did intend to practise imposed unprecedented burdens on Gray's Inn and her sister Inns. It was not easy to find sufficient competent practitioners willing to be pupil masters to the newly-called, especially as the custom of requiring 100 guineas for a year's pupillage had become obsolete. It was even harder to find tenancies for beginners after their pupillages. In both these fields the Inns bestirred themselves to secure a proper start for their young members. Chambers became overcrowded and changed their character, for whereas, when the practising Bar was small, five or six was a normal complement, it was not now unusual to pack in twenty or thirty. With so many members to provide for, the administration of chambers, once simple, cheap, easy and informal, became complex and expensive.

Education for the Bar was also revolutionised. Gone were the days when the Council of Legal Education provided gratis, in various Halls and classrooms in the Inns, lectures on the basic principles of law by highly regarded practitioners. Students might or might not attend them, as they pleased, and might or might not supplement them by private reading or instruction from other sources. In 1964 the Council opened in Gray's Inn Place the newly-erected School of Law, established on a free-paying basis. It provided regular courses of study, moots and lectures, in preparation for examinations of a much extended and more searching character than formerly. In 1978-79, training for the Bar assumed a new shape. Thenceforth the normal qualification for admission to the Inn was to be a law degree, after which the candidate must spend a year at the School of Law following a practical course of vocational training, at the end of which he sat for the Council's examination. During that year he could discharge his obligation to dine in Hall by eating six dinners in each of the four terms. This curtailed his probationary period before call, but also had the effect of much diminishing his contact with the communal life of Hall. The School of Law provided instruction but not *la formation,* the collegiate induction into the profession, with all that that implies in personal contacts, which cannot be derived from books, the recognition of corporate responsibility, the fusing of formality and conviviality, of discipline and enjoyment, which sets the seal on the continuity of the profession from one generation to the next, the comprehension of the present in the light of the immediate and remoter past, and shared experience. All this has been minimised in the hurry of acquiring a simple technical paper qualification.

The Inns of Court have also been profoundly affected by the revolution in the government of the profession implicit in the establishment in 1974-75 of the Senate of the Inns of Court and the Bar to enable the Bar to adopt and finance common policies and speak with a single voice. Practising barristers were expected to support it with prescribed subscriptions. Since the creation in 1884 of the Bar Committee, which soon became the Bar Council, there had been a confusing dichotomy in the authorities to which the Bar was subject. The further imposition of a Senate, partly elected, partly nominated, to represent the Bar, the Benchers of the Inns and the members of Hall of each Inn, erected an almost metaphysical trinity of authorities with much debatable territory between their respective spheres of action. The Senate, which established itself in Gray's Inn at No. 11 South Square, took over from the individual Inns the disciplining of barristers, but, while the internal autonomy of each of the Inns was acknowledged, the financial demands made on them by the Senate to implement the policies it had adopted necessarily circumscribed their freedom of action, particularly in the management of their property.

The changes within the Inns in general and Gray's Inn in particular were, of course, only a reflection of the changes in the world around them. Their totality was formidable: the increasing mechanisation of daily life, the cult of 'affluence', taking for granted a general diffusion of physical comfort and even luxury, the progressive retreat of the small craftsman and trader before the advance of supermarkets, chain-stores, chain restaurants and hotels, the grouping of vast commercial enterprises, swallowing up old-established businesses and diversifying the range of their own activities, the unchecked, unmanageable increase in motor traffic, from private cars and vans of all shapes and sizes to vast juggernaut containers, above all, in the post-war years, the relentless and unremitting activities of property speculators and developers, mopping up every square foot of land available, running up tower blocks, luxury offices and flats, and raising rents and real property prices far above the reach of ordinary people of modest means and causing a progressive depopulation of the centres of cities. The consequent enforced migration of daily workers to outer dormitory districts and even to places fifty miles away or more overloaded every system of transport. In the centre of towns, rents prohibitive for a family or a single person increasingly forced unrelated individuals to share flats or houses. Rates as well as rents soared as local authorities increasingly assumed the role of social benefactors and patrons of the arts as well as providing some housing (too often of the grimly 'packaged' variety of apartment blocks) for some of those dispossessed by the property developers. The Greater London Council superceded the London County Council, and the Holborn Borough Council was devoured by the Camden Council.

In the process of dislocating society, this changed the whole aspect of Holborn in the vicinity of Gray's Inn, once teeming with the robust vitality and variety of a neighbourly population living close to its inherited roots, far removed alike from the stratospheric arrogance of tower-block elevations and from

171

envious aspirations to limitless affluence for a minimum of effort. It was a community which still put into practice William Cobbett's great principle that the secret of happiness and independence, activity and ingenuity, is the art of living on little. East of Gray's Inn Road, down the slopes to Farringdon Street, had clustered the little houses of the poor, including a whole village of immigrant Italians, wrecked in the wartime bombardments, little shops, little workshops, little eating-houses, little pubs, dim little stores, long established, where a craftsman could find just the special tool, just the hook, just the screw, just the sticking preparation which he needed for a special job, all unpackaged and unexorbitantly priced. In the Georgian symmetry of Bloomsbury, the aspiring scholar or writer or artist or lawyer or medical student, young and making a start, or older and out of luck, or simply unambitious of affluence and luxury, did not have to be rich to live in quiet enjoyment of surroundings, plain, simple, pleasant and unpretentious.

To be sure, the whole area had suffered in the bombardments, but a far more determined and purposeful assault on its inherent integrity was achieved by the property developers in plausible and pitiless pursuit of the maximisation of profit and exploitation of 'market forces'. Even the academics of London University and the local authorities joined in. The devastations and intrusions of architectural brutalism were too widespread for detailed examin-ation, but the mutilations committed in Woburn Square, Brunswick Square and Millman Street must stand for all. Besides bulldozing and demolitions, there were so-called 'face lifts' in the expensive refurbishing and gutting of seemly old buildings, leaving only a delusive facade. Whatever the method, the places where the poor and the modestly endowed had hitherto made their homes and their livings were taken over and their occupants 'phased out' (in the euphemistic phraseology of the time) in an orgy of expropriation. A few examples must stand for innumerable demolitions, dispossessions and architectural outrages. Among the earliest and most odious eyesores dominating High Holborn was the monstrous State House, run up at the corner of Red Lion Street in 1961. From the western corner of Gray's Inn Road and Holborn northwards there used to stand a simple public house, a tiny, friendly restaurant-cum-sweetshop, a leather goods shop which did repairs on the premises, a stationer's shop, a little health food shop kept by a mild and earnest lady, a little ladies' wear shop, all useful, all personal. By 1956 the whole lot had vanished to make way for an office block with a great sprawling impersonal Woolworths' embedded in it. Among the shops on the opposite side of Gray's Inn Road was the little fruit, flower and vegetable shop of old Clara, born in the last century in adjoining Fox Court. In 1975, her shop and Fox Court itself were swept away to make way for the Prudential's huge new computer centre. She was much mourned by her many customers on Gray's Inn. On the opposite side of Holborn, west of Staple Inn, was Kean's Chophouse, simple, robust, unspectacular, cheap, cosy with its horsebox pews, efficient, where the proprietor and two brisk, cheerful waitresses served to scores of contented customers varied and memorable trayloads of beautifully cooked meat for ten shillings (50p). It vanished, along with its neighbours, in 1967; yet another rent-collecting office slab rose on the site. In this demolition, a very useful little tailor's shop, much patronised by members of Gray's Inn, was also destroyed. All over the area, pleasant, friendly little pubs were being closed or expensively 'face-lifted' beyond recognition, while innumerable cheap, useful little restaurants were either closed down, replaced by sandwich bars or pushed exorbitantly 'up market' to exploit expense account eating or the alien tourist boom. Leather Lane survived as a lively street market, though less robust than when its attractions included buskers, street entertainers, vendors of 'quack' medicines, a baked potato stall and a man who made sweets before your eyes in a great copper boiler.

Within Gray's Inn the worst blow to its peace and quiet was the ubiquitous motor car, converted from an optional convenience to a compulsory and dominant necessity by the depopulation of central London achieved by the developers. Now that so many of those working in the Inn or having dealings with them had to live so far on London's perimeter and beyond it, the Inn's squares became of necessity car parks. To accommodate this mass of automobiles, the pollarded plane trees which surrounded Gray's Inn Square were all removed in 1965. (Some compensation has since been made by the laying-out of flowerbeds and the planting of ornamental trees in the centre of the square.) Already in 1955 the garden gate by Verulam Buildings had been moved back to an alignment with the rear of the block instead of the front, so as to allow more road space. Gradually the porters of the Inn came to be approximated to car park attendants. In the 1980's the surrender to the standards of 'traffic flow' was consummated by the installation of electronically-controlled barriers at the entrances and exits of the Inn.

Not everything that happened in Holborn during these years was pernicious. Staple Inn, once a satellite of Gray's Inn, which had been seriously damaged in the bombardments, was admirably restored in 1955 and the occasion marked by a ceremony in which the Benchers of Gray's Inn formally participated, attended by their Head Porter, gowned and bearing his mace. Barnard's Inn, another satellite of Gray's Inn, had escaped war damage but the Mercers' School, which had occupied it, closed in 1959. Since then, its Hall has been put to varying uses, first as a canteen and later as a luncheon club. The demolition of the Midland Bank building at Holborn Circus, opening up a clear view of St. Andrew's Church (with which Gray's Inn had an historic connection) was a tremendous improvement, and now Prince Albert on horseback in the centre of the Circus appears to be saluting it and not, as formerly, the bank. The innovation of New Fetter Lane, forking north-east from old Fetter Lane to the Circus beside the enormous block of the post-war 'Daily Mirror' building (on the site of Wallis's drapery store, burnt during the bombardments) is doubtless a necessary device to relieve traffic congestion. On the opposite side of Holborn, the huge new offices and shop complex, sheathed in reflecting glass, escapes in its bizarre idiom the charge of being merely monotonous and boring. It incorporates a new public house, in neo-Tudor style, with the portrait sign of an Elizabethan Lord Chancellor, Sir Christopher Hatton. But obliterated in the redevelopment was the 'Leather Bottle' at the corner of Leather Lane, an unpretentious pub which, in an era of compulsory mechanical music, had kept alive a tradition of spontaneous singing among its customers. Obliterated, too, were several craftsmen's workshops in Hatton Garden. Most of the new structure stood on the site of Gamages, the rambling, ramshackle, labyrinthine all-purpose department store where, with persistence, anything could be found, china, live pets, clothes, toys, alcohol, household gadgets, a barber shop, the whole a tremendous loss to the shopping explorer, though not to architectural aesthetics. In justice to the project which has planted the great computer centre in Gray's Inn Road, a tribute must be paid to the group of dwellings, brick-built, modern in concept, laid out beside St. Alban's Church. Replacing a grim and gloomy range of Victorian flats for the poor, it cheers the passer by with acacia trees and miniature front flower patches.

Now, while the world was thus changing around Gray's Inn, it remained in essentials to an extraordinary degree an enchanted island and this was largely due to the loyalty and personal devotion of those who served it, acting as shock-absorbers of the day-to-day pressures which beset any learned institution, just as the dedicated NCO's act as shock-absorbers in the structure of a regiment. It is impossible to enumerate all those who in the post-war rebuilding of Gray's Inn have served it well and faithfully, but some must be remembered.

In the years of reconstruction, the Inn had the incalculable benefit of the zealous and unremitting services of Oswald Terry, its Under-Treasurer. He retained the office for thirty years, during which he put into effective execution the physical and administrative restoration of the Inn. Ever active, ever vigilant, he was seemingly omnipresent by day and by night. Tall, slender, quiet, with a very English impassivity, he was in control of every situation, whether from his office or from his flat in Gray's Inn Square. Nothing that went right or wrong in the Inn at any level escaped his observation. 'Leave it to the Under Treasurer', became perhaps too much of a habit with the Benchers. His friendships extended from the most junior to the most senior members. In 1948 he married the gracious, able and attractive Cynthia Bryant, a student of the Inn, and together they worked as a most harmonious team until her untimely death bereaved him in 1974. On his retirement in 1976, the Inn conferred on him the honour, unprecedented for a member of the staff, of election as an honorary Bencher. Since his retirement, he had

had two successors, Christopher Hughes and Rear-Admiral Christopher Bevan, a distinguished sailor, following a new trend which placed the Under Treasurerships of all the Inns and the secretaryship of the Senate in the hands of men linked with the Royal Navy.

Other members of the staff from before the war carried forward the continuity of its traditions. George Barker, the butler, restored the dignity and seemliness of dining and lunching in Hall, organising even the grandest occasions so smoothly that they seemed to unfold by a natural process. His retirement in 1957 seemed to mark the end of an era.

After the war, the multifarious services of William Holden during the years of destruction were rewarded by his appointment as Librarian, a triumph of natural genius over the concept of orthodox academic training. Bernard Cocks, the former Assistant Librarian, returning from his service with the forces, loyally and generously consented to resume his former place in second rank. The two worked together in perfect and comradely harmony, making the Library a place of warmth and friendliness for all the members, helping them beyond the call of duty in innumerable ways and participating in the life of the Inn in all its manifestations and spheres of action.

In 1961 Holden died very suddenly without any antecedent illness and Cocks succeeded him. Short, stocky, sturdy, active, friendly, cheerful, deeply, though unobtrusively, religious, he continued to administer the Library until 1968. Its unbroken traditions passed from his hands into those of Philip Beddingham, who had become his assistant in the previous year after considerable experience in the Libraries of other Inns of Court. Active, methodical, gregarious, he was a man of many interests, including heraldry, bookbinding, and, above all, bookplates, on which he was an acknowledged authority. After his tragically premature death in 1983, he left a great inheritance to his successor, Mrs. Theresa Thom, the Inn's first woman Librarian, who set herself worthily, zealously and cheerfully to assume its responsibilities, aided by a devoted staff, including Mrs. Claire Butters, Mr. Beddingham's secretary, who ably directed the Library work during the unexpected interregnum caused by his death.

One of the key offices in the Inn has always been that of Head Porter, who shouldered a daunting intermingling of duties, not only in maintaining good order within the Inn and exercising ceaseless vigilance, day and night, over its security, but also, gowned and bearing the Inn's great mace, performing several ceremonial functions, while, at the other end of the scale, he rendered personal services to members and tenants.

The Head Porter, Harry Ivey, who so distinguished himself fighting the fires in the Inn during the devastation of the great bombardments, and whose portrait in robes, painted by Henry McElwee, a barrister of the Society, hangs on the Common Room staircase, was succeeded in 1951 by another sergeant-major of the Coldstream Guards, Fred Suter. Quiet, courteous, dignified, always helpful and always efficient, he brought great distinction to the discharge of his duties. He retired in 1969. Ian Mackintosh, a forthright, convivial Scot, formerly of the Royal Marines, succeeded him, holding the office till 1973 when Kenneth Chard took it up. As quietly reliable, courteous, helpful and vigilant as his predecessor Suter, he performed his duties with unobtrusive efficiency, in perfect partnership with the then Warden (or Under Porter), Duncan Mitchell, while he was splendidly seconded by his wife, for the practical tradition of the Inn has always been that the Head Porter's wife actively co-operates with him in its service. The many interlocking duties of the Head Porter, extending over 24 hours a day for 365 days a year, were obviously too much for one man and, in the essential office of Warden, Mitchell was the perfectly co-ordinated partner. Short, fair, quiet, discreet, invariably helpful, impeccably courteous, he wore his uniform with easy dignity. In conversation one was constantly aware of an undercurrent of Scots humour. He and Mrs. Mitchell, living on the top floor of No. 13 Gray's Inn Square, were excellent neighbours to the other residents, who missed him sorely when he · retired in 1975 after a quarter of a century's service in the Inn.

In 1978 Kenneth Chard took up the post of Butler to the Society and brought to the discharge of its onerous, complex and highly responsible duties the same devoted efficiency which he had already exercised as Head Porter. The care of the Inn's silver, the management of the Hall's staff, the subtle distinctions between preparations for Grand Nights, Call Nights, House Dinners, moot nights, debate nights, and Chapel service luncheons, he coped with them all, most ably seconded by a succession of assistants, notable among whom for courtesy and ready efficiency was James Hogg. Besides that Chard, from his flat at the heart of the Inn, rendered countless services to members and tenants.

It is on the devotion of members of the staff such as these – Terry, Barker, Ivey, Suter, Mitchell, Chard – that the life and continuity of every institution with a personal human mission depends. Inns of Court, colleges, schools, cathedrals; without that unobtrusive substructure they cannot fulfill their appointed purposes. Reliance on mere interchangeable 'units of personnel', clock-watching and unattached, here today and gone tomorrow, would leave them as barren and arid as a computerised bureaucracy.

Often in Gray's Inn the ties of its staff have been hereditary. There was Henry Smith, the Hall Keeper and Robing Room attendant, who died in 1951. Born in 1890, the year his father, formerly of the Royal Marines, was first employed by Gray's Inn, he helped him there from an early age. After serving in the army in the first World War, he returned to the Inn and became absorbed in its spirit and customs. During the second World War, when the Hall was burning, it was he who organised the rescue of the great Elizabethan screen, fortunately already dismantled in preparation for removal. After him came Tom Powell, robust and cheerful, formerly of the Coldstream Guards, who served the Inn from 1945 to 1969, a magnificent asset in seconding the Senior in Hall when order had to be maintained among the students, friendly without familiarity, authoritative without rudeness, polite without being ingratiating.

One of the most remarkable examples of heredity in the Inn was Mrs. Florence Davis, who retired from its service in 1960. Her grandfather became the Inn's caterer in 1894 when the provision of dinners and luncheons was contracted for, the caterer being normally the chef. He was succeeded by the father of Mrs. Davis and, after he died, her mother took his place, retiring in 1933, when the Inn assumed direct responsibility for its own catering. Mrs. Davis then became kitchen Clerk, using the experience she had acquired from her mother. From 1947 she worked in the Under-Treasurer's office. Her husband, Mr. A. S. Davis, who retired in 1975 from the post of Chief Clerk, had worked in the Under Treasurer's Office for half a century; short, dark, quiet, self-contained, always helpful and always efficient, an unfailing source of information on every matter of detail concerning the past and present of the Inn. His long memory provided a panorama of all the changes and development he had witnessed.

Another figure in the Inn, so familiar as to be an institution, was Edward Gray, who retired in 1982. Born in the vicinity of Leather Lane, he served the Inn as long as Mr. Davis. In the Under-Treasurer's office he, like Mr. Davis, ensured the smooth running and consistent continuity of its work and the keeping of its records. Quiet, reserved, he was a keen observer and often a humorous commentator on the scenes and happenings, past and present, in and about the Inn, where his impassive expression and high complexion seemed part of its unchanging background. In his own Irish idiom, John McGaughey, who succeeded Davis as Chief Clerk, perpetuates the same spirit.

Then there was Mrs. Dorothy Heyward, who came to the Inn in 1962 as secretary to the Under-Treasurer and when she retired, twenty years later, was Deputy Under-Treasurer (Students). Short, dark, always cheerful, always efficient, always friendly, providing a ready accurate answer to any question, she was in touch with everything and everyone in the Inn, not only a guardian angel to the students but a helpful presence for everyone. Fortunately the gap she left was filled in the same spirit and tradition by Miss Margaret Chadderton, at once elegant, charming, firm and full of North Country common sense, an enthusiast for the young, wide in her interests, an ornament to the Inn in every way.

The men whose services carried on the life of the Inn from day to day crowd on the memory. Albert McManus, ('Mac'), could turn his hand to anything and knew every pipe, cable and sewer in the Inn. Polikarp Mroz, the Polish gardener, retired in 1981. Slender, upright, authoritative, severe with his military bearing and military moustache, he had experienced many adventures during the war. He was indeed King of the Walks. But happily his successor Ronald Malone assumed his responsibilities with zeal, going back for inspiration to the flowers Bacon planted. Mroz's compatriot Paul Przewdzing, with a round rosy face like the rising sun, for years the presiding genius of the Common Room refectory, famous for his omelettes, his skill at chess and the atmosphere of friendliness which he generated among the students, retired in 1983. If the Library served barristers and students as efficiently as it did, that was due not only to the talents of the Librarians but also to the patient, methodical, robust common sense and devotion to duty of those two successive assistants, Mr. Vockins and Mr. Main, who kept the records, tidied up, found books for inquirers, put books back in the right places, steadily and unobtrusively, day by day.

The services of such men and women are commonly taken for granted, but they are of the essence of the very continuance of civilised society in general and of the existence of such institutions as Gray's Inn in particular. They are the good earth in which are rooted the tall trees, the flowering shrubs, the gorgeous flowers and the useful vegetables composing the variegated whole of the profession of Bench and Bar.

It is needless to paint in detail the portraits of men whose careers are part of legal history. Since the rebuilding of the Hall, two Gray's Inn men have held the Great Seal as Lord Chancellor; Lord Kilmuir, solid in judgment, scrupulously methodical and painstaking, always reliable, a Conservative in his politics, as in his philosophy of life; and Lord Elwyn-Jones, a lifelong reformer, abundantly blessed with the charm of his native Wales, lively, witty, friendly, a man who had raised himself from simple beginnings entirely by his own efforts. While he was Lord Chancellor, the future Lord Selwyn-Lloyd, a fellow Bencher of Gray's Inn, was Speaker of the House of Commons.

The appointment of Lord Lane in 1980 to the office of Lord Chief Justice brought a fresh vitality to its tenure. A vigorous circuiteer while he had been at the Bar, he brought to the judicial office a quickness of apprehension and a robust common sense combined with complete fairness, which made it impossible to waste time in his Court. His mind derived its quality from an education based on the ancient classics. Humorous, convivial and unconventional in his private life, he never let levity or irrelevance

intrude on his judicial duties. He set himself against the domin-
ation of the Bench by bureaucracy.

To the judicial work of the House of Lords, Benchers of
Gray's Inn have richly contributed. Outstanding among them was
Lord Reid, one of the long line of brilliant Scots who left the
legal world of Edinburgh to sit as Lords of Appeal in Ordinary
and bring to the elucidation of the law of England their own
native clarity of thought and sense of relevance. Lord Reid served
for more than a quarter of a century. Living in South Square, he
very often ate in Hall. Another trinity of Scots who were Benchers
of Gray's Inn, all three notable lawyers, made their mark in the
House of Lords. Lord Kilbrandon, tall and handsome, brought a
strong social conscience to his judicial work. The learning of Lord
Fraser of Tullybelton was all the more effective in adjudication
for being wedded to a gentle and good-humoured kindliness. Lord
Keith of Kinkel, whose appearance matched his forthright good
sense and intelligence, played a very active part in the government
of Gray's Inn, for he had been called to the Bar there, as well as
in Scotland, and lived within its precincts.

Gray's Inn has always had close links with Ireland and Wales
which have held firmly since the second World War. Lord Devlin,
an intellectual and a philosopher as well as an accomplished
lawyer, sound and detached in judgment, acute in analysis,
inflexible in integrity, wide in his interests, ranging from history
to practical agriculture at his Wiltshire home, was not actually
born in Ireland. But Lord MacDermott came to Gray's Inn from
Northern Ireland when he became a Lord of Appeal in Ordinary.
This he later renounced to serve, with outstanding courage, as
Lord Chief Justice of Northern Ireland. When he died in 1979,
Lord Hailsham called him, 'a great lawyer, a great judge and a
great man'. Lord Edmund-Davies, who attained the House of
Lords from unprivileged beginnings, is one of the outstanding
Welshmen of his time. He rose by sheer mental quality, courage,
tenacity and force of character wedded to that native sense of
humour which few Welshmen are denied. Within Gray's Inn he
exercised a very strong influence.

When it comes to Benchers who have been members of the
Court of Appeal and judges of the High Court, one must resign

oneself to picking here and there almost at random. There was Frederic Sellers, the solid, kindly, hard-working Lancashire man who, after his exploits in the first World War, built up a distinguished commercial practice, sat in the Queen's Bench Division and rose to preside in the Court of Appeal. Later John Megaw and George Waller contributed their own characteristic qualities to the service of the Court, as did Sebag Shaw, short, quiet, whimsical, but formidable in his lucidity, common sense and preception of men and situations, a most pleasant companion. He, like Sellers, rendered devoted service to Gray's Inn and his death impoverished it.

To the Bench of the High Court Gray's Inn has sent judges of outstandingly varied personalities who have sat there since the 1950's. Malcolm Hilbery, already in the Queen's Bench before the war, tall, slender, authoritative, fastidious, was a dominant influence in the affairs of the Inn for many years after it, William McNair, solid in intelligence, sturdily build, dutiful, long gave the Queen's Bench Division the benefit of his mastery of commercial law. A later elevation to the Queen's Bench Division was that of Ralph Cusack, a slim, quiet, quizzical, precise Irishman whose intensely reserved personality made no histrionic display of the intellectual brilliance which made him an outstanding judge and, on his untimely death, a most grievous loss to the administration of justice. Rose Heilbron, the first woman Bencher of Gray's Inn and almost the first woman to be a High Court judge, combined striking good looks with strength of mind and tenacious industry. The handsome John Ramsay Willis, a countryman and a mountaineer, combined vigour, kindness and personal charm, carrying onto the Bench and into retirement an aura of youth unimpaired. David Croom-Johnson, like his father before him, was a judge of the Queen's Bench Division. William Mars-Jones, a vigorous and fiery Welshman, *fortiter in re*, brought to the Queen's Bench Division the forthright directness of approach which had characterised him as a naval officer in the second World War. In the Chancery Division, John Vinelott displayed his solid mental approach and strength of character.

Then there were Law Officers of the Crown, the future Lord Shawcross, handsome and incisive as Attorney-General; Dingle

Foot, dedicated law reformer, convivial companion and gifted writer of light verse, who was Solicitor-General, and Peter Archer, one of his successors in the office, lucid, friendly, modest, more apt to generate light than heat.

Of other Benchers who did not attain the honours of the High Court, only a few can be enumerated, again almost at random. Leonard Stone, gregarious, convivial and extrovert, stood, as Vice-Chancellor of the County Palatine of Lancaster, on the threshold of the High Court. His son, Richard Stone Q.C. attained the distinction, unique in the history of the Inn, of being a Bencher at the same time as his father. Lord McNair (Arnold, the brother of William McNair), Humphrey Waldock and Gerald Fitzmaurice were called to be judges of the International Court of Justice. Charles John Hamson Q.C. and Ronald Graveson Q.C. won high reputations in the academic world as legal scholars.

Nicholas Macaskie Q.C., intensely sociable and hospitable, gracious and smiling, a knowledgeable *bon viveur,* was a regular diner at the Bench table, active and young in appearance until his late eighties. When he was the senior Bencher present, his lively consultations with the chef, led ceremonially up to the High Table by the Head Porter, presented a characteristic conversation piece. David Karmel, dark, solid, lively, friendly, never yielding to the lasting effect of all but mortal wounds suffered in the war, was a devoted and influential power in the Inn and, by stealth, a most munificent benefactor to students and beginners. Sydney Pocock, cheerful, modest, universally friendly, alert, and flexible in mind and body, was the best of Resident Benchers. His sudden death in 1957 during his Treasurership was untimely, even though he was in his late seventies, for he remained lively and young to the end. Tall, fair, slender, loose-limbed, rosy of complexion, he was a key figure in the life of the Inn and also the Bar, though his practice was never large. Tireless in his work for the library, the Common Room, the Bar Benevolent Association, he was meticulously attentive to the needs and interests of all who came in contact with him. His cheerful kindness and approachableness, wedded to the soundest good sense, endeared him to all to a degree rare in any community. He knew and served Gray's Inn from its grass roots upwards.

In the unfolding roll of the Benchers, many contrasting figures claim a place in any record. Patrick Neill Q.C., tall, quietly striking, reserved, shrewd in judgment, crowned his career at the Bar first by his chairmanship of the Press Council and they be the Wardenship of All Souls at Oxford. Stephen Terrell Q.C. carried on the tradition of his family's prolific clan, stretching back in the law for a hundred years, a tradition of extrovert vitality and unconventional energy which enabled him to mix on natural terms with students and young barristers and maintained his zeal in promoting the provision of chambers for them within the Inn. He was descended from Thomas Terrell K.C., author of the classic book on patents, Bencher of Gray's Inn and convivial companion of the great Lord Birkenhead.

Again a contrasting personality, Judge Marven Everett, had been at the Bar an outstanding practitioner and authority on employers' liability, a big, burly, robust figure with the heart of a countryman. He fell sick and died in 1978, almost as soon as he had fulfilled the duties of his year of Treasurership, performed under the additional strain of the fatal illness of a beloved wife. Another contrast, Judge Esyr Lewis, a singularly gentle, reflective, quiet Welshman, very much a man about the Inn where he had long resided and where he and his wife had raised a family of four attractive daughters, the eldest of whom, Emma, was herself called to the Bar by the Inn.

In an Inn fertile in such varied characters, it was natural that distinguished men should have been happy to be elected honorary Benchers, men like the robust, resolute wartime Prime Minister of Australia, Robert Menzies Q.C., or that great individualist judge, Lord Denning, Master of the Rolls. Nor is it strange that royalty should have honoured it. After the death of H.R.H. the Duke of Gloucester, H.R.H. Charles, Prince of Wales, not only consented to become a Bencher in 1975 but also participated in the ordinary life of the Inn, dining in Hall, attending a moot, reading a poem during one of the miscellanies of music, verse and prose organised for the Christmas season.

But below the dais Hall nourishes the essential life of the Inn, of which the Benchers are only the flower and fruit. The generals have their indispensable, distinguished and properly recognised function, but the army is the rank and file whom time, for the most part, thrusts into oblivion and anonymity. The members of Hall are the life of the Inn amid the buzz of conversation, the exchange of ideas, the professional interchanges, the convivial drinking, the songs and recitations when a spontaneous party develops after dinner. Among the figures which crowded the benches, how inadequately must one choose at random among the personalities that set the tables in a roar. Charles Du Cann, author and redoubtable Old Bailey practitioner (father of a future Bencher, Richard Du Cann Q.C., also a distinguished criminal advocate) but never himself a Bencher. Short, dark, wittily incisive, one of the best Seniors in Hall, with the art of giving cohesion to a merry evening, he set a standard which later William Mars-Jones and Francis Cowper worked to carry forward.

A tremendous upholder of the customs and traditions of Gray's Inn and of the Bar was Thomas Jeffrey Hobley, dark, square of build, rubicund of complexion, a combination of the bluntly robust and the meticulously correct, formidable in rebuke to those who transgressed the customs of Hall of which he was the uncompromising guardian.

There was John Lee, long the Students' Adviser to the Inns of Court, quiet, good-humoured, tolerant, dark, smooth-haired, a lover of horses and of his little Sussex farm near Battle, with an inexhaustible fund of songs, including some about Gray's Inn which he himself composed.

Less prominent in Hall, though a resident in the Inn for many years, the business manager who kept the Inn's magazine Graya solvent in the post-war years was Conrad Walter, a late-comer to the Bar after a business career which had not dimmed his enthusiasm for history, archaeology, the classical as well as the modern languages. Small, lean, wiry, trenchant, but always courteous, he looked far younger than his years, even under the assault of a mortal malady which brought progressive paralysis.

A welcome bird of passage, when his duties in the Royal Marines permitted, was Colonel George Grover, a quiet man of keen intelligence, whimsical humour and wide experience all over the world in peace and war, typical of the men from other callings whose presence has enriched the life of Hall. Another was

Brigadier John Edney, a distinguished Sapper officer long resident in the Inn, who brought to the Bar and later to the world of international arbitrations his high talent in engineering.

A frequent diner in Hall was David Armstead Fairweather, a Scot transplanted to Wales, massive in proportions, lively in mind and wide in interests, his forcefulness emphasised by his red hair and moustache. His knowledge of life at the Bar, his hatred of humbug and meanness, his Celtic love of exaggeration in anecdotes laced with a jovial malice, his songs in German and French, his idiosyncratic rendering of Maurice Chevalier's 'Valentine', made him a magnificent table companion.

James Mulcahy, an Irishman with a native satirical talent exposing to ridicule trendy deviations from the sound traditions of the Bar, displayed genius, as Senior in Hall adjudicating on charges of breaches of the customs, in blending wild fantasy and caricature with solid knowledge of law and procedure.

Before the war, women played little part in the after-dinner proceedings over the port. From the 1950's onwards, their presence was woven into the scene. Rosalind Lawson, round-faced, blonde, whose deceptively innocent and youthful appearance and gentle tone concealed a sharp sophisticated intelligence; Jill Bannister, darkly handsome, whose unpredictability masked a knowledge of Latin and some Russian, a deep regret not to have lived in Restoration England and a passionate conviction of the innocence of Richard III; Marie Cameron, a dark, distinguished, ornament to Hall, blending liveliness with a keen intelligence; Molina Fullman, more mature when she joined the Inn than the girl students, but a great asset, especially when singing was the order of the evening, with her songs and sometimes her guitar; Rita Dickinson, also a late vocation, whose Irish songs in her sweet Irish voice always entranced. Prominent among other ladies, who pursued their profession with zeal, were Jean Southworth Q.C. who practised at the common law Bar and became a Bencher, and Elizabeth Appleby Q.C., who won distinction in Chancery.

The talents which blossomed so spontaneously after dinner in Hall often produced admirable, and sometimes boisterous, revues at Christmastide and on Call Night, when each of the newly called was expected to make a speech after the Benchers had withdrawn. There were often rendered instead songs and recitations specially composed for the occasion, many of them very funny indeed. For all these purposes Hall was versatile — moots for serious instruction in the law, debates for fluency in public speaking, ordinary dinners for sociability and the cohesion of the profession. Always it was the precious personal side of the relationships of the future Bar and Bench of England that was being fostered and developed, while men and women from every walk of life were being increasingly drawn into the circle, so that the blind son of a factory worker in the provinces might be dining with the son or daughter of a judge.

On ordinary nights when there was no moot, no debate, no talk by a distinguished person, no formal concert, no literary readings, Hall might settle down to an evening of conversation in which the pooled resources of so many different types of men and women stimulated instruction, dovetailed with entertainment, in all those things which cannot be learnt from textbooks. Charges of breaches of the customs of Hall, serious, semi-serious or frivolous, might be argued and adjudicated on by the Senior in Hall who awarded against those convicted the fine of a bottle of port, later stabilised as a 'statutory bottle' of four glasses, not oppressively punitive at a cost of a few shillings or their later equivalent in new pence. It was a way of good-humouredly maintaining order and encouraging wit and readiness of tongue. Often the evening would develop into a spontaneous party night with a rich variety of songs and recitations from all periods and of all degrees of seriousness and humour; Victorian drawing-room songs, music hall songs, folk songs, pop songs, choruses, solos. When it happened that the Senior in Hall had the talents of a good chairman, enouraging hidden talent, promoting variety, controlling the over-exuberant, the exhibitionist, good humour abounded. If (as sometimes happened) the Senior in Hall was a dull dog who regarded high spirits as childish and only wanted to mumble with his cronies about what old Mulligatawny did after he retired from practice in 1930, everything fell flat. No generation was exactly like any other generation and accordingly, as the talents of the members ebbed and flowed from year to year, Hall was lively or subdued, intelligently amusing or bibulously rowdy.

Hall, too, had its higher education. In Gray's Inn alone, if there were fewer than four Benchers at the high table they would make up their mess from the body of the Hall, barristers or students. Of late it has been invariably students. The contacts were good alike for the Benchers and their guests, providing for both an immediate personal chance of an insight into aspects of the ways of the Inn and life in the law unfamiliar to them.

So much good fellowship, so much conviviality, cost the students little. Till 1953 the price of a dinner was three shillings (15p). In that year it was raised to five shillings (25p). Twelve years later, the charge still tood at that level. In 1965 the charge for a barrister's dinner in Hall was raised to 12s. 6d. (72½p), the students paying less. By 1984, students' dinners had risen to £3.50 and barristers' to £5. Every inflationary blast blowing up the cost of conviviality has been greeted within the Hall with protest and nostalgia.

But in its voyage across the centuries Hall, like a great galleon, has sailed triumphantly through many gales and storms and fiery perils, past shoals, rocks and quicksands, endangered by members of her crew who might be mutinous or incompetent or self-seeking or ignorant of navigation and the skills to handle her. Yet she has righted herself and held her course. May she do so still.

Epilogue

WHEN the first edition of this book was published Gray's Inn was a mass of ruins only just starting to raise its head after the hammer blows of war and its accompanying devastation. Only the Hall had been re-edified in the very likeness of its historic self, an assertion of ineffaceable continuity. All the rest remained to be built again, stones and bricks and wood, but, of infinitely greater import, the corporate life of the Society. It was a long effort, requiring, above all, steadfastness. It was through the steadfastness of the Benchers, the members of Hall and the devoted staff that the Inn, after twenty years of dedication, attained heights of achievement and public recognition which could compare proudly with any period in its history.

It would be fallacious to pretend that Gray's Inn does not now face another period of crisis. It is a crisis, not of physical devastation, but of psychological, social and economic dislocation, of which perplexity before the proliferation of narcotics, the underground threat of organised international terrorism, the anarchic wave of rapacious and often hideously cruel lawlessness and the brooding cloud of nuclear obliteration hanging over our future, are only the most obvious manifestations. The euphoria of material affluence and its inherited attitudes have so inflated the expectations and therefore the demands on life of the entire population, from international tycoons down to paupers on public relief, that inflation of the economy to meet those demands has become an endemic economic disease. Self-discipline, thrift and contentment have been replaced by a debilitating self-indulgence which treats spending as a duty. The prodigal waste of a 'throw away' society, making little out of much, has replaced the art of making much out of little which the wisest men of all ages have proclaimed as

189

the precondition of happiness and independence. 'He who cannot live on little will always be a slave'.

The law is caught up in the problems of its time and so, of course, are the Inns of Court. Faced with the cancer of inflation eroding the very means by which it can fulfill its mission to personalise the practice of the law by maintaining in simplicity the community spirit of its predecessors, nothing would be more insidious than for Gray's Inn to succumb to the temptation to handle its assets by the methods of a property company, content to turn itself into a qualification factory fortified with periodical oysters and champagne banquets and regarding its staff merely as units of personnel in a commercial enterprise manipulated by text-book methods of man-management. But what shall it profit an institution if it flourishes economically at the cost of losing its sense of purpose, becoming a mere shell emptied of content?

The only thing that can bind together a regiment, a college, a religious community, a club, is the continuing loyalty which inspires its members and those who serve them in the pursuit of the objects for which they are united. Loyauté me lie. Only that inspiration moved the servants of the Inn, while the Hall was burning, to risk their lives in rescuing its Elizabethan screen, its chiefest ornament.

Throughout its long history, Gray's Inn has survived and surmounted many crises – the divisive crisis of the religious revolution in the 16th century; the Civil War, 'the Great Rebellion', in the 17th century; the extinction of formal education for the Bar in the 18th century; eclipse and almost dissolution in the 19th century under weak and negligent administration, exploited by dishonest staff and tradesmen; all but total destruction in the 20th century by fire and explosion during the bombardments of the second World War. Over all these varied catastrophes, the inherent vitality of Gray's Inn has triumphed. Fortified in the faith of such indestructibility, we can confidently expect the Society now to right herself, set her proper course and continue to fulfill a mission which will never be obsolete as long as human and impartial justice between man and man within the rule of law remains the basis of the society towards which, generation by generation, the English nation aspires.

Appendix 1

Treasurers of Gray's Inn 1951–1985

1951   SIR WILLIAM McNAIR
        (*Justice of the High Court (King's Bench Division and Queen's Bench Division)* 1950-66)

1952   SIR FREDERICK SELLERS
        (*Justice of the High Court (King's Bench Division and Queen's Bench Division)* 1947-57; *Lord Justice of Appeal* 1957-68)

1953   SIR HENRY BARNARD
        (*Justice of the High Court (Probate, Divorce and Admiralty Division)* 1944-59)

1954   H.R.H. THE DUKE OF GLOUCESTER *K.G., K.T., G.C.M.G.*

1955   SIR HARTLEY SHAWCROSS *Q.C.*
        (*Attorney-General* 1945-51; *created Lord Shawcross* 1959)

1956   SIR LEONARD STONE
        (*Chief Justice of Bombay* 1943-47; *Vice-Chancellor of the County Palatine of Lancaster* 1948-63)

1957   SYDNEY ELSDON POCOCK

1958   SIR JOHN FORSTER *Q.C.*
        (*President of the Industrial Court* 1946-60; *created Lord Forster of Harraby* 1959)

1959 HENRY SALT *Q.C.*
(*Chancellor of the County Palatine of Durham* 1960-69)

1960 HENRY GRAZEBROOK *Q.C.*
(*Special Divorce Commissioner* 1947-57)

1961 MICHAEL ROWE *Q.C.*
(*knighted* 1963; *President of the Lands Tribunal* 1966-73)

1962 PERCY LAMB *Q.C.*
(*Official Referee of the Supreme Court* 1959-69)

1963 LORD DEVLIN
(*Justice of the High Court (Queen's Bench Division)* 1948-60; *Lord Justice of Appeal* 1960-61; *Lord of Appeal in Ordinary* 1961-64)

1964 SIR DENIS GERRARD
(*Justice of the High Court (Queen's Bench Division)* 1953-56)

1965 SIR EDMUND DAVIES
(*Justice of the High Court (Queen's Bench Division)* 1958-66; *Lord Justice of Appeal* 1966-74; *Lord of Appeal in Ordinary* 1974-81; *created Lord Edmund-Davies)*

1966 SIR ARCHIE PELLOW MARSHALL
(*Justice of the High Court (Queen's Bench Division)* 1961-66)

1967 GEOFFREY TOOKEY *Q.C.*

1968 SIR DINGLE FOOT *Q.C.*
(*Solicitor-General* 1964-67)

1969 SIR JOHN RAMSAY WILLIS
(*Justice of the High Court (Queen's Bench Division)* 1966-80)

1970 DAVID KARMEL *Q.C.*

1971 SIR HUMPHREY WALDOCK *C.M.G.*
  (*Judge of the International Court* 1973-81;*President*
  1979-81)

1972 ROY BORNEMAN *Q.C.*
  (*Chairman, Board of Referees and Finance Act
  1960 Tribunal* 1960-77)

1973 SIR ROY WILSON *Q.C.*
  (*President of the Industrial Court* 1961-71;*President
  of the Industrial Arbitration Board* 1971-76)

1974 HUGH FRANCIS *Q.C.*

1975 CHARLES JOHN HAMSON *Q.C.*
  (*Professor of Comparative Law at Cambridge
  University* 1953-71)

1976 SIR JOHN MEGAW
  (*Justice of the High Court (Queen's Bench Division)*
  1961-69; *Lord Justice of Appeal* 1969-80)

1977 RICHARD MARVEN HALE EVERETT *Q.C.*
  (*Circuit Judge* 1971-78)

1978 SIR GEORGE WALLER
  (*Justice of the High Court (Queen's Bench Division)*
  1965-76; *Lord Justice of Appeal* 1976)

1979 LEONARD CAPLAN *Q.C.*

1980 LORD ELWYN-JONES
  (*Attorney-General* 1964-70; *Lord Chancellor* 1974-
  79)

1981 SIR DAVID CROOM-JOHNSON
  (*Justice of the High Court (Queen's Bench Division)*
  1971)

1982 SIR WILLIAM MARS-JONES
  (*Justice of the High Court (Queen's Bench Division)*
  1969)

1983   RONALD GRAVESON *Q.C.*
        (Professor Emeritus of Private International Law, King's College, University of London)

1984   BRIAN GIBBENS *Q.C.*
        (Circuit Judge 1973)

1985   DAME ROSE HEILBRON
        (Justice of the High Court (Family Division) 1974)

Appendix 2

Masters of the Bench of Gray's Inn 1985

H.R.H. THE PRINCE OF WALES, *K.C., K.T., G.C.B.*

THE RIGHT HON. THE LORD SHAWCROSS, *D.C.L., G.B.E., Q.C., LL.D.*
(Chancellor of the University of Sussex)

THE RIGHT HON. THE LORD DEVLIN, *D.C.L., LL.D., F.B.A.*
(A Lord of Appeal)
(High Steward of the University of Cambridge)

SIR GEORGE POLLOCK, *Q.C.*

THE RIGHT HON. THE LORD EDMUND-DAVIES, *P.C.*
(Formerly a Lord of Appeal in Ordinary)

SIR JOHN RAMSAY WILLIS
(Formerly a Justice of the High Court)

HUGH ELVET FRANCIS, *Q.C.*

CHARLES JOHN HAMSON, *Q.C.*
(Fellow of Trinity College) (Lately Professor of Comparative Law at the University of Cambridge)

KENNETH ROBERT HOPE JOHNSTON, *Q.C.*

THE RIGHT HON. SIR JOHN MEGAW, *C.B.E., T.D.*
(Formerly A Lord Justice of Appeal)

THE RIGHT HON. THE LORD ELWYN-JONES, *C.H.*
(Formerly The Lord High Chancellor of Great Britain)

HIS HONOUR SIR RUDOLPH LYONS, *Q.C., LL.D.*
(Formerly Hon. Recorder of Manchester and Liverpool)

THE RIGHT HON. SIR GEORGE STANLEY WALLER, *O.B.E.*
(Formerly a Lord Justice of Appeal)

HIS HONOUR FRANK ALLEYNE STOCKDALE
(Formerly a Circuit Judge)

LEONARD CAPLAN, *Q.C.*

THE RIGHT HON. SIR DAVID POWELL CROOM-JOHNSON, *D.S.C., V.R.D.*
(A Lord Justice of Appeal)

THE HON. SIR WILLIAM LLOYD MARS-JONES, *M.B.E., LL.D.*
(A Justice of the High Court)

LESLIE JAMES MORRIS SMITH

RONALD HARRY GRAVESON, *C.B.E., Q.C., LL.D.*
(Emeritus Professor of Private International Law, University of London)

THE RIGHT HON. THE LORD LANE, *A.F.C.*
(The Lord Chief Justice of England)

HIS HONOUR JUDGE EDWARD BRIAN GIBBENS, *Q.C.*
(Dean of the Chapel) (Circuit Judge) (Hon. Recorder of Oxford)

THE HON. DAME ROSE HEILBRON, *D.B.E., LL.D.*
(Treasurer) (A Justice of the High Court)

SIR EDWARD LUCAS GARDNER, *Q.C., M.P.*
(Recorder)

THE LORD HOOSON, *Q.C.*
(Vice-Treasurer) (Recorder)

HIS HONOUR JUDGE RAYMOND STOCK, *Q.C.*
(Circuit Judge)

SIR ALUN TALFAN DAVIES, *Q.C., LL.D.*
(Recorder and Hon. Recorder of Cardiff)

THE HON. SIR KENNETH JONES
(A Justice of the High Court)

ROBERT ALEXANDER MacCRINDLE, *Q.C.*

THE HON. SIR GORDON SLYNN
(An Advocate General of the Court of Justice of the European Communities)

STEPHEN TERRELL, *O.B.E., T.D., Q.C., D.L.*

SIR MAURICE EDWARD BATHURST, *C.M.G., C.B.E., Q.C., LL.D.*
(A Judge of the Arbitral Tribunal for German External Debts)

THE RIGHT HON. EDWARD RICHARD GEORGE HEATH, *M.B.E., M.P.* (Honorary)

SIR DOUGLAS GEORGE HORACE FRANK, *Q.C.*
(President of the Lands Tribunal) (Master of Estates)

THE RIGHT HON. THE LORD KILBRANDON, *LL.D., D.Sc., (Soc. Sci.)*
(A Lord of Appeal) (Honorary)

SIR FRANCIS AIMÉ VALLAT, *G.B.E., K.C.M.G., Q.C.*
(Professor Emeritus of International Law, University of London)

JOHN TREVOR PLUME

SIR FRANCIS PATRICK NEILL, *Q.C.*
(Judge of the Courts of Appeal, Jersey and Guernsey)
(Warden of All Souls College, Oxford)

M. ROBERT LECOURT
(Ancien Ministre)
(Ancien Président de la Cour de Justice des Communautés Européennes)
(Membre du Conseil Constitutionnel) (Honorary)

THE RIGHT HON. SIR JOHN ROSS MARSHALL, *G.B.E., C.H.*
(Formerly Prime Minister of New Zealand) (Honorary)

THE LORD WIGODER, *Q.C.*
(Master of Moots) (Recorder)

PHILIP JOSEPH COX, *D.S.C., Q.C.*
(Recorder and Hon. Recorder of Northampton)

HIS EXCELLENCY JUDGE NAGENDRA SINGH, *LL.D., D.C.L., D.Sc (Law), D.Litt., D.Phil.*
(Vice-President of the International Court of Justice 1976-1979) (Honorary)

THE RIGHT HON. LORD RICHARDSON of Duntisbourne, *K.G., M.B.E., T.D., M.A.*
(Formerly Governor of the Bank of England) (Honorary)

HIS HONOUR JUDGE STUART COLIN SLEEMAN
(Circuit Judge)

JAMES ROLAND BLAKE FOX–ANDREWS, *Q.C.*
(Recorder and Honorary Recorder of Winchester)

RICHARD FREDERICK STONE, *Q.C.*

THE HON. SIR JOHN EVELYN VINELOTT
(A Justice of the High Court)

SIR FRANK HENRY BURLAND WILLOUGHBY LAYFIELD, *Q.C.*

THE RIGHT HON. PETER KINGSLEY ARCHER, *Q.C., M.P.*
(Formerly Solicitor-General) (Recorder)

THE LORD RICHARDSON, *M.V.O., M.A., M.D., (Hon) D.Sc., (Hon) D.C.L., (Hon) LL.D., F.R.C.P., (Hon) F.R.C.S.*
(Formerly President of the General Medical Council) (Honorary)

TREVOR CAWDOR THOMAS, *M.A., LL.D.*
(Formerly Vice-Chancellor of the University of Liverpool) (Honorary)

THE RIGHT HON. THE LORD FRASER OF TULLYBELTON, *LL.D.*
(A Lord of Appeal in Ordinary) (Honorary)

Masters of the Bench of Gray's Inn 1985

M. BERNARD CHENOT
(Vice President Honoraire du Conseil d'Etat)
(Secretaire Perpetuel de l'Academie des Sciences Morales et Politiques) (Honorary)

M. LE VICOMTE GANSHOF VAN DER MEERSCH, *C.B.*
(A Judge of the European Court of Human Rights) (Procureur Général Emérite à la Cour de Cassation de Belgique) (Professor at the University of Brussels) (Honorary)

MUIR VANE SKERRETT HUNTER, *Q.C.*

EDWIN FRANCIS ROMILLY WHITEHEAD

PATRICK BENNETT, *Q.C.*
(Recorder) (Commissioner, Mental Health Act)

ALBERT CHARLES SPARROW, *Q.C.*

THE RIGHT HON. THE LORD KEITH OF KINKEL
(A Lord of Appeal in Ordinary)

THE HON. SIR MICHAEL JOHN MUSTILL
(A Justice of the High Court)

THE HON. SIR BRIAN DREX BUSH
(A Justice of the High Court)

HIS HONOUR JUDGE MICHAEL THOMAS BEN UNDERHILL, *Q.C.*
(Circuit Judge)

THE HON. SIR IAIN DEREK LAING GLIDEWELL
(A Justice of the High Court)

THE HON. SIR MURRAY STUART-SMITH
(A Justice of the High Court)

CONRAD FRANCIS DEHN, *Q.C.*
(Recorder)

FRANCIS HENRY COWPER (Honorary)

THE VERY REVD. SYDNEY HALL EVANS, *C.B.E., M.A., D.D.*
(Dean of Salisbury) (Honorary)

THE RIGHT HON. SIR ZELMAN COWEN, *A.K., G.C.M.G., G.C.V.O., Q.C., D.C.L.*
(Provost of Oriel College, Oxford, and formerly Governor-General of Australia) (Honorary)

PATRICK BACK, *Q.C.*
(Recorder)

HIS HONOUR JUDGE ESYR ap GWILYM LEWIS, *Q.C.*
(Circuit Judge)

RAYMOND INCLEDON KIDWELL, *Q.C.*
(Recorder)

ANTHONY GORDON GUEST
(Professor of English Law, University of London)

JOHN ANTHONY JOLOWICZ
(Professor of Comparative Law, University of Cambridge)

SIR JACK I.H. JACOB, *Q.C., (Hon) LL.D.*
(Formerly Senior Master of the Supreme Court and Queen's Remembrancer) (Honorary)

THE RIGHT HON. THE LORD DENNING
(Formerly Master of the Rolls) (Honorary)

THE HON. SIR ANTHONY BARNARD HOLLIS
(A Justice of the High Court)

GILBERT GRAY, *Q.C.*
(Recorder)

THE HON. SIR ANTHONY HOWELL MEURIG EVANS
(A Justice of the High Court)

THE HON. SIR THOMAS HENRY BINGHAM
(A Justice of the High Court)

HIS EXCELLENCY SIR ELLIS CLARKE, *T.C., G.C.M.G.*
(President of Trinidad and Tobago) (Honorary)

HIS EXCELLENCY THE HON. SIR DAVID BEATTIE, *G.C.M.G., G.C.V.O., Q.C.*
(Governor-General of New Zealand) (Honorary)

THE HON. SIR ANTHONY BRUCE EWBANK
(A Justice of the High Court)

THE HON. SIR ANTHONY JAMES DENYS McCOWAN
(A Justice of the High Court)

RICHARD DILLON LOTT Du CANN, *Q.C.*
(Recorder)

THE HON. SIR MICHAEL MANN
(A Justice of the High Court)

THE RIGHT HON. MARK CARLISLE, *Q.C., M.P.*
(Recorder)

RICHARD JON STANLEY HARVEY, *Q.C.*
(Recorder)

THE RIGHT WORSHIPFUL, HIS HONOUR JUDGE JOHN ARTHUR
DALZIEL OWEN, *Q.C.*
*(Circuit Judge) (Dean of the Court of Arches and Auditor of
the Chancery Court of York)*

JEAN MAY SOUTHWORTH, *Q.C.*
(Recorder)

WILLIAM JAMES KINNEAR MILLAR

SIR EVELYN CHARLES SACKVILLE RUSSELL
(Formerly Chief Metropolitan Stipendiary Magistrate)
(Honorary)

THE MOST REVEREND AND RIGHT HONOURABLE ROBERT
RUNCIE THE LORD ARCHBISHOP OF CANTERBURY
(Honorary)

JOHN MAURICE PRICE, *Q.C.*

PETER WEITZMAN, *Q.C.*
(Recorder)

JOHN MARTIN COLLINS, *Q.C.*
(Judge of the Courts of Appeal, Jersey and Guernsey)
(Recorder)

LIONEL FRANK READ, *Q.C.*
  (Recorder)

THE HON. SIR JOHN DOUGLAS WAITE
  (A Justice of the High Court)

JULIAN JEFFS, *Q.C.*
  (Recorder)

SIR SHRIDATH SURENDRANATH RAMPHAL, *O.E., A.C., C.M.G., Q.C.*
  (Commonwealth Secretary-General) (Honorary)

BARRY PINSON, *Q.C.*

RICHARD MICHAEL YORKE, *Q.C.*

THE RIGHT HON. SIR NINIAN MARTIN STEPHEN, *A.K., G.C.M.G., G.C.V.O., K.B.E., K.St.J.*
  (Governor-General of Australia) (Honorary)

JAMES WESLEY WELLWOOD, *M.A. dub.* (Honorary)

THE LORD WEINSTOCK OF BOWDEN, *B.Sc., F.S.S., (Hon) F.R.C.R., (Hon) D.Sc., (Hon) D.Tech. (Hon) LL.D.* (Honorary)

THE HON. MRS JUSTICE SANDRA DAY O'CONNOR
  (Associate Justice of the Supreme Court of the United States) (Honorary)

SIR ANTHONY DEREK MAXWELL OULTON, *K.C.B., Q.C.*
  (Master of Administration) (Clerk of the Crown in Chancery and Permanent Secretary to the Lord Chancellor)

GUENTER HEINZ TREITEL, *Q.C., D.C.L., F.B.A.*
  (Vinerian Professor of English Law and Fellow of All Souls College, Oxford) (Honorary)

SIMON GOLDBLATT, *Q.C.*

JOHN RAYMOND PEPPITT, *Q.C.*
  (Recorder)

THE HON. SIR PAUL JOSEPH MORROW KENNEDY
  (A Justice of the High Court)

THE RIGHT HON. VISCOUNT TONYPANDY
(Formerly Speaker of the House of Commons) (Honorary)

THE RIGHT HON. VISCOUNT DE L'ISLE, *V.C., K.G., P.C., G.C.M.G., G.C.V.O.* (Honorary)

PROFESSOR SIR RANDOLPH QUIRK, *C.B.E., D.Litt., LL.D., F.B.A.*
(Vice-Chancellor of the University of London) (Honorary)

PRESIDENT DEREK C. BOK
(Professor of Harvard University) (Honorary)

GROUP CAPTAIN LEONARD CHESHIRE, *V.C., O.M., D.S.O.**, D.F.C.* (Honorary)

THE HON. SIR PHILIP HOWARD OTTON
(A Justice of the High Court)

THE RIGHT HON. MARGARET THATCHER, *M.P.*
(The Prime Minister) (Honorary)

ELIHU LAUTERPACHT, *Q.C.*

HARRY HENRY OGNALL, *Q.C.*
(Recorder)

BRIAN JOHN DAVENPORT, *Q.C.*

THE HON. SIR MICHAEL HUTCHISON
(A Justice of the High Court)

ROBERT DONALD HARMAN, *Q.C.*
(Recorder)

ROBIN ERNEST AULD, *Q.C.*
(Recorder)

LEONARD HUBERT HOFFMANN, *Q.C.*
(Recorder)

Bibliography

*T*HE *Pension Book of Gray's Inn* (1901). (Edited by Reginald Fletcher.)

The Gray's Inn Admission Register 1521–1889.

The War Book of Gray's Inn (1921).

Gray's Inn Library (1929).

Gesta Grayorum or the History of the Most High and Mighty Prince, Henry Prince of Purpoole (1688).

The Black Books of Lincoln's Inn (1897–1902).

Barron, Caroline: *The Parish of St. Andrew, Holborn,* (1979).

Barton, Sir Dunbar Plunket, and others: *The Story of the Inns of Court* (1924).

Barton, Sir Dunbar Plunket: *Timothy Healy* (1933).

Bellot, Hugh: *Gray's Inn* (1925).

Bolland, William: *Manual of Year Book Studies* (1925).

Boswell: *Life of Johnson.*

Brett-James, Norman: *The Growth of Stuart London* (1938).

Chambers, R. W.: *Thomas More* (1935).

Chancellor, E. Beresford: *The Eighteenth Century in London* (1920).

Cobbett, William: *Life and Adventures of Peter Porcupine.*

Cook, Mrs. E.T.: *Highways and Byways in London* (1902).

Dickens, Charles: *The Uncommercial Traveller, David Copperfield, The Pickwick Papers* and *Great Expectations.*

Douthwaite, William: *Gray's Inn; Its History and Associations* (1886).

Dugdale, William: *Origines Judiciales* (1671).

Ewen, C. L'Estrange: *Lotteries and Sweepstakes* (1932).

Fortescue, John: *De Laudibus Legum Angliae* (1825).

Green, A. Wigfall: *The Inns of Court and Early English Drama* (1931).

Hall, Edward: *Chronicle* (1809).

Bibliography

Holdsworth, Sir William: *History of English Law* (1922).

Hope, Andree: *Chronicles of an Old Inn* (1887).

Hotson, Leslie: *Mr. W. H.* (1964).

Jones, E. Alfred: *American Members of the Inns of Court* (1927).

Kerr, Russell and Duncan, Ida Coffin: *The Portledge Papers* (1928).

Lamb, Charles: *Essays of Elia*.

Loftie, W. J.: *The Inns of Court* (1893).

Maitland, F. W.: *The Year Books of Edward II* (1903–7).

Maitland, F. W.: *The English Law and the Renaissance* (1901).

Maitland, William: *History and Survey of London* (1750).

Merrivale, Lord and Campion, Bernard, K. C.: *The Story of Gray's Inn* (1950).

Noorthouck, John: *A New History of London* (1773).

North, Roger: *The Lives of the Norths* (1819).

Oakes, C. G.: *Sir Samuel Romilly* (1935).

Pepys, Samuel, Diary.

Pollock, Sir Frederick: *The Origins of the Inns of Court* (1931).

Prest, Wilfrid, *The Inns of Court 1590–1640* (1972).

Stone, Sir Leonard: *The History of the Silver of Gray's Inn* (1950).

Stow, John: *Survey of London* (1592).

Terry, William: *Judge Jenkins* (1929).

Thorne, Professor S. E.: *The Early History of the Inns of Court*, Graya (1959) No. 50 p. 29.

Turner, G. F.: *Legal T. Leaves* (1903).

Wheatley, Henry: *London Past and Present* (1891).

Williams, E.: *Early Holborn and the Legal Quarter* (1927).

Williams, E.: *Staple Inn* (1906).

Worsfield, T. Cato: *Staple Inn* (1903).

Dictionary of National Biography.

Notes and Queries.

The files of *Graya, The Times, The Law Times* and *The Gentleman's Magazine*.

Index

Index

Index